Managing the New Public Services

Managing the New Public Services

Edited by

David Farnham

and

Sylvia Horton

MACMILLAN

First published 1993 by
THE MACMILLAN PRESS LTD
Houndmills, Basingstoke, Hampshire RG21 2XS
and London
Companies and representatives
throughout the world

ISBN 0-333-56291-7 hardcover
ISBN 0-333-56292-5 paperback

A catalogue record for this book is available
from the British Library.

Reprinted 1994

Printed in Hong Kong

Contents

List of Figures and Tables   vii
Abbreviations   ix
List of Contributors   xi
Preface   xiii

PART I   THE CHANGING CONTEXTS OF MANAGEMENT

1 **The Political Economy of Public Sector Change**
   David Farnham and Sylvia Horton   3

2 **Managing Private and Public Organisations**
   David Farnham and Sylvia Horton   27

PART II   MANAGERIAL FUNCTIONS

3 **Strategic Management**   *Howard Elcock*   55

4 **Financial Management**   *Richard Tonge*   78

5 **Human Resources Management and Employee Relations**
   David Farnham   99

PART III   CASE STUDIES

6 **The Civil Service**   *Sylvia Horton*   127

7 **Local Government**   *Howard Elcock*   150

8 **The National Health Service**   *Graham Moon and Ian
   Kendall*   172

9 **Education**   *Malcolm McVicar*   188

10 **The Police Service**   *Frank Leishman and Stephen P. Savage* 211

PART IV   CONCLUSION

11 The New Public Service Managerialism: An Assessment
David Farnham and Sylvia Horton   **237**

Bibliography   255
Index   268

List of Figures and Tables

Figures

1.1 Government expenditure as percentage of GDP 1890 to
    1990   8
3.1 Rational model of strategic management   56
3.2 Managing uncertainty over time   59
3.3 The flow of guidelines and plans in the NHS   66
4.1 Financial responsibility and accountability flow system   80
4.2 Financial planning and control system   81
4.3 Incremental budgeting model   84

Tables

1.1 General government expenditures as a percentage of
    GDP 1900 to 1992   6
3.1 Varieties of management strategies   75
4.1 A revenue budget   83
4.2 Financial and operational information   86
5.1 UK public sector employment 1961–91: selected years,
    by headcount   102
5.2 Employment in the UK public services 1979–91: full
    time equivalent   103
5.3 Employment in the UK public services 1991: sex and
    employment status   104
9.1 Categories of LEA expenditure under LMS   198

Abbreviations

ACPO	Association of Chief Police Officers
AHA	Area Health Authority
CPU	Central Planning Unit
CSD	Civil Service Department
CPRS	Central Policy Review Staff
CTC	City Technology College
CCT	Compulsory competitive tendering
CBI	Confederation of British Industry
DSO	Direct Service Organisation
DHA	District Health Authority
DGM	District General Manager
DHSS	Department of Health and Social Security
DMT	District Management Team
DES	Department of Education and Science
ER	Employee relations
ERB	Executive responsibility budgets
FTE	Full time equivalent
FPC	Family Practitioner Committee
FHSA	Family Health Service Authority
FMI	Financial Management Initiative
FMU	Financial Management Unit
GP	General Practitioner
GDP	Gross Domestic Product
GGE	General Government Expenditure
GMTS	General Management Training Scheme
GLEB	Greater London Enterprise Board
GCHQ	General Communications Headquarters (Cheltenham)
GMS	Grant-maintained Schools
HMI	Her Majesty's Inspectorate
HMI	Her Majesty's Inspector
HEC	Higher Education Corporation
HRM	Human Resources Management
HSSB	Health Services Supervisory Board
IBM	International Business Machines
INLOGOV	Institute of Local Government Studies (Birmingham)

IT	Information Technology
IHSM	Institute of Health Services Management
IAC	Interim Advisory Committee
LGMB	Local Government Management Board
LEA	Local Education Authority
LMS	Local Management of Schools
MBO	Management by Objectives
MPS	Metropolitan Police Service
MSC	Manpower Services Commission
MINIS	Management Information System for Ministers
NATFHE	National Association of Teachers in Further and Higher Education
NMS	New Management Strategy (Ministry of Defence)
NHS	National Health Service
OSPRE	Objective Structured Performance Related Examination
PBSR	Public Sector Borrowing Requirement
PI	Performance Indicator
PRP	Performance Related Pay
PRB	Pay Review Body
PES	Public Expenditure Survey
PCEF	Polytechnic and Colleges Employers Forum
PAR	Policy Analysis Review
PPB	Planned Programme Budgeting
PCFC	Polytechnics and Colleges Funding Council
PSI	Policy Studies Institute
PBO	Policing by Objectives
RPI	Retail Price Index
RIPA	Royal Institute of Public Administration
RCN	Royal College of Nursing
RHA	Regional Health Authority
RMI	Resource Management Initiative
SMTF	School Management Task Force
SWOT	Strengths, Weaknesses, Opportunities, Threats
SRB	Staff Responsibility Budget
TUC	Trades Union Congress
UMT	Unit Management Team (NHS)
UGM	Unit General Manager (NHS)
WIRS	Workplace Industrial Relations Survey
ZBB	Zero-Based Budgeting

List of Contributors

Howard Elcock is Professor of Government at Northumbria University at Newcastle. He previously taught at the University of Hull and served as a member of Humberside County Council between 1973 and 1981. Between 1975 and 1977, he was Chair of the Council's Planning Committee and was involved in the preparation of the first Humberside Structure Plan. His major publications include *Local Government* and *Change and Decay? Public Administration in the 1990s*. He also co-authored *Learning from Local Authority Budgeting* with Grant Jordan and Arthur Midwinter. He is currently Chair of the Joint University Council and previously served as Chair of its Public Administration Committee.

David Farnham is Principal Lecturer in Industrial Relations at the University of Portsmouth. He has written *Personnel in Context* and *The Corporate Environment*. He is also co-author of *Understanding Industrial Relations* with John Pimlott and *Public Administration in the United Kingdom* with Malcolm McVicar.

Sylvia Horton is Principal Lecturer in Public Sector Studies in the School of Social and Historical Studies at the University of Portsmouth. She has written mainly on local government but is currently researching into changes in personnel management in the public sector.

Ian Kendall is Principal Lecturer in Social Policy and Associate Head of the School of Social and Historical Studies at the University of Portsmouth. He has written on a number of health and social policy issues and is co-author of *Medical Negligence – Complaints and Compensation* with John Carrier. He is currently working on a book on health policy with John Carrier.

Frank Leishman entered the academic profession as a Lecturer in Police Studies, after a period in the police service. He has written in police journals and is now undertaking postgraduate work at the University of Stirling.

Malcolm McVicar is Dean of the Faculty of Humanities and Social Sciences at the University of Portsmouth. He is co-author of *Public Administration in the United Kingdom* with David Farnham. He has written widely on higher education and is currently researching into performance indicators and measurement in higher education institutions.

Graham Moon is Principal Lecturer in Health Studies in the School of Social and Historical Studies at the University of Portsmouth. He is currently seconded, on a part-time basis, to Portsmouth and South East Hampshire Health Authority as a research management consultant. He is also co-author of *Health, Disease and Society* with Kelvin Jones. His research interests are in primary and community health care management and public health. He is currently co-directing an ESRC project on community health councils.

Stephen P. Savage is Director of the Institute of Police and Criminological Studies at the University of Portsmouth. He has previously published *The Theories of Talcott Parsons* and is co-editor of *Public Policy under Thatcher* with Lynton Robins. His interests are in police studies, criminology and the public policy of law and order.

Richard Tonge is Senior Lecturer in Accounting in Portsmouth Business School at the University of Portsmouth. He was previously an accountant in local government. His research interests are management accounting and financial analysis in the public sector, with special reference to policing and trading agencies.

Preface

Britain's public services have been subjected to substantial political, organisational and managerial changes since the late 1970s. The central purpose of this book is to provide an interim account and assessment of these changes and how they have affected those managing the public services, those using them and those working in them. Within this overall task, the contributors analyse the background to these changes, including the political and economic contexts, the rationale for them and how they have impacted on the ways in which particular public service organisations are being managed. They also evaluate what is identified as a 'new managerialism' in the 'new' public services. Supporters of the new managerialism assert that the key to providing improved, efficient and 'customer oriented' public services lies in introducing more sophisticated managerial practices and more advanced management techniques into them, based largely on 'good' practice in the private sector. Critics of the new managerialism claim that it has merely expanded the numbers employed in managerial posts, at the expense of those actually delivering the services. They also contend that it has resulted in less open styles of management, while injecting a commercial element into the public services which is the antithesis of traditional public service ethics and culture.

This is not a 'how to manage' book, however. It seeks instead to explore the ideas, economic circumstances and governmental policies which have influenced the introduction of new managerial practices into Britain's public services since the late 1970s. In examining the new managerialism, the contributors seek to provide an interpretative rather than a prescriptive text, with an analytical and critical thrust.

Managing involves a complex set of human and technical activities which take place within specific organisational settings and environments. Basically, managing involves those with managerial responsibilities in organisations, whether at senior, intermediate or junior level, taking decisions about how scarce physical and human resources are to be employed and organised in order to achieve the corporate goals and objectives set by those in authority. A main theme of this book is an examination of how those responsible for making and implementing managerial decisions in the public services have had to adapt their roles

xiii

and behaviour in response to a series of radical political, legislative and organisational changes, prompted by governmental initiatives, since the late 1970s.

The public services are broadly defined as those major public sector organisations whose current and capital expenditures are funded primarily by taxation, rather than by raising revenue through the sale of their services to either individual or corporate consumers. The public services, so defined, include the civil service, local government, the National Health Service (NHS), and the educational and police services. It is these large public organisations which provide the focus of the 'new' or reformed public services over the last decade or so. This definition excludes the remaining nationalised industries and the former public utilities, such as telecommunications, gas, electricity and water, as well as public corporations such as the British Broadcasting Corporation, the Bank of England and the Post Office. It also excludes the judiciary and the armed services.

The book is in four parts. Part I examines the changing contexts of management. Within it, the editors discuss and analyse two interrelated themes: the political and economic backgrounds to public sector change since the late 1970s (Chapter 1) and the similarities and differences in the managing of private and public organisations (Chapter 2). In these chapters, it is argued, first, that the emergence and ascendancy of the 'New Right' in British politics in the 1980s resulted in the transformation of the 'mixed economy' state into a more limited regulatory state in which market forces were to play a more important allocative role than at any time in the postwar period. Second, it is suggested that there is now some convergence between how private sector and public sector organisations are being managed, with certain private sector management techniques and processes being used in the public services.

Part II focuses on the key managerial functions within and across the public services. Elcock examines the concept of strategic management as it applies to the public services. He identifies the growing emphasis placed on strategic issues in the public services and argues, using examples drawn largely from the local authority sector, that strategic choice and strategic implementation are likely to increase in importance in the 1990s (Chapter 3). Tonge analyses the nature of financial management and its changing role in the public services. He thinks it unlikely that the importance of public service financial control will diminish in the future (Chapter 4). Farnham contrasts how human resources and employee relations are now being managed across a range of public service organisations compared with the past. A main conclusion is that there has been a significant shift in public service personnel and employer practices in dealing with employees during the last decade or so and it appears that a more private sector pattern is emerging (Chapter 5).

Part III consists of five case studies of the 'new' public service management in practice. Horton looks at recent managerial and organisational changes in the civil service and concludes that, whilst change has been incremental, piecemeal and pragmatic over some 20 years, it has accelerated since 1979. As a result, the civil service is now more federalized, decentralised and managerialised than it was previously (Chapter 6). Elcock examines how local government has responded to the impact of new demands on its services in the 1980s, especially from reduced real expenditure, exposure to competition and greater responsiveness to citizen need. In his view, the move towards more professionally managed, customer friendly, responsive and accessible local authorities is now well established and is set to continue (Chapter 7). The shift towards a 'general management' model in the NHS is considered by Moon and Kendall. They also examine the role of 'internal markets' in the National Health Service and their impact on health service managerialism. They demonstrate that professional power has been weakened and the general management role strengthened since the mid-1980s (Chapter 8). The underlying theme of McVicar's analysis of policy and management in the education sector is that, prior to 1979, 'management' hardly existed. Since then, school, college and university heads are now increasingly becoming general managers, with a range of responsibilities not dissimilar from those managing comparably sized private sector organisations (Chapter 9). In examining the new managerialism in the police services, Leishman and Savage argue that 'policing' and 'management' do not sit easily together, partly because of the discretionary nature of much police work. They concede, however, that continuing pressure from government, the public and within the service itself will ensure that managerial change remains on the agenda, with further changes being inevitable (Chapter 10).

In Part IV, the editors draw the threads of the book together and provide an overall analysis of the new public service managerialism. They review the nature, origins and impact of the managerialist phenomenon in the public services and point the way to the future.

The completion of an edited book like this could not have been completed without the collaboration and goodwill of its contributing authors and publishers. The editors would like to thank their colleagues for meeting (most of!) their deadlines and our publisher, Steven Kennedy, for his support and encouragement throughout the writing of this book. Our thanks are also due to Jackie Cooper, Kellie Diggins and Cynthia Duffield for providing urgent secretarial assistance in the final stages of producing the typescript, and to Otto Germann and Robin Prior for their help with spreadsheets and other computer software. Any remaining errors of fact, judgement or opinion are ours alone.

University of Portsmouth   DAVID FARNHAM
September 1992   SYLVIA HORTON

Part I

The Changing Contexts of Management

1

The Political Economy of Public Sector Change

DAVID FARNHAM and SYLVIA HORTON

This chapter outlines developments in the size and scope of the British state and the breakdown, from the 1970s, of what has been called 'the post-war settlement'. This was the economic, social and political consensus established after the Second World War between, according to Flynn (1990, p. 6), 'the trade unions and especially the returning soldiers, the employers and governments'. It was the breakdown of the post-war settlement which opened the way for the ideas of the 'New Right' in domestic politics during the 1980s and 1990s. These ideas, and the governmental policies deriving from them, challenged the social democratic principles and values which had dominated British politics since 1945. Markets now became preferred to politics as means for allocating resources and distributing welfare in the new 'enterprise culture' of the 1980s and 1990s. The responsibility for providing public services and welfare shifted from largely monopolistic state provision to a mixture of public, private, self help, family and voluntary sources. The large impersonal and centralised state bureaucracies, created during the post-war period, came under political attack and were either privatised, or broken up, or decentralised and managerialised. Some of these changes had their origins in the period before 1979, but the effects of four successive Conservative governments elected in 1979, 1983, 1987 and 1992 were critical in their impact. The hegemony of New Right ideas and New Right governments after 1979 may be compared with the dominance of social democratic ideas and consensus governments after 1945. This chapter provides the political and

3

ideological background to the book. It puts the post-war British state, and its critics, into context and sets the scene against which changes in the managing of the public services after 1979 are discussed and analysed in subsequent chapters.

The Growth of the State Sector in Britain

Changes in the role of the state and its size and composition have occurred throughout the twentieth century. A series of incremental adjustments in the scope and thrust of state activity took place in response to changing circumstances. Political interventions of the state were also influenced by significant events, such as the First and Second World Wars. These marked discontinuity with the past but were also stepping stones to the future. It was Margaret Thatcher's premiership of the Conservative government, elected in 1979, which is likely to be seen in retrospect as heralding a new stage in the development of the state, since there have been many changes in not only the size and composition of the public sector since then, but also the ways in which its organisations are managed. However, the state sector still accounts for over 40 per cent of Britain's Gross Domestic Product (GDP), defined as the value of the goods and services produced by its residents annually, and it employs over five million people.

The boundary between the state and non-state sectors is difficult to define, as we demonstrate in Chapter 2. The former includes central and local government, the armed forces, the National Health Service (NHS), the nationalised industries and an array of public fringe bodies with administrative, regulatory, advisory and adjudicatory roles. At the beginning of the century the size and scope of the state was limited. Central government employed 116,413 civil servants in 1901 in some 14 departments, the largest of which were Customs, Excise and the Post Office (Drewry and Butcher, 1988). The provision of public services such as the poor law, policing, education and public health rested with local government, which central government inspectorates supervised. It was the Boer War in 1900 that led to an increase in general government expenditure (GGE), which is the annual combined spending of central and local government, including both capital and current spending, plus net lending. This paved the way for the Liberal Party reforms between 1906 and 1914, which laid the foundations of the Welfare State. The size of the civil service had increased to 280,000 by 1913. In the same year, GGE reached 12 per cent of GDP, as shown in Table 1.1 (on following page), but it was the First World War which marked a significant watershed in both the scope and the size of the public sector.

After 1918, the role of government was no longer confined to regulating the private sector and providing for law and order and defence. A more collectivist approach was expected of government, with the state accepting some responsibility for housing, education, health and social insurance. During the 1930s the first weakening of *laissez-faire* economic policies occurred, when governments assisted the regions hardest hit by the depression, local authority activities expanded and 'public utilities' were supplied by both public and private bodies. Public corporations were formed with the creation of the British Broadcasting Corporation and the Electricity Generating Board in 1926, followed by the London Passenger Transport Board in 1933. Figure 1.1 (on page 8) clearly shows the higher levels of GGE between 1918 and 1939, compared with pre-1914. The average for the decade before 1914 was 12.2 per cent of GDP, whilst for the decade 1928–38 it was 25 per cent.

After the Second World War, GGE rose to a new plateau. Peacock and Wiseman (1961) explain this pattern of expenditure in terms of people's changing expectations about normal tax levels. The high taxes imposed during wartime became the norm for the post-war period. This enabled governments to transfer expenditure from the war effort to social expenditures without any strong resistance. This, coupled with the catalytic effect of the war in changing social expectations, provided for the displacement to take place (Marwick, 1968).

There was a significant growth in all parts of the public sector after 1945. The Labour government, elected on a programme of economic and social reform, was committed to nationalising the major basic industries, to economic and physical planning and to establishing a full programme of social welfare. Nationalisation brought railways, the coal industry, the airlines, gas, electricity, road haulage and, for a short period, iron and steel into the public sector. This added one million employees to the public payroll. The civil service grew from 387,000 in 1939 to over a million in 1951, with about 675,000 of those non-industrial civil servants and 400,000 industrials, although by 1979, civil service employment had fallen to about 700,000, comprising 550,000 non-industrials and only 150,000 industrials. Local government grew at an even faster rate than that of central government, as it was the key

TABLE 1.1   *General government expenditure as a percentage of GDP, 1900 to 1992*

	General government expenditure	Spending on goods and services only		General government expenditure	Spending on goods and services only
1900	14.4	12.6	1940	51.9	43.3
1901	13.5	11.6	1941	60.4	49.4
1902	13.2	11.2	1942	61.1	50.3
1903	12.9	10.8	1943	61.4	50.4
1904	12.4	10.3	1944	61.4	50.3
1905	11.8	9.6	1945	58.8	44.3
1906	11.7	9.5	1946	45.5	23.6
1907	11.8	9.5	1947	38.8	19.1
1908	12.5	10.1	1948	36.3	19.2
1909	12.4	9.9	1949	34.8	20.0
1910	12.2	9.7	1950	33.8	20.1
1911	12.2	9.8	1951	36.1	21.2
1912	12.4	9.9	1952	37.2	23.4
1913	12.1	9.8	1953	35.9	23.0
1914	24.6	21.8	1954	33.8	21.8
1915	30.5	27.7	1955	33.0	20.5
1916	34.4	29.7	1956	33.4	20.5
1917	33.4	27.9	1957	34.3	20.2
1918	46.3	40.4	1958	34.4	19.6
1919	*	*	1959	34.5	19.7
1920	26.6	16.6	1960	34.1	19.4
1921	27.9	15.4	1961	35.1	19.8
1922	25.7	13.2	1962	35.7	20.3
1923	23.4	11.6	1963	35.6	20.3
1924	23.2	11.8	1964	36.0	20.6
1925	23.1	11.9	1965	36.6	20.6
1926	25.2	13.0	1966	37.4	21.2
1927	24.0	12.5	1967	40.9	22.6
1928	23.5	12.0	1968	41.4	22.3
1929	23.4	12.0	1969	40.0	21.6
1930	24.4	12.3	1970	40.1	22.0
1931	26.9	13.3	1971	40.5	22.2
1932	26.6	12.7	1972	40.8	22.4
1933	25.0	12.4	1973	41.1	23.0
1934	23.5	12.0	1974	46.8	25.2
1935	23.7	12.6	1975	48.8	26.6
1936	24.2	13.7	1976	46.9	26.0
1937	24.7	14.9	1977	42.5	23.6
1938	28.5	18.7	1978	43.0	22.7
1939	32.9	23.8	1979	43.3	22.3

1980	45.1	23.7	1987	42.0	22.2
1981	46.0	23.6	1988	39.5	21.1
1982	46.4	23.4	1989	40.0	22.0
1983	45.9	23.9	1990	40.0	22.4
1984	45.5	23.7	1991	41.5	*
1985	44.5	22.9	1992	42.0	*
1986	42.8	22.9			

* = not available.

provider of the new and expanded services in housing, education and personal social services. It was also given responsibility for environmental, physical and infrastructural development. It employed over one million people by the late 1940s and over three million by 1979. The creation of the NHS also brought into the public sector former private hospitals, doctors and health practitioners. By 1979, some seven million people were employed in the public sector and many millions in the private sector were dependent for their employment on governmental contracts, funding and state subsidies (see Chapters 2 and 5).

Alongside the increase in public employment went a corresponding increase in GGE, as shown in Table 1.1 and Figure 1.1. GGE consists of two main components, spending on goods and services and transfer payments. The former is the extent to which the nation's resources are directly absorbed by government. The latter refers to the redistribution of resources by government, amongst sections of the community. Government expenditure on goods and services increased following both major wars but tended to remain fairly stable in the intervening periods. From 1901–13 it was approximately 10 per cent of GDP; from 1919–38 around 13 per cent; and it rose to an average of 20 per cent between 1947 and 1970. It peaked in the mid-1970s at nearly 27 per cent, due mainly to changes in the prices of world commodities, especially oil, and to a fall in Britain's GDP due to the onset of world recession.

Transfer payments have tended to fluctuate much more, especially in the period after 1945. There was, however, a continual upward trend, particularly from the mid-1950s. This can be linked to a number of factors including changes in the numbers claiming benefits, increases in the range of benefits and increases in payment levels. Transfer payments rose from 11 per cent of GDP in 1954 to 23 per cent in

8

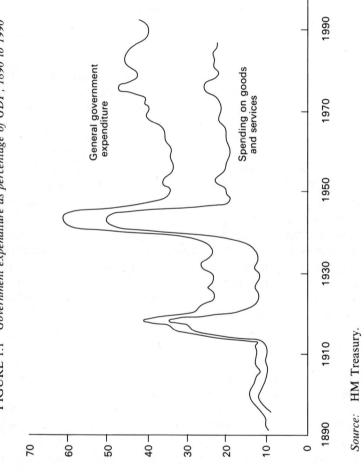

FIGURE 1.1 *Government expenditure as percentage of GDP, 1890 to 1990*

General government
expenditure

Spending on goods
and services

Source: HM Treasury.

1975. The major increases in government expenditure during the post-war period were primarily due to welfare policies of redistribution and to the provision of universal social services.

Since 1979, the patterns within GGE have changed, although there has been no significant reduction in its size or in the share of GDP that it represents. GGE averaged around 43.5 per cent throughout the 1980s, excluding the revenues from privatisation. Spending on goods and services varied by only 2 per cent throughout the period, remaining fairly steady at about 23.5 per cent of GDP. Increases in government expenditure in the early 1980s were partly the result of the government accepting the recommendations of the Standing Commission on Pay Comparability, which led to substantial pay increases in some of the public services. It was also the result of increased spending on law and order and defence. Most significantly, it coincided with the first period of economic recession, when unemployment rose to over three million.

Marginal falls in GGE in the late 1980s coincided with falling inflation, an upturn in the economy and falling unemployment. With the onset of a second recession in 1990, however, the upward trend in GGE returned. By 1992 its share of GDP was the same as when the Conservatives had taken office in 1979. As Flynn (1990) points out, even the apparent reduction of 'public expenditure as a proportion of GDP, from 46 1/4 per cent in 1984–5 to 41 1/2 per cent in 1987–8 . . . rests more on the recovery of GDP than on the reduction in spending'. Actual spending was partly concealed after 1983 by the practice of financing public spending with the proceeds of the sales of the nationalised industries. Between 1979 and 1991 more than 60 companies were sold to the private sector including the key utilities of gas, electricity, water and British Telecom. This programme raised some £37 billion which was used to increase public expenditure, reduce the public sector borrowing requirement (PBSR) and to repay the national debt.

The Post-war Settlement

It was the experiences of the inter-war depression and of the Second World War which eclipsed the economy orthodoxy of economic *laissez-faire*. This is the doctrine that economics and politics are separate activities and that the economic affairs of society are best guided by the decisions of disassociated individuals, operating in a free market economy to the virtual exclusion of state intervention. As stated above, there was a shift in economic thinking in the 1930s which supported a role for the state in economic planning. The extensive intervention of the wartime government, 1940–45, in managing the economy, demonstrated planning in practice. The levelling effects of the war experience also led to an acceptance of greater collectivism and a demand for more equality. These paved the way for new economic and social roles for the state which were the basis of what came to be called the post-war settlement.

The post-war settlement comprised three interrelated elements: a mixed economy incorporating Keynesian demand management economic policies; a Welfare State, with universal social services; and a political consensus. The Keynesian approach involved governments assuming prime responsibility for economic management and for fine tuning the economy. This aimed at creating high levels of aggregate demand for goods and services in order to maintain full employment. Governments relied on a combination of fiscal, monetary and prices and incomes policies, in their efforts to attain four primary economic goals: full employment; price stability; balance of payments equilibrium; and economic growth. To achieve these goals, governments consulted with the Confederation of British Industry (CBI) and the Trades Union Congress (TUC) in the policy process.

The Welfare State component of the post-war settlement is described by Marwick (1990, p. 45) as 'the totality of schemes and services through which the central government together with the local authorities assumed a major responsibility for dealing with all the different types of social problems which beset individual citizens'. A wide range of publicly and universally available services was provided by central and local governments including a system of social security payments and pensions, designed to ensure a minimum safety net for the unemployed, sick and elderly; a comprehensive NHS, free at the point of use; compulsory education up to the age of 15; and public housing for those who could not, or chose not to, become homeowners. This set of citizenship and social rights was the legacy of the Beveridge Report (1942).

The political consensus, sometimes known as the social democratic consensus, is described by Marquand (1988, p. 18) as the 'set of commitments, assumptions and expectations, transcending party conflicts and shared by the great majority of the country's political and economic leaders which provided the framework within which policy decisions were made'. There was a high level of agreement across political parties and political élites about the substance of public policy, especially on the roles of the mixed economy and the Welfare State. As Kavanagh (1987, p. 7) points out, the political consensus also referred to the tendency of a new government to accept its predecessor's legislation, even when, in opposition, it had opposed it. There was also an agreement on the nature of the political system and its key institutions. The political consensus, in other words, represented a 'mobilisation of bias' which favoured certain political and economic interests, issues and procedures. It did not go unchallenged but the minority who opposed it was overshadowed by the widespread support for the consensus.

By the 1970s, however, cracks were appearing in the consensus and opposition grew louder as concerns were being expressed about the post-war settlement. Crosland (1956, p. 385) had stated earlier that 'the future of socialism was dependent in part on sustained economic growth'. It was the slowing down of economic growth in the 1970s which was eventually to undermine the Keynesian-Beveridge edifice. A turning point was the onset of the long world recession triggered by the sharp rise in oil prices after then Arab-Israeli war in 1973–4. Krieger (1986, pp. 22–4) estimates that, compared with the previous 10-year period, 1973–81 saw a significant reduction in the average increase of world trade from about 9 per cent to 9 per cent. Britain, already less efficient than most of its industrial competitors, was badly hit by the recession. Britain's steady economic growth in the post-war period had reduced internal political tensions and eased the problem of governing the Keynesian Welfare State. Increased taxation and rising government spending had gone hand in hand with rising standards of living and higher consumption. With recession and the slowdown of economic growth, decisions became more difficult and the consensus was weakened. This left the way open for new political and economic ideas to take its place.

The economic crisis in the mid-1970s coincided with the Labour Party assuming office. Its response was to cut back planned expenditure and to break in part with the post-war consensus. Gough (1979, p. 128) shows that £1,700 million was taken off planned public expenditure for 1974–5, £1.1 billion for 1976–7, with two further rounds of substantial cuts totalling £2 billion in July and December 1976. Further, it was planned for the first time to have an absolute drop in total state spending in 1977–8 and 1978–9. Indeed, it became the Labour government's policy objective to reduce the total share of state expenditure in GDP by the end of the decade. It was to fall from a planned level of 55.1 per cent in 1975–6 to 48 per cent in 1978–9. The cuts in and restructuring of government expenditure were aimed at tackling three problems. One was to rectify the balance of payments deficit, by releasing resources from the public to the private sector to generate more exports. The second was to lower inflation by reducing the PSBR and taxation. The third was to reduce unemployment by releasing resources for private investment to regenerate industry, stimulate economic growth and increase job opportunities. At the same time the Labour government adopted monetarist policies of curbing the money supply in an attempt to control inflation. In the event they got public expenditure down from an out-turn of 48.8 per cent of GDP in 1975–6 to 43.0 per cent in 1978–9.

The weakening of Keynesian economic orthodoxy was paralleled by growing challenges to the Welfare State as a provider, through governmental intervention, of national minimum standards of living and a 'social wage'. These minimum standards were embodied in three types of governmental committment and state institution: full employment, universal social services meeting citizens' basic needs and measures for preventing and relieving poverty. The critiques of the Welfare State were economic and political in character. Some economic critiques blamed the Welfare State for Britain's economic problems arguing that the high taxes required to sustain it fuelled inflation, reduced incentives and diverted scarce resources out of the ' wealth creating' private sector into the 'wealth consuming' public sector. It was the expansion of the role of the state, especially the non-market sector which was seen as responsible for Britain's economic problems (Bacon and Eltis, 1976). Other economic critiques viewed elements of the Welfare State as being professionally dominated, lacking client involvement, acting as unaccountable monopolies and being under- and poorly managed.

These economic and political criticisms were mirrored in the breakdown in the social democratic consensus in politics. The view that public action was to be the preferred means for managing the economy and dealing with society's social problems was the basis for the old political consensus. But the centre ground in British politics was crumbling. Neither the old problems associated with managing the macroeconomy and alleviating poverty nor the new ones associated with the inner cities, the growing numbers of the elderly and the environment appeared capable of being resolved by the old politics. A polarisation was emerging with the right wing of the Conservative Party repudiating Keynesianism and welfarism in favour of the free market and personal responsibility, whilst the Labour Party was moving to the left with proposals for more nationalisation and more socialism. The Liberals, and later the Social Democratic Party formed in the early 1980s, filled the centre ground. But it was the Conservatives, taking political power in 1979, that finally broke with the post-war consensus and introduced a new politics based on the ideas of the 'New Right'.

The New Right

The New Right critique of the post-war settlement is an expression of economic liberalism, anti-collectivism and elements of social authoritarianism. It draws on the works and ideas of economic liberals such as Friedman (1962) and Hayek (1944, 1973), public choice theorists, such as Buchanan (1975), Niskanen (1971) and Mueller (1979), and political economists such as Lindblom (1977). The influence of American thinkers on the New Right has been dominant, with the main outlets of New Right ideas in Britain being the Institute of Economic Affairs, the Adam Smith Institute, the Centre for Policy Studies and *The Salisbury Review*.

The key values which underpin New Right thinking are individualism, personal freedom and inequality in contrast to those of collectivism, social rights and equality which were associated with the Keynesian Welfare State. The New Right emphasises the virtues and creative possibilities of the free market economy and attacks state and governmental action associated with Keynesianism and Beveridgism. They prefer markets to politics, both as a means of producing and distributing goods and services in society and as an institutional arrangement for providing social organisation and social control. They perceive political systems as being particularly unsuited for creating economic welfare. This is because of the inherent complexity of co-ordinating centrally planned economic decisions and the lack of knowledge of what people want in planned economies. Markets, in contrast, are seen to facilitate economic prosperity through their efficiency in allocating scarce resources, whilst offering choice to consumers and producers in determining their own well being and welfare.

Lindblom (1977), in addition to drawing attention to the market as an effective allocator of resources, an efficient co-ordinating mechanism and a rational decision making process, also argues that markets encourage resourcefulness and enterprise. They are flexible 'turbulent open-ended systems that can grow and change'. Further, 'they allow great room for invention and improvisation'. Through the market, total societal welfare can be obtained with social prosperity, without the state imposing specific values or prioritising economic wants or needs. The result is a 'spontaneous order' produced by the impersonal market where 'the consumer is sovereign' (Hayek, 1976).

For the New Right, the market offers freedom of choice to individuals and is a form of economic democracy. For Seldon (1990):

> The choice is between two imperfect approaches – the political process and the market process, between politics and markets, between the political and the commercial ethic – rather than between two imperfect systems, since both are necessary. But the mix can differ widely between the minimum use of government, which I describe as capitalism, and the maximum use of government and the minimum use of the market, which I define as socialism.

He concludes that markets generally serve the public interest better than do politics and that the main function of government is to make the best use of markets by letting them develop spontaneously to serve the public.

Although the New Right economic liberals prefer market to political allocation, they concede that there is a role for politics and government but that it should be a minimal one, providing only for public goods and some merit goods. Mueller (1979) puts the case for public goods arguing that defence, clean air, street lighting, policing and highways, for example, are socially necessary but that there are no economic incentives for individuals to participate in funding them, unless forced to do so. Where the market cannot operate effectively in determining an appropriate amount of a commodity to produce, nor determine its distribution, the only way of financing such goods is through collective taxation. Other cases for political intervention are: where the commodities produced within the market have externalities and social costs; where the market fails; or where the market is a monopoly. Finally, there is a case for supplying merit goods where it is socially desirable that individuals have them, because they need them to function as active and purposeful citizens. Examples here include health and education.

There is a disagreement amongst the New Right about where the boundaries of 'public goods' begin and end. But the objective is to balance the claimed efficiency of markets, and the individual freedom they provide, with the need for economic and social stability. Friedman argues that the state should provide for the less well off and those who cannot work, such as the sick, old and infirm, in addition to providing public goods such as defence, law and order and a judicial system.

Some New Right thinkers, public choice theorists, argue that markets and politics are not reconcilable. They seek to demonstrate the contradictions inherent in the social democratic mixed economy. Using economic analysis, they argue that politics is a market-place in which the politicians are the 'producers', voters are the 'consumers' and votes are the 'currency'. However, unlike the economic market, there is no cash nexus, so voters can make irreconcilable demands on politicians, such as wanting both lower taxes and more public goods, whilst the politicians can promise what the voters will buy, since they do not bear the economic costs of those choices (Downs, 1957; Buchanan and Tullock, 1962).

Other public choice theorists apply economic analysis to interest group politics arguing that, just as in the economic market, monopolies appear and a maldistribution of resources results from the irrational processes of power politics. Equally, as Niskanen (1971) argues, bureaucrats, in pursuing their own self-interest, promote the growth and expansion of governmental functions which become over-supplied and over-extended. A coalition of politicians and bureaucrats fuels the extension of political activities and this leads to inefficiency, a lack of democratic control and a concentration of power in the hands of the monopolistic suppliers and controllers of information. This 'overloaded government' thesis is not exclusive to the New Right (Rose and Peters, 1978) but it gives support to the creative possibilities of the free market economy and the need to roll back the frontiers of the state.

The New Right critics of the British Welfare State draw heavily upon these ideas and theories. First, they argue the Keynesian Welfare State creates personal dependency and weakens individuals' sense of responsibility for themselves and their families. It is supplier led, providing what the professionals and bureaucrats think people want, rather than what they need, and this makes it unresponsive to individual needs and personal choice. Second, the Welfare State is a threat to personal freedom, because it gives individuals little choice about the services provided, and it is not subject to effective democratic control. Third, since the Welfare State is the main source and provider of public services, other sources of welfare – such as the family, local communities,voluntary bodies and the market – are neglected and enfeebled.

The New Right also claims that Keynesian welfarism is fundamentally inefficient because macroeconomic management is inflationary and the Welfare State is a monopoly provider of services. It is only through market competition that economic efficiency can be achieved. Welfare State policies weaken the economy because they depend upon high rates of taxation, fuel inflation, weaken incentives and damage investment. The real sources of welfare such as individual initiative, economic growth and private enterprise are undermined. As well as weakening the economy, Welfare State policies weaken the authority of government. With government bodies becoming the focus of interest group politics, they become committed to particular welfare programmes and the captives of special pressure groups. For the New Right, and its apologists like Hayek (1973, pp. 9–10), the antidote to this 'unlimited democracy' can only be by 'limiting the powers of government' and by free market choice.

The New Politics

It would be wrong to suggest that the Conservative governments from 1979 onwards have been simply vehicles for the New Right. What is evident is that New Right ideas have had a great influence on governmental policies and that radicals in the Conservative Party have been sympathetic to New Right ideology. But many New Right proposals, emanating from its theorists and advocates, proved to be too extreme even for reforming Conservative governments. Education vouchers, funded national health insurance, the abolition of child benefit and the introduction of workfare were all rejected as politically impracticable, although some ideas, initially rejected, were subsequently implemented. In particular, privatisation in its many forms was gradually extended and internal market mechanisms became the centre-piece of major pillars of the state sector, such as in health and education by the early 1990s.

There is little evidence that the Conservative government coming into office in 1979 had a blueprint or a strategic plan which it consistently followed through. There is more evidence to support the view that its approach was incremental and pragmatic and that its policies unfolded as circumstances and opportunities permitted or as failures and problems called for new responses. What is clear is that New Right ideas and values informed the strategic policy choices and implementation programmes which the first Thatcher government and its successors pursued.

Those policies made throughout the 1980s came to be associated initially with 'Thatcherism' and were described as 'New Right' ones to signify the difference between the old and the new Conservative Party. Although the New Politics is difficult to define precisely and there are many different meanings attached to it (Gamble, 1985; Hall and Jacques, 1983, 1990; Riddell, 1983), it is usually identified as the distinctive set of objectives and economic policies pursued by the Conservative governments under Margaret Thatcher, between 1979 and 1990, and those led by John Major subsequently. Their policies incorporated macro, meso and micro objectives.

The macro objectives included reversing Britain's relative economic decline, improving the efficiency of the economy, creating the conditions for economic prosperity, 'destroying socialism' and reasserting Britain's world role. Improving the efficiency of the economy was the core objective. Disillusionment with Keynesian demand management policies and governmental *dirigisme* led the government to look for alternative macro-policy objectives and policy instruments. Underlying them were concerns for facilitating economic efficiency, increasing economic growth and raising economic prosperity. Linked with these were the aims of removing the 'dependency culture' and rolling back the frontiers of the state in order to create a dynamic 'enterprise culture' and free market economy. Socialism, in its variety of forms, was identified with social and economic equality, the suppression of personal initiative and the existence of excessive bureaucracy. Socialism was also associated with trade union power, industrial militancy, restrictions in the labour market and threats to individual freedom imposed by unrepresentative trade union leaders. Destroying socialism was a necessary condition for free enterprise to thrive. Making Britain 'Great' again had nationalistic undertones, emphasising an 'English' perception of Britain's international role in influencing foreign policy initiatives, defending the interests of the 'free world' and protecting her position in the European Community. Yet paradoxically, free market policies aimed at opening up and internationalising the British economy were paralleled by governmental attempts to protect and safeguard the UK's political sovereignty.

The meso objectives were to revitalise private enterprise, increase the competitiveness of British businesses and strengthen the right to manage. Revitalising private enterprise was linked with the goal of undermining and finally destroying socialism in Britain. Increasing business competitiveness was seen as fundamental in counteracting the growing competitive advantage of foreign firms, both domestically and internationally. This was in terms of price, quality and standards of service, in manufacturing and non-manufacturing sectors. Only by remaining competitive, it was argued, could British businesses survive and prosper and raise their share of European and world trade.

Given the Conservatives' commitment to an enterprise culture, their objective of strengthening the right to manage is hardly surprising. It complemented their aim to weaken the trade unions both in collective bargaining and in corporatist politics, as well as providing managers, in both private and public organisations, with greater authority and autonomy in enterprise decision making. This would enable managers, in turn, to react swiftly to changing product markets, to obtain flexibility from their human resources and to increase work-force productivity. In these ways companies could become 'more efficient and more competitive in the marketplace thus boosting the economy and leading to economic growth' (Farnham, 1990, p. 65). Within public organisations, managers would replace administrators and professionals in taking responsibility for using resources efficiently and effectively in the pursuit of governmental goals and objectives.

The micro objectives of Conservative governments included optimising consumer choice and consumer sovereignty in the market-place, freeing individuals from the 'dependency state' and motivating individuals to take personal responsibility for themselves and their families. These objectives were at the heart of the governments' economic and social strategy with its commitment to individualism (Walker, 1990, pp. 30–35). The state's role, by this view, is limited to facilitating the primacy of unfettered markets, to advancing individual freedom in the market-place and to drawing back the boundaries of public provision. It is a minimalist role, encouraging individual freedoms, market opportunities and private enterprise.

These tenets of market individualism within an enterprise culture were stressed by the incoming Thatcher government in its first budget statement (Hansard, 1979). They were:

First the strengthening of incentives, particularly through tax cuts, allowing people to keep more of their earnings in their own hands, so that hard work, ability and success are rewarded; second, greater freedom of choice by reducing the state's role and enlarging that of the individual; third, the reduction of the borrowing requirement of the public sector which leaves room for the rest of the economy to prosper; and fourth, through firm monetary and fiscal discipline bringing inflation under control and ensuring that those taking part in collective bargaining are obliged to live with the consequences of their actions.

These tenets were restated in the Conservative's Election Manifesto in 1992 (Conservative Party Manifesto 1992, pp. 5–7), where it was affirmed that:

In the 1990s, the Government's task will be to provide an economic environment which encourages enterprise – the mainspring of prosperity. Our aims must be:

● To achieve price stability
● To keep firm control over public spending.
● To continue to reduce taxes as fast as we prudently can.
● To make sure that market mechanisms and incentives are allowed to do their job. [and . . .]
● We will reduce the share of national income taken by the public sector.

As Walker (1990, p. 32) points out, such strategies were aimed at transforming economic and social life permanently, not just for the lifetime of a single Parliament. The strategies sought to expand the numbers working in the private sector, to promote the benefits of private housing, transport and pensions and to extend the provision of private health care, 'independent' education and capital ownership.

Deregulating the Economy

The tactical means by which successive Conservative governments attempted to implement their strategic objectives consisted of three main sets of measures. The first was their economic measures designed to increase market competition, foster enterprise and create a 'business' culture. In May 1979, for example, the Thatcher government deregulated financial capital markets by removing the exchange controls. In the following year deregulation of the labour market began with the Employment Act 1980, followed by other Employment Acts in 1982, 1988, 1989 and 1990 and the Trade Union Act of 1984. The government also weakened trade unions by abandoning the post-war commitment to full employment, allowing unemployment to rise and encouraging the market determination of wages. In addition, the government paved the way for a bigger role for the market and private enterprise by creating enterprise zones and development corporations to encourage business expansion, whilst tax cuts left more money for those who were higher income taxpayers for spending, saving and investment.

Another major initiative was reducing the size of the public sector. As later chapters in this book illustrate, various means of 'rolling back the frontiers of the state' were attempted. These included privatising public organisations by selling them off to private shareholders, hiving them off to agencies and contracting out public service functions to private providers. These policies had the triple goals of transferring the supply of these services to the private sector, providing them through the market, or at least quasi-markets, and cutting government expenditure. Privatisation had the further advantage of raising additional revenue from the sale of state assets, so avoiding increases in general taxation to fund government expenditure. During the first Conservative government from 1979 to 1983, the extent of privatisation was modest and took the form of selling off shares in companies such as Amersham International, Cable and Wireless and British Aerospace. By 1992, however, more than 60 companies had been sold to the private sector including the major public utilities of gas, electricity, water and telecommunications. The extent of competitive compulsory tendering (CCT) and contracting out in the public services was also limited in the early 1980s but was widely applied by the end of the decade.

These activities were associated first of all with monetarist and subsequently supply-side economic policy. Monetarism is predicated on the belief that governmental management of the rate of growth of the money supply can control inflation. Supply-side economics posits that governmental intervention should be limited to improving the supply side of the economy, by creating the conditions enabling markets to function efficiently. Both monetarist and supply-side policies were a complete reversal of the Keynesian orthodoxy that managing aggregate demand was the key to economic activity.

Other measures aimed at liberalising the British economy included reducing the planning and development controls by local authorities, strengthening the role of the Monopolies and Mergers Commission and encouraging self employment and the small business sector. All these were directed towards facilitating economic competition and enterprise. The statutory monopolies of many public sector bodies, such as local authority bus services, telecommunication and opticians services, were removed to allow the private sector to enter these markets and to compete with, or replace, public providers. A main advantage of expanding job opportunities to the small business and self-employed sectors was that this flagged up the the ideology of enterprise, wealth creation and self-help. It was also a useful but limited means of reducing unemployment.

A Strong State

The second set of tactical measures used by the New Right governments to implement their objectives was to create a strong state that could carry through its policies without political constraint from either local authorities or powerful pressure groups. Strengthening the role of central government involved using a range of policy instruments. These included: legislation, administrative directives and financial controls. During the 1980s there was an explosion of legislative initiatives, aimed at strengthening central government, weakening local government and making local authorities and other public bodies the agents of central government policies. Legislation was used to strengthen the powers of central government in a number of ways. These included the right to create new public bodies which could carry out its policies and to constrain or prevent other parts of the public sector from acting independently.

On the other hand legislation was used to remove or limit the powers of local authorities. They were compelled to sell council houses, allow schools to opt out of their control and to introduce CCT into a wide range of local authority activities. Examples of where local authorities, and other bodies, became the agents of central government policy were: implementing the government's community care programme after 1990; deregulating local bus services in 1983; transferring what was then non-university higher education into private corporations from 1989; and requiring the nationalised industries to prepare themselves for privatisation from 1983 onwards.

Central government also asserted its control over local government and other public bodies by the use of administrative directives and circulars. They covered areas such as managerial changes in the NHS and the national curriculum for schools. Perhaps the most important set of controls over local government and other bodies was financial. Conservative governments introduced nearly 20 changes in local government finance between 1979 and 1992. These cumulatively removed a great deal of the independence of local government and resulted in central government controlling, directly or indirectly,the expenditure of individual local authorities. 'Over-spending' authorities were initially rate-capped and then community-charge capped. The rating system was abolished and replaced by the community charge and the national business rate. By 1992 less than 25 per of local government revenue was raised locally. Furthermore, local government capital expenditure was subject to ceilings. The financing of the NHS was cash limited and the few remaining nationalised industries were controlled by financial targets and borrowing controls to keep their expenditure within planned limits.

The Conservative governments after 1979 also dispensed with many of the consultative political mechanisms which had characterised the corporatist, participative styles of previous governments. Tripartism involving government, the TUC and the CBI in economic policy making was abandoned. Major constitutional changes, like the abolition of the Greater London Council, were carried out without a public enquiry, whilst radical legislative proposals were introduced with a minimum of time for interested parties to respond (Horton, 1990, p. 182). In industrial relations, a series of green papers was used as the basis for definitive legislation, not for consultative purposes. Former negotiating forums, such as the Consultative Council of Local Government Finance, were reduced at best to information receiving bodies.

Strengthening the traditional responsibilities of the state in the area of law and order and policing, as well as shedding some of its welfare and public service roles, were other tactical means of achieving government political and economic objectives. As Savage (1990, pp. 89–91) states, prior to 1979 law and order policy reflected the consensus politics of the post-war settlement. This changed after 1979 when it was placed high on the government agenda. Whilst many other areas of government expenditure were subjected to a restrictive if not reductionist policy, the law and order budget was increased. There were increases in police manpower, police pay and prison building. There was also a major programme of legislation, reflecting a much harder line on law and order, giving more powers to the police. In parallel with these developments, the government introduced a series of reforms in welfare and public service provision. These were aimed at: encouraging the voluntary sector supply of services; making the public services more efficient through internal and external competition; forcing the public services to prioritise and ration what was provided to citizens in the community; and encouraging individuals to assume personal responsibility for themselves through private insurance.

At international level governments wanted to re-establish a powerful role for Britain, as part of their drive towards a strong centralised state. On taking office in 1979, the government committed itself to making defence the first charge on public resources. 'By 1985–6 the defence budget was one-fifth higher in real terms than in 1978–9. Britain was spending more on defence in absolute per capita terms than any other NATO power except the United States (USA)' (Carr, 1990, p. 239). Conservative governments remained committed to retaining the nuclear deterrent, partly to reinforce the claim that Britain was a world power, and partly to reinforce Britain's 'special relationship' with the USA. Britain's relationship with the European Community was more ambivalent with Conservative governments resisting all attempts to suppress the nation state and British political sovereignty.

Popular Capitalism

The third set of tactical measures used by successive Conservative governments was linked to the goal of popular capitalism. Popular capitalism is 'the term applied to a variety of policies aimed at widening property ownership and consumer choice' (Gamble, 1988, p. 138). It sought to empower individuals by weakening their attachment to the Welfare State, to undermine their belief in the concept of 'society' and to raise public consciousness of the ideas associated with the 'enterprise culture'. Widening property ownership was facilitated by a number of measures. These included enforcing the sale of council homes to their tenants; denationalising major public industries, with proportions of the 'new' shareholdings reserved for individual shareholders; and encouraging employee share ownership schemes and profit sharing in the private sector.

The means used to widen consumer choice focused on advocating the primacy of markets in both the private and public sectors. Deregulation afforded opportunities for private companies to compete with public bodies in such areas as bus transport, telecommunications, hospitals, nursing homes and opthalmic services. Assisted places gave access to private schools, whilst tax relief on health insurance encouraged use of the private health sector.

Conclusion

The politico-economic context within which the public services now operate has changed significantly over the last 20 years. The 1970s saw the weakening of the post-war settlement and the social democratic consensus. This was due, in large part, to the failure of the British economy to generate sufficient growth to support an expanding Welfare State. A new politics emerged founded on the ideas of the New Right, located in the right wing of the Conservative Party. It came to the forefront when Margaret Thatcher led the Conservatives to victory in 1979 and was strengthened by their continuity in office by winning further elections in 1983, 1987 and 1992. Throughout this period a new set of policies was put in place. These were designed to replace the old Keynesian welfarism, to redraw the boundaries of the state and to reassert the primacy of markets over politics as means of allocating resources, distributing wealth and meeting social needs. The unbroken period in office enabled Conservative governments to refine their general objectives and to claim as they entered the 1992 election, that they had transformed the British economy, rolled back the frontiers of the state and brought the best practices of the market and the private sector into public organisations.

The evidence, however, seems to contradict some of their claims. By the early 1990s the British economy was experiencing its second recession since 1979. Although there had been a short-lived boom in the mid-1980s and rapid growth, negative growth was expected in 1992, with British exports falling as a proportion of world trade and imports rising. Investment was at an all time low, private debt was the highest ever recorded and the number of bankruptcies was rising. Businesses were recording falling profits generally and it was predicted that there would be no economic recovery until after 1993. Unemployment was rising again towards the three million mark. Clearly, the government's hopes of a revitalised private business sector had not been fully realised. The evidence that the size of the public sector had been reduced was also contradictory. There had been a fall in the numbers employed from over seven million in 1979 to about five million in 1992; a contraction of over 30 per cent (see Chapter 5). This was due in the main to the privatisation programme, reductions in the armed forces and contracting out policies. However, the main public services had actually expanded and the scope of the public sector, apart from the nationalised industries, had only been trimmed, not radically cut. This was because, in spite of the many changes occurring in the public sector, changes in the economic and social environment had not abated. Cuts in services, increased use of the private sector and increased efficiency had been offset by increased demands from an ageing population for health care, pensions and personal social services. Continuing world recession had inhibited the revival of the British economy and persistently high levels of unemployment meant increases in demand for social support. In addition, public opinion had not been weaned from supporting the Welfare State, particularly the NHS, and this had constrained governments in implementing even more radical policies. As a result, real general government expenditure was higher in 1992 than it had been in 1979 and still accounted for over 40 per cent of GDP.

The replacement of Margaret Thatcher by John Major in November 1990, and his achievement of a Parliamentary majority in the General Election of April 1992, though seen by some as marking a change in Conservative policy, may be viewed more as a change of style and rhetoric than of direction and ideology. There is still the same commitment in the 'new' Conservative Party to transforming the mixed economy into a more regulatory state through implementing free market economic policies, creating an enterprise culture and facilitating popular capitalism. As the Conservative Manifesto stated before the 1992 General Election: 'The challenges of the 1990s demand a responsible and sure-footed government which understands the nature of the achievements of the 1980s and is ready to build successfully on them' (Conservative Party Manifesto 1992, p. 50). It is not too much to claim that the 'new managerialism', in the 'new public services', was and is, to some large degree, a by-product of the ascendancy of New Right ideas and of the new politics in Britain. The managerialist thrust was in part a response by successive governments to Britain's continued economic problems. Without the shift in emphases from politics to markets, from welfare to enterprise and from the 'old' post-war consensus to the 'new model' enabling state, the managerialist ideas and practices, which have been injected into public organisations since the early 1980s, based on private sector orthodoxy, would have been unlikely to have taken root as they have done. It is the issues arising from the new public service managerialism, in the context of the new political economy, which the contributors in this book seek to address.

2

Managing Private and Public Organisations

DAVID FARNHAM and SYLVIA HORTON

The debate about markets and politics and the role of the state in Britain raises the issue whether there are differences between the ways that organisations located in the 'private' and 'public' domains are structured and managed. One view is that the term 'management' refers to a rational approach to organisational decision-making, which is traditionally associated with the private sector. Managers are seen as the agents for achieving organisational goals with the most efficient use of resources. In the public sector, by contrast, the term 'public administration' has been used. This has traditionally been viewed as the process whereby public officials, employed by state agencies, implement and execute governmental policies determined by the political authorities, within a framework of law, and where the efficient use of resources is of secondary importance.

Another view is that 'management' and 'administration' are different terms for describing similar activities. A former head of the civil service has written: 'we tend to use the term administration for the public service and management for business. There is no difference' (Self, 1965, p. 8). The implication is that the practices and activities of managing are generic and that private sector managerial practices are wholly transferable to public organisations and *vice versa*.

A third view is that recent changes in public organisations have led to a new 'public management' which is different from traditional 'public administration' and private 'business management'. Perry and Kraemer (1983) claim that public management merges traditional

27

public administration with the instrumental orientation of business management. A new model of management exists, it is claimed, which reflects the unique nature of public organisations stemming from the scope and impact of their decisions and their fundamentally political character. This chapter examines these views and considers whether managing public organisations is similar to or different from managing in the private sector. In particular it contrasts managing in private businesses with the administration of the public services as a basis for assessing the changes that have taken place since 1979.

Private and Public Organisations

Organisations are social constructs created by groups in society to achieve specific purposes by means of planned and co-ordinated activities. These activities involve using human resources to act in association with other resources in order achieve the aims of the organisation. Private organisations are those created by individuals or groups for market or welfare purposes. They are ultimately accountable to their owners or members. Private organisations take the forms of unincorporated associations, companies, partnerships and voluntary bodies. They vary widely in size and scope, from small scale, local enterprises to large, multinational companies, and provide a wide range of goods and services in the primary, secondary and tertiary sectors of the economy. What basically distinguish private from public organisations, in addition to their goals, ownership and accountability, are their criteria for success which are largely economic or market in nature.

Public organisations are created by government for primarily collectivist or political purposes. They are ultimately accountable to political representatives and the law. Their criteria for success are less easy to define than are those of private organisations and include social and market measures as well as political ones. Public organisations cover a wide range of activities and encompass all those public bodies which are involved in making, implementing and applying public policy throughout the British state. They include the nationalised industries, other public corporations, central departments, local authorities, non-departmental agencies, the NHS and a multiplicity of fringe bodies which are collectively referred to as the machinery of government.

In practice, when it comes to establishing a dividing line between the two sectors, the distinction is blurred and it is difficult to determine where private organisations end and public ones begin. Dunsire (1982, p. 15) suggests that to spend time trying to distinguish private from public organisations 'is a distraction and an irrelevance'. Tomkins (1987) provides a useful spectrum of organisational types, ranging from the 'fully private' to the fully 'public without competition'. He illustrates the interdependence and interrelationships between the market and political spheres. His typology is as follows:

1. Fully private
2. Private with part state ownership
3. Joint private and public ventures
4. Private regulated
5. Public infrastructure, operating privately
6. Contracted out
7. Public with managed competition
8. Public without competition

Tomkins refines the debate of the relative merits of 'markets' and 'politics' by suggesting reasons why organisations might be located at particular points in the above spectrum. Where there are no social issues, and no specific social needs to be protected, and the ability to pay for the organisation's goods or services is seen as a fair mechanism for distributive purposes, fully private organisations are appropriate providers. Where there is potential for social issues to arise, and where governmental action may be needed to protect the public interest, part state ownership is appropriate. Joint private and public ventures are found where there are considerable commercial risks involved, and the private sector is unwilling to bear them. Governmental investment is used to develop the private sector to a point where it can take on the risks and generate its own momentum.

Private regulated organisations exist where the private sector operates within a legal framework imposing requirements and limits on their activities. Regulatory bodies such as the Office of Telecommunications and Office of Gas Supply monitor British Telecom and British Gas respectively. They control standards of provision, examine prices, and in some areas ensure supply of the service. Private regulated organisations are found where there are monopolistic or near monopolistic suppliers and where there is a need to protect consumers and the public interest from a possible abuse of market power.

Some sectors of industry rely upon a public infrastructure, with private organisations supplying and operating a service. Examples are found in transport where governments build and maintain roads or supply airports, with private bus companies, haulage contractors or airlines operating the services. This mode of private/public provision is used to facilitate a wider adoption of market mechanisms but with the state guaranteeing the necessary investment to ensure that the market responds. This underwriting or subsidising of the private sector has been a key feature in Britain.

Contracting out 'public services' to private suppliers has always been open to governmental organisations. Central and local government, for example, have traditionally used private construction companies to build 'public' schools, hospitals, civic centres and so on. They have also obtained supplies of goods and services from private wholesalers or manufacturers and negotiated research contracts with private firms and establishments. This type of market relationship enables the public body to monitor the contractor and is especially appropriate where monitoring quality is important.

There is also the option of internal markets or 'managed competition'. This is where public organisations provide services but are encouraged to compete with one another for either contracts or individual customers. The 'purchaser-provider' system introduced into the health services in 1990 is an example of this. Finally, there are public organisations which provide public goods or services without competition such as defence, policing and the administration of justice.

There are no *a priori* economic reasons why some goods or services should be provided exclusively by private organisations or public ones. Ultimately the relative configuration of private and public organisations in society reflects political choices and priorities, not economic ones. Further, as Tomkins (1987) states: 'the focus should be on the appropriate form of management for each activity rather than ideological support for its location in either the private or public sector'.

Private Sector Management

The distinctive feature of the private sector model of management is that it is largely market driven. This means that the ways in which private organisations are managed reflect the market environment in which they operate. Success, growth or even survival for private organisations depend on the ability of their managerial cadres to manage effectively the dynamic economic environment facing their businesses. Ultimately, it is 'meeting the bottom line' which counts. Unless, over time, private organisations are able to satisfy customer demand in the market, to provide a surplus of revenues over costs and to ensure capital investment programmes for the future, they cease to trade as viable economic units. Private organisations, in short, must be both profitable and economically efficient to survive in the market. The managerial function within them derives from these basic facts of economic life.

Goals and Accountabilities

Every organisation is set goals to achieve by those who govern it. Goals establish the reasons for an organisation's existence. They are important because they act as a guide for decision making and a reference standard for evaluating success. Goals in turn are translated by senior management into objectives and policies which provide the framework and parameters within which operational managers, and their subordinates, carry out their job tasks and activities.

Private organisations tend to have less complex, more easily stated and less disputed goals than those of public organisations. This is because they are basically market centred. Private businesses, for example, have the economic goal of creating a profit both for distributing as dividends to their shareholders and for reinvesting purposes. Second order goals such as organisational growth and expansion, business reputation, market domination, brand leadership and product diversification may be set by managers but these goals are also mainly market driven. They are 'for profit' organisations.

Large business organisations generally have corporate plans detailing how their goals are to be operationalised into specific objectives, over three, five or even ten-year periods. It is this planned, rational approach to objective and target setting, within the boundaries of business goals, which is often singled out as the distinctive feature of the large business sector and of private sector management. Other managerial activities associated with business organisations include: identifying the total business and its markets; forecasting likely changes in the environment; acting to take advantage of market opportunities or averting market threats; and focusing on the needs of the organisation's customers.

Not for profit private organisations, or voluntary bodies, have goals generally concerned with mutual help, the interests of their members or social welfare. Their managements too have to ensure a surplus of revenue over costs or at least break even. They are actively involved in generating funds to finance their activities and, like their profit centred counterparts, have to be organised and managed efficiently and effectively. But their criteria for success are not profit related. In this sense, they have more in common with 'not for profit' public services than private commercial organisations.

All organisations, whether private or public, are ultimately responsible, through their governing bodies, for the actions they take, in seeking to achieve their goals and objectives. They have a duty to use the resources they employ responsibly, and to provide goods or services responsibly, taking into account their obligations to a variety of organisational stakeholders. In the private sector, these include shareholders, employees, suppliers, customers and the community. The principle of organisational or corporate accountability is that the collective responsibilities of private organisations may be enforced by a mixture of market, legal, social and moral imperatives.

Private organisations are held accountable in a number of ways. They are legally accountable to their shareholders who may attend meetings and vote on issues affecting company policy. Shareholders also have the rights to appoint and remove directors, to receive annual reports and accounts and to share in corporate profits. Private organisations are also legally accountable, in part at least, to their employees, suppliers and consumers. Employees, for example, have a set of common law and statutory employment rights. The legal obligations of private organisations to their suppliers are embodied in the law of contract which provides a legal framework around which business organisations build their mutual commercial activities. As far as consumers are concerned, corporate legal accountability is largely through the Office of Fair Trading, which publishes information, proposes new laws and takes action on behalf of consumers. 'Citizen charter' rights are aimed to extend that accountability.

The legal accountability of private organisations to the community incorporates a variety of measures, relating to controls over land use and development, pollution control and noise abatement. The law covering land use and development, for example, attempts to achieve a satisfactory balance between the interests of people within the community and those of business organisations. Pollution control is aimed at minimising the potentially hazardous impacts of effluents and noxious substances released into the air, land or waterways. Legislation is also geared to preventing the damage done to individuals and households by excessive noise levels from factory machinery, motor vehicles, aircraft and so on.

The social and moral accountabilities of private organisations have become more important in recent years as businesses have accepted that they have social responsibilities. These have to be taken into account when their managements take decisions about production, pricing, resource utilisation and the distribution of profits. Private organisations are becoming increasingly customer aware and environmentally conscious. Not to do so can result in lost customers, fines and loss of reputation. Ultimately, however, the accountability of all commercial for-profit organisations is to the market. If they do not satisfy the market they can eventually go bankrupt and cease to do business.

The Managerial Function

In response to their needs to meet the market demands placed upon them, private organisations tend to have a managerial function which is based on 'economistic', 'rationalist' and 'generic' principles. The economistic nature of private sector management is reflected in the market goals and accountabilities of private organisations and in the dominance of economic efficiency as the criterion of success. It also explains why it is that the 'value added' areas of functional management, such as finance, production and marketing, have such high status and standing in them. It is these functional areas of management which are seen as providing the keys to: profitability, efficiency, cost control, productivity, product design, product quality, product innovation, sales growth, market share and market potential. It is success in the market which is ultimately the measure of effective private sector management, nothing else.

The rationalist nature of private sector management derives from the ideas of 'scientific management' and classical management theory, where management and appropriate managerial techniques are allocated a special and crucial role in organisations (Taylor 1911; Urwick, 1944; Fayol, 1949). That role is to achieve the organisation's goals and objectives through planning, organising, staffing, directing, co-ordinating, reporting and budgeting. Managers are expected to take decisions ensuring that the resources needed to achieve market goals and objectives are used economically and efficiently. They claim the right to take these decisions because of their technical skills and on the basis of 'the right to manage'.

The rationalist approach to management also claims that there is a body of managerial knowledge, techniques and skills which managers need to apply to make their organisations successful. Armed with this knowledge and skills, managers can determine appropriate organisational structures, technical systems and division of work. They are also responsible for creating the necessary communication, co-ordination and control systems, integrating the organisation and providing measures of performance. In the rationalist approach to management, managers are the systematic planners and controllers of organisations. As Drucker (1989) writes, management as a system 'expresses the belief in the possibility of controlling [humankind's] livelihood through systematic organisation of economic resources'.

The view of management as largely a generic set of activities and structures common to all organisations had its origins in the early classical school of theorists. But a range of American and other writers in the post-war period created a body of 'modern management principles' which they applied to both private and public organisations (Drucker, 1954, 1974; Herzberg *et al.*, 1959; McGregor, 1960; Rice, 1963; Lawrence and Lorsch, 1969; Mintzberg, 1973). They asserted that management is a universal activity, across organisations. It does not take the same form in all situations and there is no 'one best way' of organising businesses. However, all managers are faced with similar tasks and perform similar roles and managing is a mix of rational decision-making, problem solving and intuitive judgements. This generic approach to managing dominated management theory from the 1950s, and has been reflected in managerial practice in much of the market sector, in both Britain and North America, ever since.

A 'new wave' generic management emerged in North America in the 1980s and found its way into some 'leading edge' British companies during the decade. This focuses on the managing of 'culture, quality and excellence'. It derives from the ideas articulated largely by a series of American managerial 'gurus' who were seeking to provide sets of prescriptive answers to managers for corporate success in increasingly competitive product markets. Their ideas have had a major influence on business education and business literature. One focus is on corporate culture developed by Deal and Kennedy (1982) and Schein (1985). Deal and Kennedy, for example, argue that 'strong culture' is an important element in business success, stating that companies with clearly articulated values and beliefs are often outstanding performers. The concept of 'total quality management', borrowed heavily from Japan, is basically a simple one. It asserts that all work processes are subject to variation which reduces quality and if the level of variation is managed and decreases, quality standards improve. The emergence of excellence as a managerial philosophy is particularly associated with the writing of Peters and Waterman (1982), Peters and Austin (1985) and Peters (1987). In identifying what they perceive to be 'excellent' companies, Peters and Waterman claim these have a number of features. These are: getting on with the job; believing that customers come first; encouraging innovation; treating people as a source of quality and productivity; having leaders who tell employees about corporate values; staying close to the business they know; having simple structures with small corporate centres; and being centred on 'core values'. Peters (1987) also addresses the problem of change, arguing that companies now require flexibility and 'love of change' to replace mass production and mass markets. The latter were based on relatively stable environments which have now vanished. His recipe for corporate success is more quality and flexibility, supported by training of the highest order.

Variants of the economistic, rationalist and generic views of management are observable in many private organisations, rooted in the belief by their managers that these precepts are soundly based in managerial theory and good practice. These approaches are necessary, it is believed, to meet the market demands of economic efficiency and to optimise the chances of organisational success. They derive from the predominantly market goals and market accountabilities of private organisations. To what extent these prescriptive approaches to the managing of resources within organisations actually deliver what they promise, however, has yet to be satisfactorily demonstrated. Managerial practice in the private sector may well be a much more pragmatic and contingent set of activities than the theoretical literature leads us to believe.

The Public Administration Model

The public sector consists of many diverse organisations and it is difficult to generalise about their goals, structures and styles of management. What they have in common is their creation by governments to achieve political goals and to support political objectives and policies. It is this political context which is the driving force behind public organisations and is reflected in the ways they are managed.

Goals and Accountabilities

Managing in the public sector contrasts with the market driven nature of management in private businesses in a number of ways. First, the goals are set by politicians. Second, the criteria of success are relative to the goals set by the politicians and cannot be reduced to a 'bottom line' of profit or loss. Public organisations, it is said, cannot go bankrupt because they do not rely on the market for their revenue. Governments command taxation and public bodies are generally financed wholly or in part from these funds. There is no cash nexus between the suppliers of most public goods and services and their consumers. Commercial public bodies like the nationalised industries, and trading departments of local authorities which charge the public directly, can still be subsidised if they incur deficits. It is often asserted that the absence of market discipline results in inefficiency and waste and that the management function in public bodies is therefore a dilution of the private sector model.

Public organisations are given goals which reflect the purposes for which they exist but, in contrast to those of private bodies, they tend to be complex, vaguely defined and often conflicting. The goals of public organisations are also sometimes unattainable. The reasons are identified by Pollitt (1990, p. 121):

First, there is the need to build and maintain coalitions of support. . . . Second, a broadly-based objective is less likely to give immediate hostages to fortune. . . . [and] it is easier to argue that it has been, at least in part, successful. . . . Third, vague wording . . . [or] 'woolly wording' is . . . attractive in the sense that it provides endless opportunities for defence, evasion and apparent innovation during the process of political debate.

In a liberal democracy, politicians have the task of trying to satisfy many different and disparate interests and integrating these into the policies which public bodies pursue. Therefore, the more general the stated goals, the wider their appeal. It is because of the many different areas of concern for government that their goals may often conflict. For example, a government may be committed to reducing taxation and at the same time expanding education. Governments pursue multiple goals which are also continuously disputed as sectional interests challenge them. Public officials, unlike private sector managers, are also faced with frequent changes of goals as either political pressures force a new negotiated order or changes in political leadership result in new priorities.

The division of responsibilities amongst public organisations is also a consequence of political considerations rather than of logic, economics or organisational principles. It is not uncommon for one level of government to set goals and policies and for another level to implement them in detail. Policies developed by the Department of Education and Science, for example, are carried out by the universities, colleges and local education authorities. The size and complexity of public organisations, and the frequent separation of goal setting and policy implementation, mean there is often a lack of control by policy makers over those carrying out policy. Here a power-dependency relationship emerges in which skill in exploiting political resources replaces any rational process of decision-making or direct form of control.

A further consequence of the multifunctional and interrelated nature of public organisations is their complex structures. Central and local government are both characterised by complex systems of interdepartmental committees and multiple consultative and communication channels. Those responsible for managing these complex systems are often managing the interface between their own organisation and others. Again this is as much a political as a technical role.

As political organisations, public organisations are ultimately accountable to the 'public' which they serve. The 'public' are especially interested in what these organisations do and how they do it. This is because, first, public bodies are often monopoly providers, leaving the public no choice but to take what they supply. Second, public bodies can exercise power to ensure compliance of public laws and regulations, by fining people or even depriving people of their liberty. Third, they provide public and merit goods which directly affect the quality of people's lives. Fourth, they levy compulsory taxation to fund governmental activities. Fifth, they regulate many areas of social life from licensing drinking, driving and entertainment to controlling building designs and land use. Therefore as citizens, consumers and taxpayers, the public are interested in the use of public power, the values reflected in the decisions made, the efficiency with which public money is used and the quality of the services provided.

It is this exercise of public power that necessitates public organisations being held accountable in a democratic society. Public officials are expected to act as stewards of the public interest and of the public purse, as well as being the providers of goods and services. The forms that public accountability takes vary according to the type of agency, the political salience of its activities, the level of government and its particular functions. As Lawton and Rose (1991, p. 17) state, it is difficult to generalise about the process of accountability in the public sector. 'The mechanics of accountability in local authorities are different from those in central government, which in turn vary from those in the NHS'. In practice, public sector accountability takes place in four contexts: legal, political, consumer and also 'professional'.

All public bodies operate within a strict legal framework. Unlike private organisations, which can do anything which the law does not specifically forbid or prevent them from doing, public ones can only do what the law permits and prescribes for them. This legal rule, known as *ultra vires*, means that public officials must be able to point to legal authority for all their actions. Failure to exercise their legal responsibilities, or actions which are in excess of their legal authority, can be mandated or restrained by the courts. Unlike most European countries, there is no system of public courts in Britain. It is the ordinary courts that hold public organisations to account, both for their actions and for the procedures which they use. Public officials are required to demonstrate that they have complied with the substantive law, the procedural law and the rules of natural justice.

Political accountability manifests itself in a number of ways. All public officials are directly or indirectly accountable to a political person or body. Civil servants are accountable to a minister, local government officers to elected councillors and boards of the nationalised industries and the Management Board of the NHS to the appropriate ministers. This model assumes that powers are vested in ministers who are responsible for what public servants do and are accountable, in turn, to Parliament for their actions. Similarly, power is vested in the elected local authority council which is responsible to the public for the actions of their officials. The reality of ministerial responsibility has long been disputed and civil servants are now more directly accountable to Parliament, through its specialist committees, than they were in the past (Drewry, 1989). Local officials also deal directly with the public. In both instances, the ultimate accountability to the public, as the electorate, is through periodic elections and the ballot box. Between elections, the press and pressure groups keep public organisations alert and inform the public of what is happening.

Accountability to the consumers and clients of public organisations is through institutions established to deal with complaints and grievances. Various tribunals deal with appeals against administrative decisions. Where complaints are about maladministration they are dealt with by the Parliamentary, Health Service or Local Government Commissioners. In addition to these external institutions, each public body has its internal complaints procedures. During the 1980s the rights of consumers came to the fore and all public organisations had to look at ways in which they are responsive to and accountable to the public. The *Citizen's Charter* proposes many radical changes including giving limited statutory rights to certain public consumers, thus taking accountability to consumers from the administrative and political realms into the legal one (Farnham, 1992).

Professional accountability is particularly pertinent to the public sector as many public organisations are dominated by professionals such as doctors, nurses, teachers and social workers. Professionals seek not only to control entry to their occupations but also to determine their own methods of work and to police their members. They claim professional autonomy, clinical freedom or academic freedom. It has been argued that they are not accountable to either their clients or their managers and the politicians responsible for the policies they carry out. Professionals claim, in turn, that they are accountable to their professions and to their internal codes of ethics. Complaints against doctors are dealt with by the British Medical Council and against lawyers by the Law Society. During the 1980s there was an attack on public professional bureaucracies, with the imposition of internal managerial structures subordinating the professionals to hierarchical controls. They are now being held increasingly accountable to 'public managers', who may or may not be drawn from among the professionals they supervise.

Administering or Managing?

A dominant perception is that public organisations are administered, whilst private organisations are managed. Both types of organisations have goals, however, both use resources to achieve those goals, and both are held accountable to their stakeholders for the decisions they take and for the ways they use resources. The people responsible for taking the decisions and carrying out the policies and objectives, in both types of organisation, are clearly performing the same role: they are planning, organising, co-ordinating and controlling, in other words, managing. Administration in both types of organisation involves establishing procedures which are designed to link policy with practice, to ensure consistency and to facilitate control. In public organisations, it is these administrative processes that tend to dominate. This gives public organisations their distinctive nature, although this varies from one organisation to another.

An earlier analysis by Keeling (1972) identified a large number of 'systems' within public organisations, reflecting the diversity of their tasks. He argued that only a minority of the systems had the primary task of making the best use of resources. He called these 'management systems', which were found notably in the nationalised industries. Other systems he classified as 'judicial', 'diplomatic' and 'administrative'. These differ in their structures and operational styles from management systems. The latter bear a closer resemblance to private business organisations than do the other systems. The key contrasts between administrative and management systems which he observed were that:

1. Objectives tend to be expressed in very general terms in administrative systems and are rarely reviewed or changed. In contrast management systems have more clearly identified goals and objectives, with specific time scales and targets.
2. The main criteria of success for administrative systems are avoiding mistakes and getting things right. In management systems, the criteria are achieving targets, usually expressed quantitatively.
3. The economical and efficient use of resources are secondary tasks in administrative systems but of primary importance in management systems.
4. Administrative systems tend to have role cultures where responsibilities are precisely defined and there is limited

delegation; structures tend to consist of long hierarchies and there is a tendency to caution and to refer problems upwards. In management systems there is more of a task culture, shorter hierarchies, more delegation and a willingness to take decisions.

5. The role of the administrator is more one of arbitration and rule interpretation. In contrast the manager is a protagonist, looking for opportunities, fighting for resources and taking initiatives.

The key features of administrative systems which Keeling highlighted were that they have mechanistic structures, with long chains of command and narrow spans of control. They are heavily bureaucratised and foster defensive and passive behaviour. Role and status are routinised to constrain discretion. Managerial systems, on the other hand, he suggested, tend to have more flexible structures with less hierarchy. They are task oriented and maximise individual discretion and there is a high level of decentralisation and wider spans of control. The criteria of success in public administrative systems are mistake avoidance, satisfying public expectations of equity and fairness, averting political controversy and achieving consensus, conformity and consistency in practice. The criteria of success in management systems, in contrast, hinge around achieving the goals set for the organisation. Making the right decision is less important than making an appropriate decision, given the elements of risk and uncertainty involved. Managers are judged by their ability to recognise and seize opportunities, to react quickly to changed circumstances and to make profits or avoid losses.

Although both management and administrative systems are found in the public sector, it is the administrative system that has traditionally dominated. This is in part because historically the public services emerged as administrative bodies, supporting political policy makers and law makers and ensuring that the law was implemented. The civil service is still dominated by an administrative élite whose perception of their role is that of policy advisers to ministers and guardians of the public interest. The Fulton Report (1968) confirmed that they did not see themselves as managers, which had an effect on the way in which the service was managed.

The traditional administrative culture is also a consequence of public systems of accountability. Public bodies have monies appropriated by Parliament or local authorities for specific purposes annually. They are required to account for the regularity of their expenditures each year.

This invites a cautious attitude to the use of funds and close scrutiny over each commitment of resources. Any decision to change the use of funds has traditionally required to be vired by the finance department. Bureaucratic administrative structures and systems are also in part a consequence of the size of public bodies, of their dispersal throughout the country and of the need to ensure standard and uniform practices. The law requires that all those entitled to social or welfare rights should receive equal treatment. It also sets down the rules and procedures to be followed. Only bureaucratic practices can ensure that this occurs.

Administrative systems are concerned about the use of resources in so far as they constrain what can be done, but they do not assess success in terms of a narrow economic definition of efficiency – the ratio of resource inputs to product outputs – but in terms of goal effectiveness. As Dunsire (1973) argues, public organisations have to achieve a balance between resource efficiency and goal effectiveness. Self (1971) asserts that those public organisations operating in the market can use 'resource tests' of efficiency but those not operating in the market have to use 'goal tests'. For some operating in the market, but committed to political goals, a mix of policy/resource tests is appropriate. Policy tests are ultimately qualitative and judgemental. They imply a qualitative judgement about not only the goals but also the relative priority to be given to different goals. It is politicians in the final analysis who decide on both the goals and the resources to be used in pursuing them. There is no objective way of determining what the right policies or right amount of resources are. In the market it is the price mechanism which arbitrates, in the public domain it is political choice.

How public organisations are managed derives from these fundamental facts of political life. They are predominantly administratively driven, not management driven. Traditionally, their management systems have emerged out of their administrative systems, not vice versa. In the private sector, the management function precedes the administrative one. In public organisations, because of their primarily political goals and accountabilities, and the priority given to procedures, it is the administrative function which is prior to the management one.

The Managerial Function

The consequences of this are that the managerial function in most public organisations has tended to be 'bureaucratic', 'incrementalist' and 'particularist'. The characteristics of bureaucratic management are specialisation and hierarchy, impersonality and expertise. Those in managerial positions have clearly defined roles within a specialised, hierarchical and horizontal division of labour. Their responsibilities are narrowly defined and circumscribed by rules, with limited discretion. The implications of this are that individual managers do not control the resources used to carry out managerial tasks and responsibilities. Managers cannot vary the mix of resources and are bound by human resource allocations and appropriation budgets determined centrally. Bureaucratic management leads to narrow spans of control and decisions are taken at a high level in the organisation, leading to centralisation. All these features result in slow decision making and delays in responding to the demands made upon them, including the demands of the public as consumers and citizens.

The impersonal nature of bureaucratic management is reflected in the ways that managerial tasks are carried out according to prescribed rules. This is done without arbitrariness or favouritism, with written records kept of each transaction. Public managers are expected to ensure that employees, suppliers and members of the public are treated fairly, equitably and within 'the rules'. This results in predictability and standardisation of procedures and outcomes, although it can produce inflexibility and unresponsiveness to particular needs.

The expertise of public managers has traditionally derived from their skills as either generalist administrators or specialist professionals. The civil service, for example, has traditionally been dominated by the 'administrative generalist', whose expertise has been rooted in understanding the machinery of government and the political process. This has been acquired through experience in various parts of the service as their careers progress. Lower-level managers have also tended to be generalists, with the managers of professional groups, such as lawyers, economists or statisticians, accountable to the generalists. In contrast local government managers, at all levels, have tended to be specialist professionals. Chief officers have normally been drawn from the professional groups they manage such as education officers, directors of social services and town and country planning officers. In the National Health Service (NHS) it has traditionally been the professionals, especially the medical profession, that have dominated the managerial processes. In both these sectors, administrators have provided supportive roles to the managers of professionals.

The incrementalist nature of public management reflects the fact that the perspective of public managers is short term. Planning in public organisations takes place through small changes and limited adjustments to existing policies (Hogwood and Gunn, 1984). The system of financial planning tends to be based upon the annual budget cycle, although most public bodies since the 1960s have produced three-year expenditure surveys. These tend to be little more than forecasts, however, and are not binding. External changes of policy and intra-organisational changes of priorities are constantly confronting public managers. Public organisations, as we have seen, work in a context in which they are interdependent and rely on other public bodies. Local authorities, for example, depend upon the Department of the Environment and Parliament to grant them money each year and to determine the powers and responsibilities they have. The NHS has to accept the pay awards of the Whitley councils and Pay Review Bodies, which are again decided on an annual basis. Operating in a politically dynamic environment also makes rational long term planning difficult for public managers (see Chapter 3).

Changes in political leaders often mean substantial changes in policies. Although there have been some attempts by public organisations to adopt rational decision-making strategies and longer term plans, these have generally been short lived and unsuccessful in the past. The introduction of planned, programme, budgeting and policy analysis reviews in the civil service during the early 1970s, for example, fell victim to the new Labour government and the International Monetary Fund after 1974. The movement to 'corporate management' in local government, following its reform in 1974, was abandoned within a few years after the introduction of cash limits. The problem of rational long term planning is greatest where the process of strategic choice and strategic implementation is separate, as in the cases of education, housing and social services.

Public management is particularist in the sense that there has traditionally been a noticeable absence of general managers in public organisations. Although the managerial structures in the nationalised industries bear a closer resemblance to those in the private sector, and a general management orientation is more evident, this itself is particular to these more market-oriented, commercial bodies. Management in the civil service, local government and the NHS is also particular to those bodies. In local government, for example, there is a tradition of specialist management. In some departments there are professional bureaucracies, as in social service departments. In others there are administrative bureaucracies, as in finance departments. As Chapter 7 points out, specialist management structures, based on particularist traditions, make co-ordination, planning and the rational use of resources difficult in local government and results in managerial fragmentation. Professional managerial bureacracies tend to put service to their clients above resource considerations and resist external controls infringing their autonomy. This has been especially evident in the NHS where doctors have traditionally managed the use of resources and have claimed clinical autonomy in doing so. In the Family Practitioner Services the General Practitioners have arguably not been managed at all.

From the 1960s there was increasing criticism of the managing of public organisations because of their alleged inefficiency and ineffectiveness. This focused on their absence of financial management systems, measures of performance and cost control. In addition, some commentators argued that public managers, particularly top civil servants, did not see themselves as managers and that they lacked appropriate managerial skills. Although some changes occurred during the 1960s and 1970s, no radical reforms took place. It was the election of the Conservative government in 1979 which provided the political impetus to try and bring about a new style public management.

The New Managerialism

There is no generally agreed and precise definition of the term 'managerialism'. A succinct one is provided by Pollitt (1990, p. 1) who sees 'managerialism [as] a set of beliefs and practices, at the core of which burns the seldom-tested assumption that better management will prove an effective solvent for a wide range of economic and social ills'. He identifies five elements in managerialist analyses. These are: social progress requires continuing increases in economic productivity; productivity increases come from applying sophisticated technologies; the application of these technologies can only be achieved through a disciplined work-force; 'business success' depends on the profession-alism of skilled managers; and to perform their crucial role managers must have the right to manage.

The 'new managerialism' which emerged in Britain during the 1980s is not simply a public sector phenomenon. It pervades both private sector and public organisations. As the then Secretary of State for the Environment wrote: 'Efficient management is a key to the [national] revival. . . . And the management ethos must run right through our national life – private and public companies, civil service, nationalized industries, local government, the National Health Service' (Heseltine, 1980). In the private sector, the growth of the new managerialism has been essentially market driven. With the opening up of both British manufacturing industry and financial services to increasingly fierce European and international competition, the corporate sector had to adapt to these new market conditions. In reaction to these forces, private businesses looked to increases in productivity, greater job flexibility, more investment in the new technologies, more job restructuring and better management to help them cope with turbulent, unstable market conditions.

These changes have sometimes been enforced upon frightened and reluctant work-forces by 'macho' styles of management. In other cases, managements have used more sophisticated styles of managing aimed at getting greater employee commitment to corporate goals and enterprise success, through improved performance and quality programmes. In all cases, it is the skills and competences of their professional managerial cadres which are seen to be the key to organisational survival and success. Their position was strengthened during the 1980s and early 1990s by rising unemployment, weakened trade unions and changes in employment law, which shifted the balance of bargaining power away from employees towards employers (see Chapter 5).

In the public sector, the thrust towards managerialism has been politically driven. In essence it is predicated on the view that private sector economistic, rationalist and generic management is the ideal model of management to be aimed at. It is seen as being superior to the public administration or public management models and, if the efficiency and quality of public service provision is to be improved, then private sector management practices and ideologies need to be imported into public organisations. There is also a political agenda underpinning public service managerialism. As Pollitt (1990, p. 49) writes, for the New Right

better management provides a label under which private-sector disciplines can be introduced to the public services, political control can be strengthened, budgets trimmed, professional autonomy reduced, public service unions weakened and a quasi-competitive framework erected to flush out the natural 'inefficiencies' of bureaucracy.

The new managerialism, in short, was a distinctive element in the policies of the New Right towards the public services.

Throughout the public services, since the early 1980s, there appear to have been three main managerialist thrusts, although there were variations of them within each of the services. First, there was tighter control of spending, involving cash limits and 'manpower budgets', constraints on spending and financial and staff cuts. Second, there has been a movement to decentralise managerial responsibilities and functions. This has resulted in more devolved budgetary systems, giving more responsibility to line managers, more emphasis on organisational responsiveness to 'consumer' and 'client' interests and a growth in management education and training. Third, a strengthening of the line management function has taken place by introducing new planning systems, emphasising the achievement of concrete, short term targets. These have been accompanied by the development of performance indicators, stressing economy and efficiency, the measurement of the achievements of these targets, and the provision of merit pay awards or promotion to those individuals getting results. The introduction of individual staff appraisal, on a more formal and extensive basis than had existed before, has been linked with this.

Implicit in the shift towards managerialism in the public services has been an assumption that a bureaucratic, incrementalist and particularist managerial function should be superceded by a more economistic, rationalist and generic model. The economistic nature of the new managerialism is reflected in the increasing importance paid to accountancy procedures within the public services (see Chapter 4). The desire to make public expenditure go as far as possible to produce efficiency and 'value for money' is one indicator of this. Another is the financial responsibilities increasingly being delegated to civil service agencies, local authority services, hospital trusts, schools, colleges, universities and other bodies. Such changes have been facilitated by the application of modern information technologies, sophisticated software systems and 'hi-tech' capital investment. There is also the introduction of compulsory competitive tendering across the public services, with its emphasis on costing, quality service provision, economic efficiency and value added.

For the first time, many middle and lower level public officials have responsibilities for identifying costs, monitoring the way that money is spent and accounting for the financial performance of their units or sections. Containing and controlling spending has become a major objective for public managers. Public managers are also having to devise criteria for measuring and evaluating the efficiency of their organisations. Such quantifiable measures and criteria include: unit costings; efficiency indicators; productivity ratios; service quality indicators; and numbers of transactions completed.

The rationalist nature of the new managerialism is demonstrated, amongst other things, by the introduction of mission statements, strategic goals and corporate plans into public service organisations. Mission statements, for example, set out an organisation's ground rules for 'doing business', whilst corporate and business plans provide targets to be aimed at and achieved. An example of a mission statement is provided by the Department of Social Security before it became an agency. It stated that 'Our Business is Service' which is 'Fair', Efficient' and 'Responsive'. 'All customers must be treated equally', with efficiency meaning 'being on time, and right first time' and staff being responsive 'to the public's need' (Central Office of Information, 1989). Reference was made to 'value for money', providing clear explanations of 'how decisions on claims are reached' and having 'a business-like atmosphere . . . for customers whenever necessary.'

The rationalist context within which public management increasingly operates is further illustrated by the framework document of the Driver and Vehicle Licensing Agency of the Department of Transport (Department of Transport, 1990). The Agency's stated goal is 'to secure a progressive increase in efficiency and effectiveness in the registration and licensing of drivers and vehicles and the collection of vehicle excise duty'. Its aims are:

- to improve customer service;
- to secure value for money through the optimum use of technology, material resources and investment;
- to help staff give of their best.

To achieve these aims DVLA will produce and effect Corporate and Business Plans including measures to:

- reduce unit costs and maximise efficiency;
- improve speed of turnround of transactions and other measures to improve the quality of service to customers;
- improve the collection and the enforcement of Vehicle Excise Duty;
- assist the pursuit of the wider transport policies of the government in the UK and Europe;

- provide a full (IT) service to meet its own requirements and those of agreed clients;
- develop the skills, efficiency and job satisfaction of its staff through training and development, effective management practices, communication and good working conditions.

The shift from particularist management to generic management in the public services is demonstrated by a number of changes which have taken place. Four key ones are: first, public management is increasingly dominated by general managers, rather than by specialist managers or professionals; second, it is more objective driven, rather than problem driven; third, its managers are now more prepared to facilitate change, rather than to resist it; and, fourth, managers now behave as if the public are their main concern, rather than other groups such as their staff. Chief executives, for example, head more than 70 'Next Steps' agencies in the civil service. General managers with programme or directorate responsibilities now populate the new style local authorities. General managers have been appointed throughout the NHS since 1984. And headteachers are now managers of their schools, rather than administrators. Although many of these general managers have professional qualifications, they are appointed for their general management skills. Mobility between public sector organisations and between the public and private sectors is increasing, although it has not been as great as governments have wanted. General managers have responsibility for budgets, operations and personnel. And line management has been strengthened at the expense of consensus management, at least below top strategic levels.

General managers are now driven by objectives, plans, budgets and performance indicators. Individual performance reviews, merit pay and performance related pay ensure that staff also focus on agreed objectives. Although managers still respond to problems, they are now expected to be proactive in anticipating and avoiding them. Managers are also at the centre of managing change in the public services. There have been significant changes within and across the public services since the early 1980s. Managing cultural change has been a major responsibility of the new general managers. Without changing the values, beliefs and expectations of those working in the public services, managers cannot achieve the objectives set for them. The cultural, behavioural and structural changes which have occurred have had considerable impacts on managerial, employee and client attitudes and in the ways in which the public services are being delivered. A new 'public service ethos' has become the focus for much of the public sector. The emphasis is on doing things right and providing services which meet the needs of the customer, not of the organisation. Public service managers are now much more 'customer aware' and client oriented, compared with the past. They are less concerned with worker-related problems than with other issues, such as keeping their customers happy. Quality of service has become a major concern for most public managers.

This was reinforced by the publication of the White Paper, *The Citizen's Charter* (Prime Minister's Office, 1991). It has four themes: quality, choice, standards and value. It seeks to achieve: published standards of service; consultative arrangements with the public; clear information; courtesy and efficiency from named staff; user-friendly complaints procedures; and independent validation of performance. *The Charter* provides a set of principles and a programme of specific measures aimed at improving public services during the 1990s. Its proposals are wide ranging and cover the Post Office, benefits offices, job centres, the railways, roads, the police, courts, town halls, council houses, hospitals, schools and prisons. It is primarily about the standards of customer service provided to people using the public services. The success of *The Charter* will depend, to a large extent, on managers in the public services and their staff. It envisaged that it is at the point of delivery, where the individual citizen comes directly into contact with public workers, that *The Charter* will become a reality. It epitomises the shift towards generic management principles in the public services during the 1980s and the move to a more service-oriented culture.

Conclusion

This chapter has set out to demonstrate the similarities and differences between managing private and public organisations. The similarities are that managing each type of organisation involves operating within strategic choices, determining goals, providing means to achieve them, using resources efficiently and ensuring the quality of their outputs. Both have their administrative systems and both are held accountable to their principal stakeholders.

Public service management remains distinct and separate from much of private sector practice, however, because it is contingent on factors which are unique to public organisations. These factors include: control by elected politicians; the specific legal framework of public service organisations; their relative openness; and their accountability to a diverse range of public watchdogs. All these factors constrain managerial discretion, structures and styles in the public services. The differences between managing private and public organisations derive, ultimately, from their contexts and orientations. The context of the private sector is that it is market driven, whilst that of the public services is that they are politically driven. Private sector orientation is towards meeting consumer demands, as a means of making profits, and public sector orientation is towards satisfying political demands, as a means of achieving political integration and social stability. Outputs can be quantified in the private sector but they are more qualitative, and less easily measured, in the public domain.

There is evidence, however, of some convergence between managing private and public organisations since the early 1980s. This has been described as the 'new managerialism' or the new 'public management'. Many private management techniques are now being widely used in the public services and the language and practices of 'business' are becoming common to the public sector. Compared with the past, public service managers are now increasingly concerned with marketing their services, measuring their inputs and outputs, achieving customer satisfaction and being financially accountable. The 'new' public service management is becoming distinctly managerialist in the sense that the responsibility for achieving organisational efficiency and success, and carrying out public policy, is being firmly placed upon public managers, especially the new genre of general managers, and their management structures. Public managers are increasingly seen by political policy makers as the agents of resource efficiency, enterprise initiatives and 'business' effectiveness. Their managerial role is still limited, however, by the fact that, as public managers, they are constrained by the overall resource decisions and policy boundaries made by the politicians in the first place.

It is this subordination to politics rather than to the market which is the essential distinction between public and private organisations. Managing public organisations can never be exactly the same as managing private companies. The convergence which is happening is in the ways that: organisational resources are being managed, emphasising economy and efficiency; public service organisations are becoming more 'customer' and 'client' centred; many operational decisions, such as financial and staffing ones, are being devolved to senior, middle and lower tier managers. It is these themes which are explored in the next part of the book and the case studies.

Part II

Managerial Functions

3

Strategic Management

HOWARD ELCOCK

What organisations do and how they do it are the results of decisions
taken about goals and objectives and the means of achieving them.
These major decisions affect the performance of an organisation and
influence its success and survival. 'How these major or strategic
decisions are made and how they are implemented can be defined as the
process of strategic management' (Bowman, 1990, p. 1). Strategic
management is basically concerned with two main types of activity.
The first is the making of strategic choices – setting the directions in
which the organisation is to move in the future. The second is strategic
implementation – ensuring that the organisation has the right
structures, processes and culture to carry out the policies determined
by the strategic choices its governors have made. Both of these
activities imply planning, together with an attempt to identify and
achieve stated organisational goals and objectives within a given
environment, over time.

There are a number of approaches to strategic management ranging
from the highly rational, logical and structured approach associated
with corporate planning to the *ad hoc*, opportunistic or reactive
approach associated with crisis management. As Bowman (1990, p. 2)
suggests: 'Between the extremes of corporate planning, on the one
hand, and completely *ad hoc*, reactive decision making on the other
there lies a range of strategic decision-making styles'. Small
organisations operating in a fast changing, unpredictable environment
would be most likely to adopt the reactive, *ad hoc* approach. Larger
organisations needing to take a longer term view, because of the lead-
time involved in investment or the high cost of not planning, will be

more likely to choose the rational systematic style and approach outlined in Figure 3.1.

FIGURE 3.1   *Rational model of strategic management*

Analysing the problem

↓

Identifying coorporate objectives
and values

↓

Identifying alternative programmes
and options and evaluating against
objectives

↓

Costing alternative options

↓

Taking a strategic decision

↓

Drawing up plans and budgets
to implement strategy

↓

Monitoring and control

Approaches to and styles of strategic management are contingent upon various factors. One of these is the location of the organisation in the public or private sector, another is the fundamental purpose or objective of the organization. A significant factor is whether the organisation is 'for profit' or 'not for profit'. If the purpose is to make a profit, then managing the organisation's strategy is more straightforward, as all choices and options can be evaluated against the profit objective. In not for profit organisations, especially those in the public domain, there is no unattested goal which provides a criterion for choosing options. As Chapter 2 shows, there are many stakeholders in public organisations and their goals are multiple and complex and frequently disputed. The absence of a bottom line (like profit) means that strategic management in public organisations lacks clarity and certainty in making decisions and the process inevitably involves making political judgements in seeking to satisfy or integrate the multiple and disparate interests involved. Goals will have to be constantly adjusted if those political judgements are strongly disputed. In the public services, until fairly recently, most attention has focused on how strategic choices are made, partly because of the statutory obligations imposed on public authorities to prepare strategic plans of various kinds, but above all because of the political direction to which all public service organisations are subject. In recent years, more attention has been given to problems of strategic implementation, partly because of the record of failures to achieve strategic policy goals and partly because of the increased pressure on resources. Use has been made of various techniques and models such as Strengths, Weaknesses, Opportunities and Threats (SWOT) analysis which have been developed in the private sector. This chapter traces a process of development, decline and revival in strategic management, in which an almost total concentration on strategic choice has become a more balanced consideration both of how strategic choices are made and how their implementation is to be assured.

Reducing Uncertainty

There is one fundamental problem which must be faced by all those involved in or advocating the development of strategic management: how to avoid trying to do too much while still producing plans which commend themselves to those who must accept and implement them as a better way to develop their organisations and activities than simply applying the 'Science of Muddling Through' (Lindblom, 1959). This need to secure support exists even, or perhaps especially, on the many occasions when a plan is prepared to meet a statutory obligation, such as the duty imposed on local authorities to prepare structure and local plans under the Town and Country Planning Act 1968 or to prepare transport policies and programmes under the Transport Act of the same year (Hampton 1991). Again, the National Health Service Reorganisation Act 1972 required health authorities to prepare strategic plans covering the next ten years, together with operational plans covering a three year period (Brown, 1978; Elcock and Haywood, 1980).

There have been many instances of strategic planning systems which have failed or lost their credibility because they have tried to tackle too many issues, analyse too much information or appease too many conflicting interests. Prominent among them were the attempts on both sides of the Atlantic to introduce planning, programming, and budgeting systems into the financial management of public authorities (Wildavsky, 1980). In consequence, some of strategic planning and management's more recent advocates have sought consciously to restrict the ambitions of planners and their systems. For instance, Bryson (1988) has encouraged strategic managers in the public sector to aim to achieve a series of 'small wins' as steps towards the eventual achievement of a 'big win', rather than aiming directly for the latter.

One way of restraining strategic managers from over-ambitious and therefore unrealistic approaches to their task is to encourage them to adopt a selective approach to making strategic choices such as that offered by Friend and colleagues (Friend and Jessop, 1969; Friend, Power and Yewlett, 1977; Friend and Hickling, 1987). They regard strategic choice as essentially a process of solving the problems posed for the organisation by its environment, by reducing uncertainty about them. Since the strategist's task is always essentially to look into the future in order to develop policies and management approaches for coping with it, uncertainty is inescapable.

One must not overdo scepticism about the value of strategic planning based upon the inevitability of uncertainty. It may be possible to reduce uncertainty in many ways. For example, population projections indicate problems which are likely to require attention, such as the consequences for managers in the National Health Service (NHS) and local authority social services departments of the 'age explosion' generally or in specific locations such as seaside resorts which are turning into 'sunset cities'. Again, current birth-rates provide an indication of the likely demand for primary school places five years hence, secondary education in around 11 years' time and higher education in 18-20 years' time. However, one must always be aware of the dangers in assuming that the future will always be like the past.

Because strategic choice must in essence be a process of trying to make statements about the future on the basis of which strategic management can be predicated, uncertainty needs to be reduced. Organisations can move towards the taking of strategic (or indeed other) decisions by considering the reduction of uncertainty along three dimensions, as illustrated in Figure 3.2.

FIGURE 3.2 *Managing uncertainty over time*

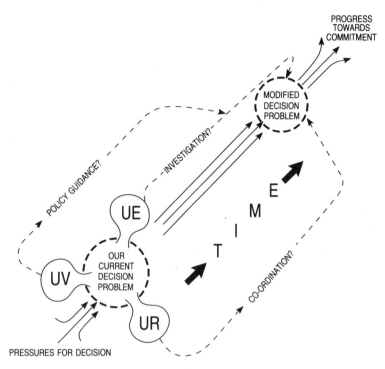

Source: Friend and Hickling (1987).
Key: UE = uncertainty about the environment
UV = uncertainty about values
UR = uncertainty about organisations

Uncertainty about the Environment

Here the need is to acquire more information, whilst remembering that collecting information is both costly and time-consuming. Furthermore, it is likely that the closer we attempt to get to complete certainty, the costlier our search for it is likely to become. Thus a systematically drawn sample of between one and two thousand individuals can offer up to a 98 per cent probability of accurately reflecting the views or attributes of a much larger population at a small fraction of the cost of conducting a census of the entire population. Information is not only expensive to obtain but also time-consuming for the policy-maker to absorb.

Government departments and other government agencies have been supplied with information by the Central Statistical Office since 1941 and each also has its own statistical division. Local government has its own statistical service provided by the Local Government Management Board. The statistical services are a source of data on the basis of which forecasts, projections and estimates about the future can be made. There is much evidence, however, that the statistical services have not always supplied information which is in a form that is useful and that more often there are gaps in what information is collected.

An indication of a felt need within the central government for the systematic collection and analysis of information was first referred to in the Fulton Report (1968) which recommended that government departments should have policy units responsible for major long-term policy-planning and the assembly and analysis of information required for its planning work. Although most departments set up such units their role was very limited. In the 1980s the need was still felt and this led to the development by all government departments of management information systems. Their purpose is to enable managers at all levels, but especially ministers, to see where resources are being spent and what they are being used for, in the expectation that both ministers and managers will be able to redirect resources so that they may be used more efficiently and effectively. Michael Heseltine's MINIS (Management Information for Ministers) system, which he introduced at the Department of the Environment in 1980, is the best-known one, but every department now possesses such an acronym and the management information system that it denotes (Hennessy, 1989). They provide a top management system able to review the department's aims, examine its 'businesses' and the 'customers' it serves and set objectives and establish priorities. However, their main purpose so far has been to increase the efficiency and effectiveness of resource use rather than to develop strategic plans.

Uncertainty about Values

Strategic and indeed all managers need to know what they are expected to achieve. They therefore have to obtain from those responsible for setting organisational goals, who in public service organisations are ultimately elected representatives, what values they hope their managers are seeking to realise and what objectives they should be seeking to achieve. This may be relatively straightforward in one-party states or in local authorities where one party is assured of perpetual control of the council, but it is more difficult where power is shared, as in coalition governments or hung councils or where control changes hands frequently. These cases pose particular problems for strategic planners and strategic managers, whose work is essentially long term, because the values preferred by elected members may change, perhaps drastically, every few years or more often. In consequence, strategic managers may adopt consensual policies which are likely to survive changes in control (Elcock 1975, 1979a, 1985).

Uncertainty about Related Organizations

It is very rare that any single organisation possesses all the means to achieve its objectives and secure the implementation of its policies (Pressman and Wildavsky, 1973; Barrett and Fudge, 1982). The co-operation of other departments, other public agencies, private firms and voluntary bodies is likely to be needed if strategic plans are to be carried out, but that co-operation cannot be automatically assumed. Other organisations may be pursuing different values or have to take cognizance of conflicting interests. For instance, county councils can take a strategic view about where sites for travelling people ought to be provided but district councils are likely to resist proposals to establish sites in particular locations because of pressure from local residents upon whose support their members are more dependent than are the members of the county council (Elcock, 1979b). Here, the strategic manager must assume the role of the 'reticulist', assisting individuals and organisations to communicate and negotiate with one another. This role is described by Friend, Power and Yewlett (1977, p. 364) as follows:

> Whatever his formal status, [a reticulist] must first be able to appreciate the patterns of interdependence between those present and future problems which may impinge significantly on his own current field of concern. . . . At the same time, he must be able to appreciate the structure of relationships, formal and informal, between roles in the decision process, so as to understand the political costs and benefits of activating alternative forms of communication with other relevant actors, both in his own and other organisations.

Hence reticulists are individuals or organisations that facilitate communication among the actors involved in a decision area, negotiating agreement to common approaches to the problems with which the actors must deal. Otherwise, nothing will happen despite the pleas of the strategists.

Reticulist roles become even more important as local authorities and other public bodies become increasingly reliant upon other organisations to provide services for them, instead of providing those services themselves. The contracting out of much local government and NHS work entails the establishment of a series of relationships between the public authority which has the responsibility for ensuring that the service is provided to an adequate standard, and the contractors that have been allocated the task of actually providing it. This web of relationships will be especially complicated in the field of community care when the government's community care policies are implemented. Under the new arrangements the care of many client groups, including the mentally and physically handicapped and the infirm elderly, will be undertaken by health authorities, voluntary agencies, private contractors and others and co-ordinated by local authority social services departments. In order to maintain communication and ensure the development of coherent care for a wide range of weak and vulnerable clients, members of social services departments will need to develop considerable reticulist facilities and skills.

This kind of analysis leads to three conclusions about what constitutes a realistic approach to strategic management. The first is that we cannot plan or proactively manage everything all the time. Instead, we must adopt 'key issue' approaches to making strategic choices under which planners and managers confine themselves to tackling those issues which are most urgent and important at the present time, by seeking to reduce the uncertainty surrounding them. It follows that today's strategic plan is not immutable because tomorrow new key issues may emerge to which managers must attend. Equally, some current key issues may lose their importance if, for example, the scale of values to be implemented is changed. Second, it becomes apparent that the strategic management process is at least as important as the final outcome or, as Eddison (1973) states, 'planning is more important than plans'. The process of collective learning produces benefits beyond those offered by the final plan document itself (Schon, 1975). The third conclusion is that strategic management is a repetitive learning cycle not a linear progression towards a clearly defined final destination. We may have final goals in mind but we move towards them, perhaps erratically, by going through a series of learning cycles, not by a straight line progression through a series of intermediate states. Strategic management is therefore not like a train journey. It is rather like trying to find the right exit from a traffic island – which then only feeds us into the next island!

Making Strategic Choices

The object of the strategic planning process and hence of strategic management is not, then, simply arriving at a final definition of an ideal state, coupled with a route map of how to get there. It is rather an attempt to produce by processes of reducing uncertainty a series of statements which will guide individuals, groups and organisations in their day-to-day and detailed decision-making. Hence, the propositions promulgated by strategic planners and managers should have three attributes.

First they should be general statements about the policy objectives to be sought and the major future developments which are to be encouraged, which command sufficient support to have some assurance of implementation. A set of such propositions constitutes a strategic plan, which should also possess an overall logic which gives the individual choices coherence. That logic must be heavily influenced by the political environment and values within which strategic choices are being made. There is no point in expecting a Conservative government to implement collectivist goals. Equally a Labour-controlled council is unlikely willingly to accept policies which promote unrestricted free markets. Also, to secure implementation, strategic propositions must at the very least not be opposed by any interest or group of interests which have sufficient power to impede or block implementation of the proposition (Banfield, 1961).

Second, strategic propositions need to be statements about the future which raise actors' eyes beyond their immediate preoccupations. Thus a financial plan worthy of the name should extend beyond the present or immediately coming financial year. The Public Expenditure Survey (PES) as advocated by the Plowden Report (1961) and established in 1963 was precisely such an attempt to project forward the consequences of present spending decisions beyond the immediate budgetary horizon, so as to indicate what resources are likely to be available for new initiatives in years to come (Heclo and Wildavsky, 1973; Gray and Jenkins, 1985). This aspiration remains theoretically on the books despite the degeneration of the Public Expenditure Survey system into a 'formidable bulwark of inert incrementalism' (Hayward, 1975, p. 291) in which it is used to strike a series of bargains between the Treasury and the spending departments each year. We should also note that in 1980 the Thatcher government shortened the PES planning horizon from five years to three.

Third, strategic propositions are also contextuating. Etzioni (1968) argues that the decisions that individuals, including managers, groups and organisations need to take can be divided into two classes. The first is general or contextuating decisions which determine the policies to be pursued. Within these contextuating policies, routine or 'bit' decisions can be taken incrementally until increasing protests or other indications of policy stress suggest that a new or revised contextuating policy should be set. Hence the strategic plan also provides a means for co-ordinating the activities of the different departments which make up a government, a local authority or other public agency, as well as a set of propositions which can be used to negotiate co-operation among the different organisations whose powers, resources and capabilities must be used to secure the implementation of the policies of the strategic manager. It sets the framework within which reticulists must manage individual and organisational relationships. However, Etzioni leaves unresolved the question of how initially to identify the appropriate issues to be regarded as contextuating. Such an approach to strategic planning was developed in the Town and Country Planning Act 1968. Under the 1968 Act, district councils are required to prepare local plans covering particular areas or issues within the policies laid down by county councils in their structure plans. The latter plans alone require approval by the Secretary of State for the Environment. The policies laid down in the structure plan therefore provide the setting both for the preparation of more detailed local plans and for the determination of individual planning applications.

It follows that strategic management consists in developing the procedures needed for the consistent resolution of individual questions and grievances, as well as for the preparation of plans for smaller spaces and lesser issues than those dealt with as the 'key issues' which have been identified as requiring treatment in the strategic plan itself.

Strategic Failures and their Consequences

Much of the above must seem self-evidently desirable to many students of public policy and management. Yet strategic policy planning suffered a major loss of support and credibility which resulted in its eclipse for much of the 1980s (Vidal, 1990). Thus in 1983 the government decided that the Greater London Council and the six metropolitan county councils ought to be abolished because their establishment in 1972 had reflected 'a certain fashion for strategic planning, the confidence in which now appears exaggerated' (Department of the Environment, 1983). Strategic planning went into decline for several reasons. In the first place, it took too long to prepare strategic plans. Many of the development plans prescribed by the Town and Country Planning Act 1947 took between 15 and 20 years to prepare, from initiation to gaining ministerial approval. Although the Department of the Environment (1974) urged the new county councils to adopt a 'key issue' approach to preparing their structure plans, many of these plans were not completed until the early 1980s (Caulfield and Schulz, 1989), although a few were completed much more quickly (Elcock, 1985).

Again, the strategic plans which Regional and Area Health Authorities were required to prepare under the 1976 NHS Planning System took several years to prepare and seemed to consist largely of defences of local interests and priorities against the Secretary of State's policy priorities (Elcock and Haywood, 1980). The plans were to be prepared within sets of guidelines prepared by the Department of Health and Social Security (DHSS) and elaborated by Regional (RHAs) and Area Health Authorities (AHAs) in their turn. The preparation of strategic plans then began with the District Management Teams (DMTs), whose plans were aggregated and added to by the AHAs. The Area Plans were then brought together and again added to by the RHAs for transmission to the DHSS. The process is illustrated in Figure 3.3.

Unfortunately, the DHSS was unable to produce either the planning system blueprint or the first sets of guidelines until 1976. By then the health authorities had already been operating and developing their services for two years. In consequence, the first strategic plans were not prepared until 1978. The DHSS attempted to use the NHS planning system to bring about a reallocation of resources in favour of underfunded services, such as primary care, geriatrics and the care of

FIGURE 3.3   *The flow of guidelines and plans in the NHS*

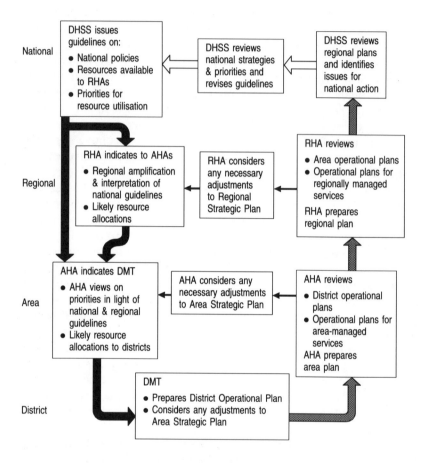

Source: Department of Health and Social Security (1976) *The NHS Planning System*, Her Majesty's Stationery Office.

the mentally ill and handicapped, by procuring reductions in spending on acute and maternity services. However, this policy was widely resisted by the health authorities and DMTs, largely because it was unacceptable to the medical profession and above all to the hospital consultants (Elcock and Haywood, 1980). In 1982 the NHS planning system was simplified, after the abolition of AHAs and the replacement of both AHAs and DMTs with 192 District Health Authorities (DHAs). Planning now consists chiefly of annual review meetings between the Secretary of State and the RHA chairpersons. At these meetings, the minister requires to know how far the RHAs have complied with government policies. RHA chairpersons, in turn, ask the same questions of their District Health Authority chairpersons at annual review meetings held in each region. The future of this system is itself uncertain as radical changes are taking place in the NHS, which are examined in Chapter 8.

The seemingly interminable delays in preparing strategic plans, together with often publicised disputes over their content among the various agencies involved in their preparation, caused increasing disillusionment. In consequence, the public came increasingly to support the 'New Right' policies of the Conservative Party under Margaret Thatcher's leadership, which concentrated on limiting the role of the state, including its interference in citizens' lives, as well as securing increased economy and efficiency in the provision of such public services as could not be privatised or otherwise exposed to market forces. Both as a matter of ideological conviction and one of personal predilection (Blackstone and Plowden, 1988), the Thatcher governments heavily discounted attempts at long term planning in the public services – as indicated by their early reduction of the PES planning horizon from five years to three. Nicholas Ridley, when he was Secretary of State for the Environment, proposed in 1986 that county council structure plans should be abolished, partly on the ground that they took too long to prepare (Department of the Environment and Welsh Office, 1986). It was also because authoritative state planning conflicted with the government's preference for market-led action.

A second issue was that although local government planning authorities accepted the recommendations of the Skeffington Report (1969), about the need to encourage public participation in the preparation of strategic plans, many citizens still see 'the planners' as a sort of high priesthood which stands aloof from the concerns of ordinary people (Wildavsky, 1973). Furthermore, planners sometimes appear to be pursuing planning ideologies which are unsympathetic to the views and aspirations of their local communities (Gower Davies, 1973). Disillusion with planning was only an extreme case of a more general public disenchantment with the paternalistic professionalism which dominated many public services, which new approaches such as the 'Public Service Orientation' have sought to correct (Stewart, 1986; Clarke and Stewart, 1988).

Third, strategic planning must by definition be corporate planning, therefore it challenges the established professional interests and views of those working in central government and local authorities, including those of the planners themselves. Equally, many of the senior officers who are responsible for major public services tend to regard corporate meetings with colleagues in other departments with whose activities – as they see it – they have little concern, as a waste of time and an unnecessary distraction from the job of providing the service for which they are responsible. In consequence, even after the appearance of the Bains Report (1972) and its widespread formal adoption by local authorities after reorganisation in 1974, corporate management met with a great deal of resistance, and by the end of the 1970s many of its advocates had lost their enthusiasm for it (Haynes, 1980).

The strategic planner may be an arrogant high priest in relation to the ordinary citizen whose planning application has been refused, but he or she is also regarded as an irrelevant nuisance by a director of social services who is swamped by a succession of crises about child abuse or neglect of old people. However, there is some evidence to show that in the early 1990s some local authorities are again increasing their capacity for strategic and corporate planning, often by the creation of chief executive's departments which can pull together financial, legal and other expertise, as well as exerting more influence over the service departments (Isaac-Henry and Painter, 1991).

Fourth, uncertainty was in any case greatly and sometimes deliberately increased by the Conservative governments after 1979. Indeed, it can be argued that if perfect competition is established as the desirable model to be copied by public policy-makers, uncertainty becomes a value to be promoted: it becomes a 'good thing'. The repeated shifts in the local government grant distribution rules which occurred during the Thatcher years, with nine major changes being made in the first five years, created such a climate of uncertainty that most local authorities abandoned their efforts at developing financial planning systems (Elcock and Jordan, 1987). This uncertainty actually caused local authorities to retain extra sums in their balances as insurance against future changes in the grant allocation rules – at a cost of £1.2 billion to rate-payers between 1979 and 1983 (Audit Commission, 1984). This was clearly not a planned but an unintended consequence of the government's effort to cut local government expenditure. The outcome of high uncertainty generally, however, has been a tendency towards more short term, reactive decision-making and crisis management.

The last factor causing strategic planning to go into decline was that strategic plans have often been excessively long and detailed. This has resulted in policy-makers and managers alike being unable to absorb the amount of information presented to them by strategic planners. The limits on policy-makers' span of attention was well illustrated by Stirling District Council's attempt to introduce zero-based budgeting, a form of financial strategic management in which all activities have to be scrutinised before they are included in the budget for the coming financial year. This resulted in a document of over 600 pages describing the activities of an authority whose total budget was only some £10 million (Charlton and Martlew, 1987). In consequence, the document was not used to prepare the budget and the authority retreated towards incrementalism in subsequent years.

The combination of these factors, together with increasing public alienation from the massive, alienating bureaucracies which were the public face of the public sector (Hoggett and Hambleton, 1987), produced the intellectual and popular climate of the early 1980s, in which the value of strategic planning was largely discounted. This was reflected, not only in the justification already quoted for the abolition of the Greater London Council and the metropolitan county councils, but also in the virtual abandonment of local authority structure planning after 1980 and its proposed abolition in 1986. Only the replacement of Nicholas Ridley at the Department of Evironment by the less doctrinaire Chris Patten, followed by Michael Heseltine, coupled with increasing concern about such environmental issues as acid rain and global warming, saved structure planning from abolition, although its future is still not entirely clear. In any case, the primary focus of local authority managers and their advisers had by then shifted to a preoccupation with bringing local authorities 'closer to the customer', rather than continuing to develop strategic plans (Stewart, 1986; Clarke and Stewart, 1988). We have also seen that in the NHS a perhaps excessively sophisticated cyclical planning system, which was intended to procure the interaction of national policies with local needs and circumstances, was replaced in 1982 with a set of 'top-down' policy review meetings. The object of these meetings appears to be confined largely to securing the implementation of the government's policies, for instance, in compelling all health authorities to put their domestic and maintenance services out to competitive tender.

In central government, the attempts at improving strategic choice and planning in the 1970s were also shortlived (see Chapter 6). Only the PES system survived into the 1980s and its time span was reduced to three years. It had also changed from a mainly planning system to one in which short-term cash control predominated.

Strategic Planning becomes Strategic Management

There are clear indications that because private business organisations – especially the larger ones – recognise the need to develop strategic capabilities, public service organisations have increasingly sought to revive their strategic plans and planners to help them cope with the uncertainties surrounding them, under a new guise of strategic management. It is possible, for example, to plan strategically in ways that will reduce the damage caused to a company's or an authority's staff and services by expenditure cuts or in order to prepare for the introduction of a major innovation such as the community charge (Elcock, Fenwick and Harrop, 1988). In a very real sense, it has become apparent that the lessons of the 1970s now need to be relearnt in a new context, that of the strategic implementation of the values and policies which are being set by ministers, councillors and others.

This new incarnation of strategic management consists of two main features. The first is renewed interest in the reiterative planning cycle as a tool for the development of relevant policies – making strategic choices – through a series of cycles which we might call the 'whirling dervish' effect. The second is an increasing concern to analyse an organisation's relationship with its environment, and with its own members, in order to determine whether it is capable both of achieving its objectives and of satisfying its customers: strategic implementation. SWOT analysis was an early private sector example of such an approach to strategic implementation. It requires organisations to examine their internal strengths and weaknesses in relation to the external opportunities and threats confronting them. In essence, the two essential tools of strategic management are the strategic choice cycle, in which planning is still more important than plans, and the organisational matrix to assess the likely effectiveness or otherwise of strategic implementation.

The planning cycle consists of a series of responses to external demands for action, the lessons derived from the organisation's own experience or, usually, both. The cycle generates a series of general, long term, contextuating policies within which routine problem-solving can take place and individual cases can be resolved. In theory, these strategic propositions need not be collated into a formal planning document but in practice they often are. This is done either to comply with a statutory requirement such as the obligation for a county council to prepare a structure plan for approval by the Secretary of State, or in order to give the organisation's members, customers and collaborators both a sense of direction and a handy reference guide to the strategic propositions at present in force as they plan their own strategies and actions. These are sometimes referred to as mission statements or position statements.

In preparing formal plan documents, two sets of dilemmas need to be resolved. One set of problems concerns the plan's longevity, the other the extent of the detail strategic plans should contain. The length of time for which a plan or its constituent policies can or should remain valid cannot be prescribed, except to say that they should provide guidance beyond the immediate concerns of the organisation and its members, whilst not unduly inhibiting their ability to respond to changing opinions or circumstances. Increasing dissatisfaction with a plan or one of its component policies indicated by, for instance, attacks in the media, questions in Parliament or debates in the council chamber, as well as adverse comments by interested pressure groups, may all indicate policy stress and hence a need to revise or replace part or all of the strategy. It will probably be beneficial to review it after a fixed period, say every five years as is required for structure plans. We may also 'roll forward' the plan each year for a further fixed period, as is common practice in financial planning, including PES. Kent County Council has a policy strategy plan covering three years with one year operational plans which include finance plans (budgets), business plans (activities) and personal action plans (targets) which translate the strategic plan into action. It also undertakes a ten-year 'futures' exercise every one or two years. (Lavery and Hume, 1991). However, in some cases the plan may result in or take account of major capital investments, such as reservoirs or hospitals, which take years to construct and then constitute a long term commitment of resources. For example, one RHA told the DHSS in its first Strategic Plan in the late 1970s, that its ability to adjust its policies to take account of

ministerial instructions to transfer resources from the acute medical
sector to the 'Cinderella' services was severely constrained. This RHA
was about to open a new and very large district general hospital in its
regional capital which would commit almost all the RHA's growth
monies for several years. (Elcock and Haywood, 1980, pp. 73–5). In
such a case there may be no point in carrying out more than a limited
review of the organisation's strategy for quite a long time. In such
circumstances there may indeed be little scope for making strategic
choices.

One development which has resulted from the Thatcher era's
concentration on economy, efficiency and effectiveness – the 'three
Es' – which should assist strategic managers in reviewing their strategic
choices has been the development of increasingly sophisticated
approaches to the evaluation and review of public policies. The
government's concern to improve evaluation can be seen at one level in
the Joint Management Unit's instruction to ministers and departments
that any new policy proposal to be put to the Cabinet must include a
statement as to how it is to be evaluated (Joint Management Unit,
1987). At another level, large batteries of performance measures and
performance indicators have been developed for public services,
notably for local government by the Audit Commission (Elcock,
Jordan and Midwinter, 1989) and for the NHS by the DHSS (Pollitt,
1985). Admittedly, the effect of performance measures and indicators
in influencing the behaviour of managers within the organisation or
service, who seek to maximise their performance under the indicators
even if this distorts the service or produces suboptimal results, must be
carefully monitored (Pollitt, 1989). None the less, effective evaluation
and review is critical to the success of the planning cycle because only
in this way can the organisation determine what issues its own
experience suggests should be considered for inclusion in the next
version of the strategic plan. It should also assist in the early
identification of incipient policy stress.

The second set of dilemmas with which the strategic manager must
deal concerns the amount of detail which strategic plans should contain.
We have seen that many strategic planning exercises, apart from taking
too long to prepare, have failed and become discredited because they
produced plans which were too long and too detailed for policy-makers,
let alone the public, to comprehend and use effectively. Equally, a
strategy which does not provide guidelines for dealing with the
problems confronting a government, a local authority, a health

authority or other public agency, which also cause concern to its citizens, is no use. Hence the first major step in the planning process must be to identify a limited range of key issues on which the organisation's strategic managers can be requested and required to concentrate their attention. The strategic manager must also consider how well the organisation is likely to implement the strategic choices once they have been made and what co-operation from other individuals and organisations is likely to be needed – a dimension which, as we have seen, is increasingly important as public organisations become increasingly dependent on private contractors and voluntary agencies for the provision of their services. He or she must also consider whether the strategies adopted require that the organisation's culture needs to be changed (Johnson and Scholes, 1988).

In doing this, strategic planners in the public services have increasingly copied their colleagues in the private sector by developing matrix analyses which tease out those issues which are posed by their external environment from those which are generated internally. SWOT analysis is a case in point, since it requires the identification both of internal strengths and weaknesses, as well as external opportunities and threats, as the preliminary to planning how to deal with them.

In applying such a technique to the public sector, Royston Greenwood (1987) offers a matrix analysis of a sample of local authorities whose dimensions are based on the following variables:

(a) High or low differentiation: the strength of the central management and policy-making function relative to that of the service departments.

(b) The extent of decentralisation and the use of divisional or functional groupings within the authority's structures.

(c) Orientation towards the external environment rather than internal problems: how far the authority is aggressive, entrepreneurial and proactive in dealing with the outside world.

(d) How well the authority meets the changing demands being made upon it.

Greenwood identifies among his sample examples of:

(a) Defenders: which prefer stability to experimentation and concentrate on the provision of statutory services. Their major preoccupation is with the authority's own efficiency.

(b)   Analysers: which are authorities which seek to learn how other authorities perform similar functions and use this knowledge to improve their own performance.

(c)   Prospectors: which actively seek new opportunities and challenges.

(d)   Reactors: which are authorities which value stability but introduce changes as circumstances require.

(Greenwood, 1987, pp. 310–11)

A similar analysis of public authorities in the North-East of England (Elcock, Fenwick and Harrop, 1988) resulted in a comparable set of conclusions illustrated by the matrix set out in Table 3.1. This classifies organisations in terms of their proactive or reactive managerial stances relative to their inward- or outward-looking relationships with their environment. Briefly, the authorities in this study were analysed as follows:

A.   **Proactive/outward-looking organisations**. These carry out market research, are sensitive to community needs and develop Public Service Orientations (Stewart 1986, Clarke and Stewart, 1988). They are much concerned with developing strategic plans. They will need to identify whether their concern is primarily with the provision of one or several services, or with the wider welfare of a local or regional community. They are also likely to have strong central control units (Isaac-Henry and Painter, 1991).

B.   **Reactive/outward looking organisations**. These are likely to be reactive in part at least because of the nature of the demands made upon them, for instance, the emergencies with which police forces, fire brigades and hospitals must cope. However, they also seek to influence the environment, for instance, through preventative health campaigns, community policing or fire prevention work. Such activities will entail at least a degree of strategic management, although central control may be relatively weak because the organization's chief concern is with the effective delivery of its services to its customers (Isaac-Henry and Painter, 1991).

C.   **Proactive but inward-looking organisations**. These often respond to problems by reorganising themselves (Elcock, 1991) and are concerned with protecting their staff and activities. They are not likely to engage at all extensively in strategic planning and will have relatively weak organisational centres.

D. **Reactive inward-looking organisations**. These are mainly concerned with containing their budgets and activities within the limits of externally set budgetary and other constraints. These bodies too are unlikely to develop much in the way of strategic plans or to have significantly powerful corporate centres.

TABLE 3.1 *Varieties of management strategies*

	Managerial stance	
Relationship to environment	*Proactive*	*Reactive*
Outward-looking	A	B
Inward-looking	C	D

Source: Elcock, Fenwick and Harrop (1988).

An organisation can make use of such models as these to identify key issues concerning the organisation's structures, culture and processes. They help strategic managers to secure effective strategic implementation, by asking two sets of questions: First, 'In which box of the matrix are we located?' If we are in the appropriate box, how can we improve our performance? Second, 'Do we need to move to another box?' If so, what means do we use? For instance, developing a Public Service Orientation is likely to make a local authority both more proactive and more outward-looking (Stewart, 1986). The organisation's culture may need to change too, perhaps radically. There is no essential virtue in being in one box rather than another. Indeed we have seen that the nature of the organisation's functions may determine its location in one box rather than another. Emergency services, for example, must by definition be at least in part reactive. However, answering these questions should provide the basis for developing a set of key issues which can then be addressed through the planning cycle, in the form of three further questions, the answering of which should assist in improving strategic implementation.

The first is whether organisational structures should be changed. The development of a network of decentralised offices or teams of workers based on small areas such as electoral wards, for example, will enable a local authority department to become both more accessible and more responsive to its customers' needs. The decentralised offices will also provide better information about what problems policy-makers should be addressing if they are to increase citizens' support for them, electorally and otherwise (Elcock, 1986b). Alternatively, a desire to develop a plan for the economic development of a community or the improvement of the health of its population will require the creation of a central unit. This must be able both to prepare appropriate policies and secure their implementation, both throughout the organisation and through other individuals and organisations (Isaac-Henry and Painter, 1991).

A second issue area concerns the authority's internal management: industrial relations may need improving or more appropriate office accommodation may be needed, especially if managerial developments are to accompany structural changes. Third and last, review processes must be developed in order to ensure that strategic managers and policy-makers can check whether the new policies are achieving the objectives determined at the beginning of the planning cycle, perhaps by use of a matrix analysis. This was the point which the Joint Management Unit was making when it insisted that new proposals coming before the Cabinet should include a statement of how they would be evaluated. Effective evaluation entails developing the appropriate capacity at the organisation's centre.

Conclusion

Strategic choice and strategic implementation are certain to increase in importance in the 1990s, for several reasons. The first is that both business people and public officials have increasingly recognised the usefulness of strategic management in coping with uncertainty and dealing with major long-term problems. Second, budget-makers in particular have realised that they can develop strategic plans which enable them to meet governmental or other demands that are made on them, for example, for spending cuts (Midwinter, 1988a) or for coping with increased demands resulting from demographic change (Lavery and Hume, 1991). These demands can be more effectively met through the development of coherent resource collection and allocation policies than simply through the annual battle between 'Advocates' and 'Guardians' (Wildavsky, 1979). Third, reviving concern about the environment is generating public support for the development of long-term policies to restrict pollution, slow down the destruction of natural environments and cut the wasteful use of natural resources. Lastly, and in part consequent upon growing environmental concern, people are coming to recognise the need for and value of regulation and control. This development is likely to be encouraged as the regulators present more acceptable faces to the regulated, for instance as local authorities, Next Step agencies, health districts and other organisations develop various forms of public service orientation. Effective strategic management is dependent, however, on reliable and comprehensive information. It also requires good strategic analysis and appropriate organisational systems, structures and personnel policies. Strategic managers must encourage public involvement in the preparation of plans and seek to maintain a consensus of support for their work from individuals and collective interests alike. If this can be done, the many valuable lessons learned in the 1960s and 1970s, and pushed to the back of most people's filing cabinets in the 1980s, can be reapplied to produce better societies, less frustrated public servants and more contented citizens in the 1990s.

4

Financial Management

RICHARD TONGE

The public services have seen a significant increase in the importance placed on financial issues and priorities throughout the 1980s. These have ranged from the introduction of competition on the basis of cost and profit, to the setting of specific financial targets or objectives at the strategic level of the organisation. At the same time the role and provision of financial information as an aid to decision-making has been enhanced. The impact of these measures has been felt within all public service institutions including the National Health Service (NHS), the universities, local authorities and central government.

The part played by finance has taken a variety of forms, reflecting its flexibility as both an economic and a managerial tool adapting to the culture, characteristics and objectives of a particular organisational setting. One financial mechanism used as a management control device has been the cash limit. This has been used where the outputs or services provided could not be readily measured in financial terms. As a result, expenditure on resources consumed was perceived as the only effective financial measure or control device available, to restrain or reduce the growth of public spending, and to achieve better 'value-for-money'. By contrast, 'rates of return' have been used as the financial target in those public sector organisations most resembling trading or business organisations and where output can be measured in financial terms, permitting a profit or surplus to be calculated as a representation of financial value. This profit or surplus can then be compared to the amount of financial capital invested and a financial return computed. With such control measures exerting financial pressure, there is the commensurate need to assess the quality of the financial information systems to ensure that these make an effective contribution to the decision making, control and planning process. This chapter seeks to identify what is meant by the term financial management before identifying the changes attributed to its increased influence on structures and processes within central government, the NHS and local government, during the Thatcher and post-Thatcher period. These changes are then considered within the context of the new managerialism and its implications for the public services in the 1990s.

The Nature of Financial Management

There is no universally accepted definition of financial management. However, Hill and Rockley (1990) find a measure of agreement amongst writers that financial management involves: 'specifying and obtaining objectives, safe-guarding and making optimum use of resources, achieving aims, and enabling something to happen according to plans and budgets'. The ethos for this is based on the notion of financial stewardship, where financial responsibility is entrusted to the senior management of an organisation by its owners. The management is charged with the responsibility of protecting and safeguarding its owners' funds and using them to the benefit of the provider. In this context, management has to make decisions on the various resources at their disposal. These include people, equipment, technology, land, raw materials, information and money. The resulting mix, in terms of quantity and quality of each resource consumed, should result in a rational decision-making process in the pursuit of set objectives.

There is a need for the provider of funds to receive reassurance that the management has applied the funds in an appropriate and efficient manner and is accountable for its decisions or actions. Feedback, as part of a monitoring or a control system, is essential, and can take the form of a verbal or written report to the provider of funds. Management can then be held accountable for decisions taken both in the planning phase and the delivery phase of service provision. The reporting of budget proposals is in the form of a financial statement about management plans and an annual report provides financial information on what has been undertaken or achieved.

Financial information systems are an important element within the whole process of organisational planning and decision-making. In addition, they provide the means which link resource inputs to service outputs and as a result provide a rudimentary, financial based measurement of performance. The key aspects of financial management as they relate to delegated responsibility, accountability and the role of management are summarised in Figure 4.1. It is the lines joining the various elements which are of crucial importance as they form a linkage and represent the channel of communication between the various elements. It is financial information as a representation of organisational behaviour, activity and decision-making which provides a common thread acting as a link between the various elements. To that end, financial management is the process and techniques which link delegated financial responsibility to financial accountability.

Managers are accountable to the fund providers external to the organisation. Due to the complex nature of many organisations, and given the resulting hierarchical structure, senior managers delegate responsibility for operational matters to middle and junior managers and hold the latter accountable for the discharge of those responsibilities.

FIGURE 4.1   *Financial responsibility and accountability flow system*

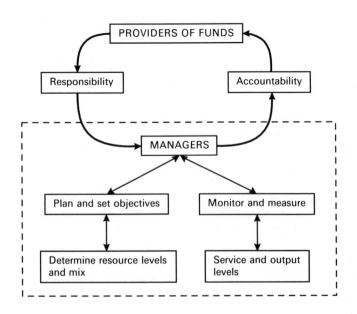

Hence, senior managers translate their own objectives into more specific or detailed objectives, financial or otherwise, for middle or junior management to fulfil. The easiest communication device that requires little additional translation is the language of finance and as a result financial management is geared towards ensuring that the concerns of senior managers regarding subordinate task fulfilment are satisfied. This is achieved through a series of planning and control procedures, illustrated in Figure 4.2. It is the role of finance in decision-making which is important here. To obtain decision-making of the highest quality, it is necessary to provide appropriate information and finance has spawned a wide variety of information sources that can help. These include annual financial statements, audit reports, periodic budget statements and *ad hoc* performance reports, all incorporating an appropriate package of financial performance indicators.

FIGURE 4.2   *Financial management planning and control system*

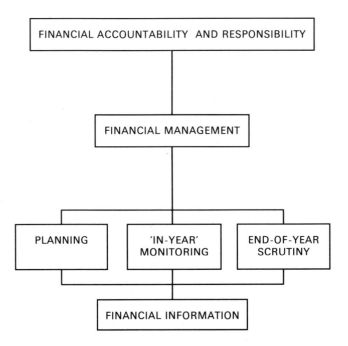

One of the key financial techniques that helps in planning and controlling is the budget. Its flexibility as an information system to aid decision making is unquestionable. It can be adapted to whatever time horizon is felt appropriate, it can be structured to reflect organisational needs by reflecting the willingness of senior executives to delegate decision-making responsibility, and in the absence of the market mechanism it is a means for aligning resource consumption with service requirements. By and large, the public services have tended to budget for revenue, income and expenditure on an annual basis, primarily to establish tax revenues for the subsequent 12 months. What this means is that a snap shot or financial picture is being established, over a 12 month period, for something which is in reality an on-going process in terms of service delivery.

The kind of budget information compiled in the public services follows very closely the example shown in Table 4.1. This revenue budget establishes the amount to be expended and income collected for a particular service heading. The net balance, or difference between expenditure and income, if in deficit (£32,360 for next year) will be borne out of a tax levy. When the estimate or budget is approved, it is the authorisation for the managers responsible to carry out the objectives and targets set for that unit. The format or layout of the budget is referred to as a 'line-item' budget, where expenditure and income have been assigned to specific items of responsibility. Generally, as a result, managers will be required to keep within the financial requirements laid down for each category. If, however, the delegation of responsibility over management of the service and its associated resources includes the ability to switch resources in pursuit of service provision, the individual lines become less a cost constraint or a restrictive control feature and more an information source which aids managerial flexibility.

Another major feature of the illustration above is the method used for constructing the budget. In the private sector, where there is a clearly-defined relationship between physical inputs and output activity, then the planned output can be the starting point for the construction of the budget, given the assumption of a clearly-defined input/output relationship. In situations where it is difficult to make that assumption about the relationship, as in many areas of the public sector, then 'incremental budgeting' is utilised. For example, the cost of the police service is not necessarily a function of a measurable output such as the level of arrests – but of a number of complementary or

TABLE 4.1 *A revenue budget*

Service Area ....

| | Current year | | Next year |
	Original estimate (£)	Revised estimate (£)	Original estimate (£)
EMPLOYEES			
Salaries	10,000	10,500	11,200
Wages	22,000	20,600	23,000
	32,000	31,100	34,200
PREMISES			
Repairs	1,200	1,010	1,500
SUPPLIES & SERVICES	970	900	1,200
ESTABLISHMENT EXPENSES	540	530	570
	34,710	33,540	37,470
LESS:			
INCOME	(4,030)	(3,720)	(5,110)
	30,680	29,820	32,360

conflicting factors including the state of the economy, individuals' willingness to report crimes and offences and the level of training provided.

Because the causal relationship between resource and product or service is difficult to determine, the emphasis within incremental budgets is to analyse changes in relation to an established base. Each year the budget is adjusted to reflect the changes in the provision of a particular service in terms of the quantity or quality of resources consumed, their relative mix and any adjustments required for price changes in the light of the latest available information. Figure 4.3 illustrates this position. It is a form of 'exception reporting' where attention is focused on the incremental changes that have or will occur since the original budget was prepared. It can be regarded as inherently flawed in that the process of compiling a revised estimate for any given year, and an original estimate for the following year, assumes that the

FIGURE 4.3   *Incremental budgeting model*

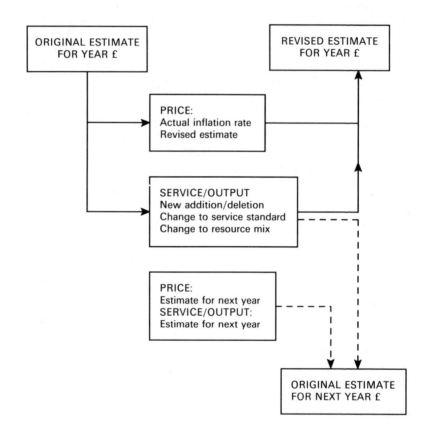

original estimate for the base year was correct. Any error contained within the original estimate for the base year has a distinct possibility of being repeated if not compounded in the estimate or budget for the subsequent year(s). This is seen by many to be a completely irrational approach and contrary to good management, due to its lack of critical review.

An alternative method of budget construction, resolving the problem identified above, was identified in a system called 'Zero-Based Budgeting' (ZBB). Phyrr (1970) describes ZBB as follows:

Customarily, the officials in charge of an established programme have to justify only the increase which they seek above last year's appropriation. In other words, what they are already spending is usually accepted as necessary, without examination. Substantial savings could undoubtedly be realised if [it were required that] every agency . . . make a case for its entire . . . request each year, just as if its program or programmes were entirely new.

Such an approach looks for the justification of all the money shown under the budget head, including existing or 'on-going' expenditure commitments as well as any 'year-on-year' changes. Essentially it makes for greater demands of managers as they need to review the need, role and resourcing of all service areas. This includes the objectives for a particular service, the activities needed to fulfil the objectives, priority ranking and establishing the appropriate resource mix. Such a methodology assumes that managers have the decision-making responsibility to withdraw a service or cut resource consumption (including human ones) where appropriate. One of the major criticisms made of the approach relates to the time and the resources needed to critically assess all the various activities and services within the budget timetable (see Chapter 3). Some supporters of its application in the public sector have proposed that it should be a biannual event. This would enable more time to be spent critically evaluating rather than just controlling to a figure and provide for greater certainty in future planning.

In practice, public service managers find themselves in situations where the budgeting system has not been converted to the ZBB approach, but organisational changes are requiring them to use the rationale of 'Zero-Basing', for example where there is an internal market or compulsory competitive tendering. The client/purchasing authority determines service objectives in the light of policy and prepares a specification of how those objectives are to be fulfilled. The contractor/provider evaluates the specifications/requirements and available resources and submits a price as to how much it will cost. To provide for an appropriate contract specification, managers have to be clear about objectives and how these are best achieved. The fixed contract period instils this need for an ongoing review.

While budget construction and the information derived can be seen to make an important contribution to the overall management process, financial information must be used in conjunction with other operational information. The purpose of 'in-year' monitoring of service levels and costs against objectives requires that managers look beyond purely the budget figure for an assessment of the achievement of objectives. If objectives expressed in the form of a budget were the sole criteria for monitoring performance, then this would ignore associated variations in activity levels of an operational nature. In fact, such a narrow focus of attention can result in a blinkered interpretation of actual organisational activity and financial information for management purposes, which produces results which are potentially erroneous, as shown in Table 4.2. On the basis of purely financial information, attention focuses on the Service *X* area, as this is the subject of an overspend. However, when this is considered in conjunction with operational/management information, the picture changes and Service *Y* becomes the focus of attention. The 'cost per customer' could be taken to be a performance indicator as it invites the manager to investigate or explore the reason for its occurrence. For example, why is the actual cost per customer £8 as against a budget figure of £2?

TABLE 4.2   *Financial and operational information*

	Service X		*Service Y*	
	Budget for year (£)	*Actual spending (£)*	*Budget for year (£)*	*Actual spending (£)*
FINANCIAL INFORMATION	100,000	120,000	100,000	80,000
	Estimate of customers to be seen	*Number actually seen*	*Estimate of customers to be seen*	*Number actually seen*
MANAGEMENT INFORMATION	50,000	80,000	50,000	10,000
	Estimated cost per customer (£)	*Actual cost per customer (£)*	*Estimated cost per customer (£)*	*Actual cost per customer (£)*
	2	1.50	2	8

Likierman (1988, p. 98) highlights the complexity with which performance measurement in the public sector is trying to grapple.

It is not easy to define performance measurement in relation to public expenditure. And even if performance is defined, there are still problems in how best to measure it. One means, increasingly developed in recent years, has been to devise performance indicators. These are potentially a means of relating plans to outcomes, justifying the use of resources, assessing the overall effectiveness and efficiency of the activity, providing a basis for calculating rewards and incentives and helping to establish whether value for money has been obtained.

The range of performance measures adopted in the public service is extensive. They include: staff productivity, cost per unit of output, cost per hour of human input, and cost per head of the population. All provide a different emphasis linked to resource inputs, service outputs or a ratio relating the two. The information generated through the performance measurement process is seen as helpful in assessing the following:

1. **Economy**   – measuring how well the organisation acquired its resources.
2. **Efficiency**   – measuring how well the organisation has utilized its resources in pursuit of the service or activity.
3. **Effectiveness** – measuring how far the organisation has fulfilled its key objectives.

A major debate exists regarding the last category, where output, in many public service areas, is acknowledged as being very difficult to measure and results in undue emphasis being placed on economy and efficiency. However, all three aspects should be viewed as being of equal importance when trying to draw some conclusions about overall performance.

The role of performance measures or indicators is to provide managers with information on areas within their responsibility and to encourage them to investigate items, both of a positive and negative nature, to establish the 'what' and 'why' of the occurrence. They are meant to be indicative rather than definitive and to acknowledge best practice as well as bad practice. Indicators can of course be criticised because they are often inaccurate or out of date, can be manipulated and only deal with what can be quantified. Nevertheless they are useful in providing comparisons of what is happening elsewhere. The positive benefits of the use of performance measurement are given authoritative support by the Chief Secretary to the Treasury who is on record as saying (Hansard, 1987, vol. 31):

> I see three main benefits from better measurement and targeting. By relating outputs to the costs involved, managers can make better choices. By setting out in advance what a programme is expected to achieve, by when and at what cost, subsequent review and evaluation is improved. By telling this House and the outside world what has been achieved and how that relates to previous targets, Departments are made more accountable.

It should be evident that the success of financial management within the public services is very dependent upon the quality of the management function within the organisation. This includes: effective delegation of responsibility, clear lines of accountability, effective planning and control systems, good communications and a supportive culture. These factors influence the quality of the information systems in use and those under development. Ultimately, the financial information system has to be flexible and adaptable to a wide variety of organisational situations. The information must be structured to represent a financial view of the organisation as a whole, a department, a work group, a unit or an individual as required.

The use of financial information as an aid to management within any organisation is only possible if its role is relevant to individual managers. This can be influenced or shaped by two important factors. First, there is the willingness of senior managers to delegate responsibility and decision-making, without feeling that their own position of authority is weakened. Failure to deal with the adequate delegation of operational decisions, for example, increases the perception of financial information being used as purely a control mechanism. Managers will tend to feel disillusioned when they are held accountable for things over which they have not been given decision-making responsibility. Financial information, most commonly in the form of a budget, becomes the focus of attention for misdirected blame. Second, the position of individuals within an organisational hierarchy, in conjunction with its culture, determines the extent to which planning or control decisions are seen as an integral part of the job managers perform. Operational managers generally view financial management as principally a control device over them and to be used over resources at their command. In this case, it would be more correct to call the situation one of resource management, within a financial constraint. Financial planning, revenue raising or income generation increase in their importance and relevance as managers obtain promotion, to higher level positions.

Financial Management since 1979

The Conservative government, elected in May 1979, gave a major political commitment to increasing the efficiency and effectiveness of the public services, especially the civil service. The economic position inherited in 1979 offered an appropriate environment not only to pursue that commitment, but also to control public expenditure and to reduce it, thus lowering the burden, it was claimed, that it represented for the private sector. A central aspect of the changes was to switch the emphasis of senior officials away from administration towards management. This demanded an improvement in the quality of management decision-making. Strategies aimed at providing the thrust for such a change focused on two approaches to begin with. First, there were scrutinies of aspects of service delivery or resource utilisation within departments. Second, there was the establishment of information systems geared towards strategic, financial and operations decision-making.

The role of the scrutinies is summed up quite well by Metcalfe and Richards (1987a, pp. 29, 30) who state:

> These quick action oriented analyses of, and prescriptions for, management systems were carried out by a young official in each of the Departments concerned. The emphasis was on asking fundamental questions, and on proposing a solution direct to top management so that the bureaucratic middle layers – the 'cotton wool' zone – would not have the opportunity to water down the recommendation.

There is no doubt that the scrutinies programme afforded a degree of legitimacy and authority to the Prime Minister's commitment to a radical overhaul of the civil service administration and management. Scrutinies provided a means of highlighting some of the themes for improving management in government. The lack of adequate management information for instance, was demonstrated through the MINIS (Management Information for Ministers) scrutiny in the Department of the Environment. This lack of information recurred in a number of the studies. The emphasis they placed on the financial consequences of decisions ensured that scrutinies gave value for money as well as raising financial awareness in the areas concerned. The Rayner Scrutinies were also concerned with the long-term problem of reducing cultural resistance to the notions or themes being expounded. They wanted to turn administrators into managers who would be concerned about the resources under their control and who would have responsibility for the impact, cost and use of those resources. It was such ideas and perceptions, when added to the political and ideological commitment of the government, that helped to pave the way for making the civil service more receptive to the ideas of the Financial Management Initiative (FMI).

The FMI reflected many of the management principles and processes contained in the official reports of the scrutiny pro- gramme. These principles were embodied in the 1982 White Paper (Cmnd 8616):

1. Managers should have a clear view of their objectives and a means to assess their performance in achieving them.
2. Managers should have clearly- and well-defined responsibilities for making the best use of resources.
3. Managers should have access to information (particularly concerning costs), training and expert advice that they need to exercise their responsibilities effectively.

The objectives of the FMI were far wider than just the financial issues. The FMI was concerned with a fundamental change in the approach to managing central government operations, requiring changes in attitude and not changes related solely to technique or presentation of financial information. According to Humphrey (1991, p. 172):

> the FMI is propounding a very traditional management by objectives view of organisational control. Management is portrayed as a scientific activity involving the specification of objectives, the measurement of and monitoring of performance in relation to the chosen objectives and the taking of corrective action where appropriate.

For the process to work and ensure successful implementation, there needed to be an improvement in the quality of financial information. Hence, managers within departments had to design and implement new systems based around the utilisation of decentralised financial and operational information and, as a result, 32 central government departments were asked to submit plans to the Treasury early in 1983 indicating how they proposed to satisfy the demands of the FMI within their departments.

Generally it was found that the plans contained four main elements. First, a top management system which represented a need to clarify objectives and priorities at a senior departmental level. Second, a financial information system relating expenditure to the main departmental activities. The third element looked to improving management information on operational issues, through quantifying performance and introducing quality control. Finally, in many of the departmental proposals, attention was focused on the need for internal monitoring, along the lines of a management audit. This covered such things as internal audit, organisation and method studies, operations research and staff inspection.

An example of a major department where the FMI was implemented was the Ministry of Defence (MoD). Michael Heseltine, the Secretary of State for Defence during the period in which the FMI was initiated, decided that MINIS should be introduced into the MoD in the early 1980s. The purpose of MINIS was to record detailed information about a department's activities, costs and performance to provide a basis for ministers and senior officials to review the work of the department and to decide on future courses of action in pursuit of policy objectives. Such decisions would take into account any organisational or structural changes necessary, as well as the quality, quantity and mix of human, physical and financial resources to be deployed in any particular situation. The whole process was aimed at enabling top management to manage positively rather than reactively. The approach resulted in a number of significant changes within the MoD. Initially, a fully unified and integrated defence staff reporting to the Chief of Defence Staff was created. An Office of Management and Budget was established to strengthen central control over MoD corporate planning matters, the commitment of resources and the monitoring of departmental financial and management systems.

The second major change was the move towards more accountable management with delegated managerial responsibility. This objective was realised through the introduction of two kinds of responsibility budgets:

1. **Executive Responsibility Budgets (ERBs)** – these covered all types of expenditure attributable to individual units or establishments.
2. **Staff Responsibility Budgets (SRBs)** – these were expressed in terms of staff numbers and the associated financial provision.

What started as a response to the FMI developed into a major programme of change referred to as the 'New Management Strategy' (NMS) which was an attempt to get better value for money within the MoD. At the heart of the new strategy were three main features:

1. The introduction of a formal planning system.
2. The establishment of a system of delegated budgets to align financial and managerial responsibility.
3. The enhancement of a system of performance monitoring and review.

As a result of NMS, the Ministry of Defence is endeavouring to shift the emphasis towards an output or service-based approach for management responsibility, which is informed by finance, rather than by the more traditional approach of planning and controlling on an input cost basis. It is hoped, as a result, to put greater flexibility in decision-making in the hands of the budget holders or managers responsible for providing the service or activity. To that end it is seen as a natural extension of the FMI.

On a more general level, the Financial Management Unit (FMU), a joint unit involving the Treasury and the Cabinet Office, reporting in 1984, was quite clear that the collection of financial data is only one element in the overall management process of planning and control. For delegated budgetary control to be effective, it requires that decision-making be based upon sound interpretation of such data or information. The Report supported the idea of the flexibility of the system, pointing out that its implementation in widely-differing departments had led to different systems of delegated budgetary control. These varied in the extent to which individual managers were permitted to divert resources between budget heads and the extent to which virement arrangements could be used to balance an over-spending on one budget head with an underspending on another.

There can be no doubt that the desire to improve the quality of management within the public services is partly dependent upon the commitment to and successful implementation of an appropriate financial and management information system. As a result it can be seen as a vehicle supporting the broader political ambitions of government in the area of public service spending and staffing levels. It was an essential prerequisite for the successful transformation of the FMI philosophy into a broader organisational thrust, based on the 'Next Step' agencies. As Richards (1990) writes, the Ibbs Report, published in February 1988, had recommended that the civil service should move to a different form of organisation. 'The rationale behind this approach was to make a reality of the model of devolved management implicit in the Financial Management Initiative (FMI)'. Within a year, recognition of the importance of the Next Step initiative was producing the following observation (Collins, 1991):

> 1990 was important for the gathering momentum of the Next Step initiative in the Civil Service. . . . In many respects the government's approach relied on extending measures which had been introduced following the launch of the Financial Management Initiative (FMI) in 1982. . . . The FMI principles – clear objectives, performance measurement, value for money, managerial information systems – continued, though the FMI label itself has passed into history.

The impact of financial management was not felt solely in central government departments. The themes and practices it encapsulated were felt in other parts of the public services, in particular the NHS and local government. In the NHS, the Griffiths Report (DHSS, 1983) recommended the appointment of general managers and argued for greater delegation of financial responsibility, with improved accountability mechanisms and financial management. It placed great emphasis on management budgets and the involvement of clinicians in resource decisions. There was clearly a need for a new managerial approach if the benefits of financial management were to be realized. A natural development of Griffiths was the Resource Management Initiative which focused on the need for better financial information to support the management changes. The Department of Health and Social Security (DHSS) set up a Steering Committee on Management Budgets (1985) 'to enable it (NHS) to give a better service to its patients by helping clinicians and other managers to make better informed judgements about how the resources they control can be used to maximum effect'. For this to be successful it was recognised that there were three essential prerequisites: clinicians had to be involved in budget setting; budgets had to be devolved; and budgets had to reflect strategic priorities.

In addition the 'Korner Reports' produced by the NHS/DHSS Steering Group on Health Services Information identified that a plentiful amount of data existed but it was poorly structured, lacked consistency and resulted in weaknesses in information systems. This impaired effective decision-making. Korner argued for information being provided about activities, workloads, manpower and finance, within minimum data sets. The theme of the Korner reviews drew attention to the need for improvements in both financial and management information systems. These were required both on an individual basis and on an organisational basis to provide information essential to efficient and effective decision-making (DHSS, 1984).

In local government major changes have occurred in financial management, organisational structure and culture. As Leech (1988) states:

> local government has been a major testing ground for free market ideas. Cynically it might be suggested that reigning back the state is easier in areas outside direct central government responsibility. It is frequently noted that public expenditure has not been cut overall, but restructured and local government services have been amongst the principal victims of the restructuring.

Two specific aspects of financial management illustrating its impact in local government are performance indicators and the role of the Audit Commission. The importance of performance indicators cannot be understated. The operational information generated can relate to a variety of issues including: quantity of items produced, units of service provided, number and range of clients seen, resources employed and time available. When combined with the relevant financial information, they provide many of the basic unit cost measures for assessing performance in terms of efficiency and effectiveness.

Such information is also used to control local government through the work of the Audit Commission. The Commission appoints the external auditors who undertake the scrutiny of year-end financial statements of local government (and the NHS), to ensure the financial stewardship function complies with the relevant legislation. The Commission also reports on the management of significant service/ operational areas, including an assessment of the reasons behind variations in the level of spending between authorities. It identifies best practice as well as bad practice. The performance measures generated contribute part of the information basis for coming to some kind of assessment. The identification process involves statistical analysis and the production of league tables. The philosophy behind this type of analysis comes in for significant criticism as it appears to be cost-orientated with little attention being given to quality of the service.

By the late 1980s, the Audit Commission (1989) felt that 'value-for-money' had been too narrowly defined as 'cost-cutting' and a change in emphasis is now evident. The Commission stated that

> Councils are also under political pressure to provide more responsive services than in the past to more demanding consumers. And traditional financial systems are not as good at encouraging effective management as they are at controlling the level of spending.

In fact in an earlier document, the Audit Commission (1988b) criticised local authority financial systems for placing unnecessary constraints on detailed management and giving insufficient emphasis to overall performance. The need to align financial and managerial responsibilities was seen as central to improving the situation. The financial management changes recommended included:

1. every budget to have a budget holder;
2. front line managers to be budget holders for the items under their control;
3. items excluded from the front line to be controlled elsewhere;
4. senior managers to supervise the financial management of those reporting to them.

Conclusion

There is little doubt that an integral aspect of the 'New Management' within the public services has been the increased emphasis placed on the financial consequences of actions and decisions. This is reflected in the organisational changes and revision to management systems that have been undertaken within the public services since the late 1970s. The financial aspect of 'New Management' can only be called new, however, in the context of the public services since efficient use of resources, value for money and competitive tendering would be taken for granted within the business community. It is the experience gained in that cultural environment that has been imported into the public services. The growth in the importance placed on the role of finance is rooted in the New Right ideological perspective discussed in Chapter 1. Armed with this view, the Conservative governments from 1979 sought to redress the imbalance between the private and public sectors. Their aim was to shift the whole economy back in favour of capitalism, the private sector and individual choice. They used a number of measures to put this into effect. These included privatisation through share issues where the organisation has to compete on the basis of product, price and profit. Some public services were introduced to the discipline of the market-place by competing for work. But, in those areas where there is no obvious private sector competitor, the approach was to raise the financial awareness and cost consciousness of the managers involved. This was achieved through the development of internal markets, the use of budgetary controls based on cash limits, performance measures to assess service delivery and resource use and the role of external review agencies.

A number of these strategies have highlighted weaknesses in management processes and these had to be rectified if financial management was to have any chance of success. The FMI was built upon the need for managers to have a clear view of their objectives, the means to assess performance, clearly-defined responsibilities and access to appropriate information and advice. FMI was really only a part of a broader 'Management Initiative', one aspect of which was providing better information about the likely costs of decisions. The development of Next Step Agencies and the New Management Strategy for the MoD are other parts of this ongoing management initiative or reform. This perspective is echoed in the work of the Audit Commission on local government and more recently the NHS. As a result, there has been a very significant strengthening of financial accountability within the public services, making it as important as democratic and legal accountabilities. Managers within the public services are now required to demonstrate that their decisions provide value for money. The management of resources and provision of goods and services have to be 'informed by cost' so that decision-takers are financially aware when setting priorities and making choices. In many cases this requires public service managers to demonstrate that they can offer value for money, by subjecting their service to compulsory competitive tendering.

Financial management has been given a central role in facilitating change but this has not been easy. There has been hurried and limited training giving individuals no time to understand the underlying principles and techniques of financial management. Central departments, including the Treasury, have been unwilling to devolve responsibility. The continued practice of no carry over of under spending has given no incentive for managers to make savings whilst restrictions on *virement* have denied managers the flexibility which FMI implied. Finally, there have been weaknesses within the management information systems including objectives not being specific, poor communication and over-simplistic measures of performance. An analysis of these problems reveals that they have little to do with purely financial management and are more related to the general management culture of the organisation. For example, the *virement* problem and lack of flexibility regarding over-spending is a remnant of earlier periods of tight financial controls from the strategic centre. These practices have no place in the 'new world' of the public service manager. Next Step agencies, Health Service Trusts and Local Management of Schools are all designed to remove such problems.

Looking to the future of financial management within the public services, we would argue that it will continue to be high on the agenda of public organisations. The return of another Conservative government will see more public services distinguishing between the client/purchaser and contractor/provider roles, as the discipline of the 'market' spreads. Bidding for contracts on the basis of cost will continue being required at the operational level by the service providers, and in many areas separate agencies will be providing services subject to contracting arrangements for which they compete. There are no conflicts amongst the discipline of the market, the pursuit of contracting in the public sector, the need for managers to be more aware of the financial implications of spending decisions and the commitment to a programme of high quality social welfare and care, as the latter would form the basis of the standard specification in a contract. It is just as important to ensure value for money in public services as in private businesses. Good management is a necessary condition of good government. The problem arises when government policy towards social welfare programmes is not in accord with its willingness to commit the necessary financial resources to fund them.

Once the options for improving value for money, through various procedural, managerial and financial initiatives, have been exhausted, then the overall level of public services funding is the only variable that can be adjusted. In such circumstances, politics replaces managerial rationality in decision-making.

5

Human Resources Management and Employee Relations

DAVID FARNHAM

This chapter examines the changing nature of what have traditionally been called personnel management and industrial relations in the public services. It seeks to demonstrate, first, that there has been a move away from a predominantly 'soft' welfare-centred, 'model' employer approach in the public services since 1979 to a 'harder,' market-centred, human resources management approach. Second, there has been a shift away from the dominant Whitley model of industrial relations, which legitimised the role of national collective bargaining, to a more flexible, partly-decentralised bargaining model. Third, there has been a weakening of collectivist approaches to the managing of people in the public services, based on common standards of employment and joint machinery between employers and staff, to more fractional, individualist initiatives. Whilst these changes must not be exaggerated, they provide a distinctive shift in the styles and practices of managing the work-force in the public services since the late 1970s. The major personnel management and industrial relations issue facing employers, unions and employees in the public services during the 1990s is the extent to which these developments are permanent and irreversible and to what extent the changes outlined below are likely to be extended.

Employment in the Public Services

We start by examining the changing structure of employment in the public services. In 1991 the estimated UK work-force in employment was approximately 26.2 million. This comprised some 19.9 million, or 76 per cent of the total, in the private sector, with around 5.9 million or 22.4 per cent in the public sector. The public sector, in turn, is normally classified as comprising those employed in central government, the local authorities and the public corporations, including the nationalised industries. In 1991 there were estimated to be some 2.2 million employees in central government, three million in the local authorities and 700,000 in the public corporations (Central Statistical Office, 1991).

As can be seen from Table 5.1, total public sector employment in 1991, by headcount, was about the same level as it had been in 1961. Public sector employment had peaked in 1979 at some 7.5 million, falling to just under six million by 1991. Between 1961 and 1979, employment in all three major parts of the public sector was on a slowly rising plateau. Between 1979 and 1991 it was on a slowly declining plateau, apart from the local authorities, where it oscillated around three million for the whole decade. The decline was especially noticeable in the public corporations, which was largely accounted for by the privatisations of the former 'public utilities', such as telecommunications, the National Bus Company subsidiaries, electricity and gas. There was also a significant fall in the numbers of civil servants after 1979, from a total of some 738,000 to about 580,000 by 1991. Civil service employment was reduced, for example, by: contracting the size of establishments; privatising some areas such as the Royal Ordnance Factories in 1985 and the Ministry of Defence Dockyards in 1987; and hiving off staff into non-civil service agencies such as the Victoria and Albert, and Science Museums in 1984.

Turning to the major public services, we observe from Table 5.2 that total employment fell from over four million full-time equivalents (FTEs) in 1979 to about 3.7 million in 1991. This represented an overall decrease of some 342,000 employees or 8.4 per cent over the 12-year period. There were, however, considerable variations of employment change within the public services during these years. Two public services, the police and personal social services, for example, increased their FTEs between 1979 and 1991. These rose by 25,000 and 52,000, or by 15 and 22 per cent, respectively. FTE employment in the NHS rose by 70,000 or by 7 per cent between 1979 and 1983 but it fell by 44,000 or four per cent between 1983 and 1991. In 1991 there were 101,000 people employed in National Health Service (NHS) trusts. In the civil service and educational services, by contrast, there were decreases in FTE employment of 166,000 and 128,000, or by 23 and 12 per cent respectively, over the 12 year period. Although there was a minor recovery of employment in education between 1986 and 1988, this fell back again by 64,000 or by six per cent between 1988 and 1991.

The structure of employment in the public services by sex and employment status, using headcounts, is shown in Table 5.3. This shows that, in 1991, 55 per cent of all full-time employees in the public services were males and 45 per cent were females. When we turn to part-time employment, only 11 per cent were males, compared with 89 per cent who were females. Looked at another way, 37 per cent of all public service work in 1991 was male full-time employment, 30 per cent female full-time employment and 29 per cent female part-time employment. Only 4 per cent was male part-time employment.

There were wide variations in the structure of employment amongst the various services. The NHS, for example, was dominated by female full-time and part-time employment, at 42 and 36 per cent respectively. Only 19 per cent of NHS employment consisted of male full-time workers. This pattern was duplicated in the personal social services where 49 per cent were female part-time workers, 32 per cent female full-time workers, with only 14 per cent male full-time workers. In the educational sector, the largest proportion was female part-time workers at 42 per cent, followed by male full-time workers at 29 per cent and female full-time workers at 21 per cent. Only 8 per cent of part-time workers in education were male. The situation differed in the police services, where 83 per cent of those employed were male full-timers, 13 per cent female full-timers, 2.5 per cent female part-timers and 2 per cent male part-timers. In other parts of the local authorities and central government, there were also relatively low proportions of part-time employees, both male and female. In local government, 66 per cent of all employees were male full-timers and 19 per cent female full-timers. In central government, 41 per cent were male full-time employees and 36 per cent female full-timers. Twenty-two per cent were female part-timers.

From the above analysis it is clear that the public services underwent considerable structural and employment changes after 1979. These structural features of public service employment provide the back-

TABLE 5.1 UK public sector employment 1961–91: selected years, by headcount (thousands)

Mid-year	Central government				Local authorities						Public corporations			Total public sector	(civil service)
	HMF	NHS	Other	Total	Education	Social services	Construction	Police	Other	Total	Nationalised bodies	Other	Total		
1961	474	575	741	1 790	785	170	103	108	703	1 870	2 152	48	2 200	5 860	672
1964	424	627	743	1 794	925	200	124	116	724	2 088	1 949	130	2 079	5 961	683
1969	380	716	794	1 890	1 189	257	132	141	787	2 505	1 916	125	2 041	6 436	701
1974	345	911	884	2 140	1 453	272	135	160	762	2 782	1 777	208	1 985	6 907	705
1979	314	1 152	921	2 387	1 539	344	156	176	782	2 997	1 849	216	2 065	7 449	738
1984	326	1 223	810	2 359	1 430	368	126	187	871	2 942	1 416	195	1 610	6 911	630
1988	316	1 228	778	2 322	1 504	405	125	194	853	3 081	798	126	924	6 327	593
1991	297	1 092	788	2 177	1 416	414	106	202	810	2 948	516	107	747[1]	5 872	580

Note: 1.   included 124,000 in NHS trusts.
Source: Derived from CSO (1991) Economic Trends.

TABLE 5.2 Employment in the UK public services 1979–91: full-time equivalent (thousands)

Mid-year	Civil service	NHS	Education	Police	Social services	Other local authorities	Total public services
1979	724	977	1 110	172	235	851	4 069
1980	700	1 001	1 087	176	235	845	4 044
1981	684	1 038	1 058	180	240	828	4 028
1982	659	1 047	1 041	180	241	812	3 980
1983	643	1 047	1 034	182	246	816	3 968
1984	619	1 036	1 027	182	251	815	3 930
1985	596	1 030	1 021	182	256	814	3 899
1986	597	1 018	1 029	184	263	800	3 891
1987	584	1 016	1 043	186	271	805	3 905
1988	577	1 017	1 046	190	277	799	3 906
1989	567	1 013	992	191	282	790	3 835
1990	559	1 009	990	194	288	708	3 748
1991	558	902[1]	982	197	287	801	3 727

Note: 1. There were also 101,000 employed in NHS trusts.
Source: Derived from CSO (1991) Economic Trends.

TABLE 5.3   *Employment in the UK public services 1991: sex and employment status (thousands)*

| | Male | | | Female | | | Total |
	Full-time	Part-time	Total	Full-time	Part-time	Total	
NHS	206	33	239	460	393	853	1 092
Education	407	112	519	298	599	897	1 416
Social services	58	21	79	131	204	335	414
Police	167	4	171	26	5	31	202
Other local authorities	608	27	635	176	104	281	916
Central government[1]	889	33	922	779	476	1 255	2 177
[NHS Trusts	23	4	27	52	45	97	124]

Note:
1. Includes civil service and non-departmental agencies but excludes HM Forces and NHS.
Source: Derived from CSO (1991) *Economic Trends.*

ground to the human resource and employee relations issues emerging during this period. The main features were: overall employment contraction, although there was a modest expansion in some areas; the relatively high proportions of part-time employees in certain of the services; and the relative gender balances between males and females in the different services.

The Public Services as Model Employers

It is generally recognised that the public services traditionally viewed themselves as 'model' or 'good practice' employers. As model employers, the public services aimed to provide terms and conditions of employment which would act as examples for all other employers to follow. As good practice employers, they wished to provide terms and conditions of employment in line with those of the best private sector companies.

The model employer approach, and the different shades of meaning attached to it, was articulated as early as 1929 in the evidence of the Civil Service Clerical Association to the Tomlin Commission. According to the Association (White, 1933, p. 60):

from conditions such as to provide an 'example' to private employers throughout the country . . . we have passed in our experience to 'conditions equal to those given by the best employers outside the Service.' From this we have passed to 'conditions as good as those afforded by good outside employers.' At a still later stage, the criterion became as 'good as those provided by good outside employers, regard being had to the advantage enjoyed by Civil Servants in the matters of hours, sick leave, pensions, etc.' Finally, the doctrine has become that 'the State should afford conditions not "out of scale" with those of outside industry'.

The good practice employer model was summed up in the report of the Priestley Commission (Royal Commission on the Civil Service, Priestley Report, 1956, p. 39) where it stated that:

> The 'good employer' is not necessarily the one who offers the highest rates of pay. He seeks rather to provide stability and continuity of employment, and consults with representatives of his employees upon changes that affect both their remuneration and their conditions of work. He provides adequate facilities for training and advancement and carries on a range of practices which today constitute good management, whether they be formalised in joint consultation along civil service lines or not. Such employers are likely to be among the more progressive in all aspects of management policy.

There are, then, a number of different, but related, strands of model and good employer practices that can be identified in the traditional public services. They resulted in distinctive features of personnel management and industrial relations practices which were essentially collectivist, paternalist and bureaucratic.

One characteristic was the commitment of public service employers to union recognition and to collective bargaining as the best method of conducting industrial relations. Union recognition is a necessary condition for conducting effective collective bargaining. And, until recently, there has never been a serious problem of union recognition in the modern public services. Unions were recognised in the civil service, and in parts of the local authority sector, soon after the Whitley reports were published towards the end of the First World War in 1917–18. After the end of the Second World War, with the expansion of the Welfare State, union recognition was extended to the NHS, the newly-nationalised industries – which already had well unionised work-forces – and other public corporations.

In the Workplace Industrial Relations Survey (WIRS) of the early 1980s, it was shown that nearly all public service establishments at that time recognised at least one union, compared with only half of those in the private sector (*Public Money*, 1984). Seventy-nine per cent of all the public service establishments recognised manual unions,compared with 50 per cent for the private sector as a whole. The figure for central government establishments was 49 per cent, local government 79 per cent, the NHS 87 per cent and education 77 per cent. In the case of non-manual unions, 92 per cent of all public service establishments recognised them, compared with 30 per cent in the private sector. In central government, the figure was 93 per cent, local government 92 per cent, the NHS 95 per cent and education 87 per cent. From this evidence it may be concluded that public service employers have normally been far more likely to recognise both manual and non-manual unions than have private sector employers. Moreover, public sector organisations tend to recognise unions in establishments with lower levels of membership than do private sector managements.

In addition to national pay bargaining arrangements, the public services have also been more likely to agree joint disputes and disciplinary procedures with trade unions than has the private sector. In local government and the NHS, for example, the WIRS shows: 52 per cent and 58 per cent of the establishments had disputes procedures on pay and conditions; 60 per cent and 77 per cent disciplinary procedures; and 41 per cent and 54 per cent consultative committees. The overall private sector figures by comparison were 28 per cent, 31 per cent and 33 per cent respectively. In the private service sector, the figures were even lower at 20 per cent, 26 per cent and 28 per cent.

The WIRS also shows that bargaining took place over a wider range of non-pay issues in the public services than in the private sector. For both manual and non-manual workers, much higher proportions of public service establishments were involved in negotiating on pensions, recruitment, internal redeployment, redundancy, and manning levels, for example, than were private sector establishments. Only on production methods and capital investment was the private sector marginally ahead of the public services. The public services as a whole were also more willing to pay full sick pay and to take care for the health and safety of the work-force. Moreover, in their assumption of the role of model employer, public service enterprises traditionally adopted a co-operative and paternalistic approach to their employees. This contrasted with a more confrontational stance typical of British industrial relations in parts of the private sector in the 1960s and 1970s.

Other features of model and good employment practices in the public services have been a positive commitment to equality of opportunity at work. Many public services, such as the civil service and the NHS, for example, had equal opportunities policies long before most private sector organisations had them. These related to recruitment, selection and promotion procedures, equal pay for work of equal value, and career development for staff at various levels of responsibility and skill. Public service employers have also sought to provide fair terms and conditions of employment to their staff. These have included: stability and security of employment; pay comparability; career structures; reasonable holiday entitlements with pay, often based on seniority rights and length of service; sick pay benefits; occupational pensions; and opportunities for training and development for career advancement.

It is on the basis of these and related activities that the traditional public services sought to be model and 'best practice' employers. They attempted to follow these underlying principles to produce harmonious, efficiently-run public services and to provide examples for other employers to follow. The extent to which these practices have been modified and remodelled on private sector ones in recent years is explored below.

Emerging Styles of Personnel and Industrial Relations Management

Personnel management is normally associated with the techniques and activities used by personnel specialists to facilitate the effective recruitment, deployment, rewarding, utilisation and training of people at work. In the traditional model of personnel management, it is line managers who manage people and personnel specialists who provide them with personnel advice, monitor personnel policy and manage the personnel management systems. In these circumstances, personnel specialists are sometimes put in an ambigious position. This is because they have not only managerial roles, and are ultimately accountable for their actions to senior management, but also a mediatory role between the organisation's employees and their employer. This happens, for example, where they try to ensure equity, fair play and consistency in the application of employment rules and policies as they affect employees, both individually and collectively.

Industrial relations is normally associated with the ways in which the substantive and procedural rules of employment are determined between employers and trade unions in the collective bargaining process. These rules are then incorporated into the contracts of employment of individual employees and their employers. Industrial relations, so defined, are largely pluralist in character. This implies that conflict between employers and employees is endemic in the employment relationship but that joint negotiation is a problem identification and conflict-resolving process which, with concessions by the negotiators on both sides, enables compromises to be reached and ultimately benefits both parties to the wage-work bargain.

There is little doubt that variants of the personnel management and industrial relations approaches to the managing of people were the dominant ones in the public services after the Second World War. Since 1979, however, there have been qualitative shifts in the employers' emphases in their dealings with employees individually and collectively. These have arisen from new, employer-led employment practices – underpinned by governmental policies – weakened trade union resistance and corresponding developments in the private sector. This is why the terms 'human resources management' (HRM) and 'employee relations' (ER) are increasingly being used rather than personnel management and industrial relations. We use them here because they reflect the neo-managerialist and renascent unitary values that have emerged in dealings between employers and employees in the public services during the 1980s. In practice, of course, mixed styles of managing people coexist within most employing organisations and there are no pure styles of HRM and ER. But the ideas supporting these approaches have been influential in modifying employer policies, practices and behaviour in the managing of public service workers since the late 1970s.

In outline, HRM has four main features compared with personnel management. First, it is concerned with employees as 'human resources' and the ways in which they are to be proactively managed. Its direction stems from corporate and managerial strategies within organisations and it presupposes an integrated approach to the management of people. It is an approach where HRM activities, such as recruitment, selection, appraisal, rewards, communication and training, are more aligned and integrated than is often the case with traditional, paternalistic personnel management. Second, HRM seeks to elicit the commitment of employees to organisational goals and objectives, not merely compliance with them. Third, HRM is owned by line managers rather than by personnel specialists. Fourth, managerial attention is shifted from relying exclusively on collective forms of accommodation with their 'labour force' to more individualistic ones with their 'human resources' (Storey, 1989, p. 20).

ER activities do not necessarily preclude managerial dealings with trade unions and employee representatives. But they do emphasise that these activities are employer-led, not union-led. They also imply a more proactive managerial approach to handling employer-union relationships. Clear distinctions are sometimes made between matters for negotiation, consultation and information. And emphasis is placed on effective communications between employers and employees, with a willingness of management to deal with and inform staff directly and individually, rather than collectively, where they feel the need to do so. The managerial style is essentially one which asserts the right to manage and is overtly defensive of the managerial function and managerial rights.

Recent Developments in HRM and ER

There have been a range of developments in HRM and ER in each of the public services, and across them, since the election of the first Thatcher government in May 1979. Although some commentators argue that these developments were rooted in earlier shifts in employment policy and practice, and are therefore not wholly original, two things are apparent. First, the speed and rapidity of these changes throughout the 1980s were faster than they had been hitherto. Second, they have produced a post-Thatcher legacy so that it is likely that a 'ratchet' effect will result, with little likelihood of former paternalist personnel practices and cultures being restored. Within this context, a number of distinctive changes are discernible. The ones outlined here are: the strengthening of the right to manage; innovations in HRM practices; and changes in collective bargaining and the role of trade unions.

Strengthening the Right to Manage

Strengthening the right to manage was a central plank of governmental policy during the 1980s. In the private sector, the 'freedom to manage' was seen as providing the opportunity for managers to be increasingly autonomous in corporate decision-making, thereby enabling the 'wealth creating' sector to become more efficient and more competitive in the market-place, both at home and abroad. This, it was believed, would regenerate the British economy, leading to economic growth, the creation of new jobs and national prosperity. In the public services, strengthening the right to manage was to be a means for increasing economic efficiency in state enterprises and a critical element in controlling and even reducing public expenditure. This, in turn, it was hoped, would facilitate cuts in personal taxation, divert resources to the private sector, result in economic innovation and create an 'enterprise culture'.

Strengthening the right to manage in the public services was to be achieved by two major strategies. These were: asserting greater political and managerial control over public enterprises and importing private sector management techniques into them. The first strategy was implemented by a mixture of legislation and ministerial directives and the second by relying heavily on the use of management accountancy and other managerial techniques, borrowed and adapted from the corporate sector, supplemented by HRM practices. The situation is typified in the civil service where, according to Blackwell and Lloyd (1989, p. 75), 'ministerial control over key processes of policy-making and strategic departmental management [was] tightened, while at the same time line manager discretion to manage resources [was] increased although often within stringent budgetary constraints'. There are parallels across the public services reflecting what has been described as a 'new managerialism' or 'a strategy designed to integrate and institutionalise efficiency programming and political control'. Its aims were, it is claimed, 'to deploy optimally declining resource inputs within constraints acting as proxies for market forces'.

The main HRM and ER implication of the strengthening of the right to manage is that public service managers became less restrained in implementing their personnel policies and practices than in the past. Formerly they were constrained by time-consuming bargaining and joint consultative arrangements involving union and staff representatives. Now the union role is more collaborationist or it is marginalised. Public service managers are also becoming increasingly affected by the financial parameters within which they operate. This is because public sector management accountancy now relies heavily on the concepts of value for money, measured against the criteria of economy, efficiency and effectiveness (see Chapter 4). It encapsulates detailed management information systems, the setting of financial targets and the measurement of performance against targets. It is a tradition which is biased towards controlling costs and eliminating waste. But, as one public sector accountant has concluded, 'at the very time that the private sector is showing greater interest in social and self controls, based on a corporate ethos, the public sector ethos is being weakened by a preference for more formal economistic modes of control' (Hopper, 1986).

In their attempts to create a new managerial culture in the public services, governments not only facilitated renewed confidence by managers in their right to manage; they also tried to create a new culture of management. This means that governments aimed to get public service managers, especially their higher echelons, committed to their political and organisational changes. They sought to do this: by emphasising the managers' key role in achieving public service efficiency; individualising their contracts of service; providing them with reward packages with private sector type fringe benefits; and initiating performance-related pay (PRP) arrangements for public servants.

At a seminar organised by the management consultants, Peat Marwick McLintock, and the Royal Institute of Public Administration, in December 1987, for example, constant reference was made by speakers to the importance and value of bringing together the public services and the private sector so that each could learn from the other's experiences. As Sir Robert Armstrong, Head of the Home Civil Service from 1983 to 1987, said: 'This is especially so in matters of management where the public service has learnt and will, I hope, continue to learn from experience in industry and commerce' (Armstrong, 1987, p. 11). A director of another firm of management consultants added that three of the five objectives set by the Institute of Directors, for making the enterprise culture an enduring reality, related directly to breaking down the barriers between the two sectors. 'And a fourth – "treat employees as individuals" – is something the civil service can learn from' (Taylor, 1987, p. 35).

Individualised contracts of employment are now provided for a range of public service managers including, for example, general managers in the NHS and senior managers in local government. Some senior managers, such as those in local government, also have fringe benefits including private medical care and 'company' cars. But one of the most widely-copied private sector practices used to reward public sector managers, and to get their personal commitment, is PRP. PRP provides for periodic increases in pay which are incorporated into basic salaries, resulting from assessments of individual performance and personal value to the organisation. Such increases may determine the rate of progression through pay scales or pay ranges. They are expressed as percentages of basic pay, as pre-determined cash increments or as unconsolidated lump sums. Supporters of PRP argue that where scope for increasing salary budgets is severely limited, PRP enables the money which is available to be distributed in the most cost-effective way. It is also claimed that PRP enables the employer to reward excellence and to retain those staff upon whom continuity of service and operations most crucially depend. Critics of PRP, on the other hand, argue that these systems decay, managers and employees often pay 'lip service' to appraisals linking them to rewards and employees sometimes regard them as being unfair.

The first PRP scheme introduced into the civil service was on 1 April 1985. It involved an experimental, unconsolidated lump sum merit bonus for those in the grades from principal to under-secretary. Under this scheme, a maximum of 20 per cent of eligible staff were to receive a minimum bonus in any one year of £500. Despite the mixed reception given to the scheme, PRP has since been extended to other management and non-management grades, although the Review Body on Top Salaries did not feel that PRP was appropriate for those in politically sensitive roles, including permanent secretaries, the judiciary, senior officers in the armed services and senior staff in the foreign service. In local government, chief officers' pay scales are now sufficiently flexible to provide performance rewards. PRP appears to be especially supported by Conservative controlled local authorities. They use variations of discretionary increments in existing scales, merit bonuses or awards for exceptional performance. In the NHS, the arrival of Len Peach in the mid-1980s, seconded from International Business Machines (IBM), signalled changes in the remuneration policies for senior managers. Further, the recommendations of the Griffiths' Report required action on PRP and in autumn 1986 PRP was introduced for the service's 800 general managers. Its key features include: the setting of objectives; individual performance review to assess how far these have been achieved; and financial rewards for those where meritorious performance in achieving these objectives has been demonstrated (Murlis, 1987, pp. 29–33).

Innovations in HRM

One of the developments in HRM practices in the public services during the 1980s was the introduction of flexibility in pay and flexible personnel management practices. In the civil service, for example, significant steps were taken to introduce greater flexibility into the payment system in 1985. Central pay assumptions were abandoned with the introduction of Special Pay Additions which were aimed, it was claimed, at meeting acute recruitment and retention difficulties in particular localities and for specific skills shortages. The April 1990 pay settlement for clerical, secretarial support and executive grades was the first under revised pay determination arrangements incorporating the introduction of flexible pay. For the following year, a new performance-based payment system was introduced for some grades, under which all pay increases were to be performance related. Similarly, under agency status, 'Next Steps' agencies can develop their own pay policies best suited to their specific employment and 'business' needs.

In the educational services, following the Education Reform Act 1988, all local education authorities (LEAs) had to submit schemes of 'local management of schools' (LMS) by the end of September 1989 (see Chapter 9). The phasing in of LMS schemes began in April 1990 and it was planned that all secondary and larger primary schools would have delegated budgets by April 1993. LMS passes certain managerial and HRM responsibilities to individual governing bodies. These include: appointing staff; determining the number of teachers and other staff at the school; and controlling the school budget. National agreements conferring individual contractual entitlements to teachers, such as sickness, periods of notice and maternity rights, remain binding on all governing bodies. Governors were also initially bound by the terms and conditions laid down in the Teachers' Pay and Conditions Act 1987, together with existing employment protection legislation. Where local agreements, negotiated between LEAs and the teacher unions, confer individual rights on teachers, these continue to apply after financial delegation. These cannot be unilaterally changed by governing bodies where this would breach individual contracts of employment.

Existing pay allowances, above the main scale, are not affected by LMS. However, one of the key changes under LMS is that discretion on new incentive allowances is moved from the LEA to the governing bodies with delegated management. In these schools, the governors have power to decide the number of allowances and who is to receive them. They are also able to accelerate incremental progression by giving additional increments at any time on the main scale to both existing and new staff.

Evidence of governmental support for implementing flexible working arrangements in the public services, during the late 1980s, is especially provided by the civil service. The Treasury set out the wide range of flexible working arrangements available to managers and staff in the service (HM Treasury, 1990, p. 5), arguing that these measures were to be part of the development of the modern civil service. Two major features were stressed. One was that the service is a very varied organisation dealing with an enormous range of activities. This means that 'management must be flexible'. The second was, given this background, that the civil service, like other employers, had to reach out into the labour market to ensure that it gets the 'best' people and those which it needs. 'This involves managers adapting themselves to what people out there actually want'. This move towards flexible working was accompanied by other employment practices designed to modernise the way the civil service operates. These included: flexible pay deals; part-time working; term-time working; special leave; reinstatement; career breaks; fixed-term appointments; working at home; recurring temporary appointments; and on-call arrangements.

Staff appraisal systems are now a common feature across the public services. Where they existed earlier, such as in the civil service, they focused less on job-related qualities than on more personality-based ones. Now the public services, borrowing heavily from private sector practice, are using annual staff appraisal systems which principally assess staff performance in current jobs, in many cases related to targets and objectives set annually in advance. Such systems place considerably more emphasis on the assessment of individual performance than on personal promotability. Procedures are generally open, allowing employees to see and comment on what is written about them. Such reports form the basis of an appraisal interview, between employee and line manager, focusing primarily on improving performance in the current job. These reports are usually retained by both the employee and manager concerned.

Another innovation in HRM practices in the public services is the creation of further pay review bodies (PRBs) for certain groups of staff.

These represent a move away from collective bargaining arrangements and a more employer-centred pay determining process. PRBs have been long established for the armed services, senior civil servants, the judiciary and Members of Parliament, and doctors and dentists in the NHS. What is new is the extension of PRBs into other areas of the public services during the 1980s. Mailly and his colleagues (1989, pp. 127–8, 260) argue that the creation, in 1983, of a PRB for nurses and midwives and health visitors and for the professions allied to medicine dealt a severe blow to the notion of a Whitley bargaining structure, which had been designed to cover all staff groups in the NHS. These pay review arrangements, together with that for doctors and dentists, 'mean that the pay of over half the staff in the NHS is decided outside the Whitley structure'. In establishing a PRB for nurses and midwives and the professions allied to medicine, the government was treating these groups of staff in a special manner. It was made on the promise that the professional body representing nurses, the Royal College of Nursing, would not become involved in industrial action. Its members accepted involvement in the PRB since they saw it as the best means for maintaining their professional status and for improving their conditions of employment, though with what success is open to debate.

The removal of pay bargaining rights for schoolteachers in England and Wales took place for essentially different reasons than those for nurses, midwives and related staff. The rationale for this grew out of increasing disillusionment by the then Secretary of State for Education and Science with the lack of progress of negotiations with the teacher unions, in the Burnham Primary and Secondary Committee, and by the prolonged industrial dispute with the teachers in 1985–6. As a result, the Burnham Committee, which determined teachers' pay under the Remuneration of Teachers Act 1965, was abolished by the Teachers' Pay and Conditions Act 1987. This Act set up a teachers' PRB, known as the Interim Advisory Committee (IAC). Its terms of reference were to make recommendations on the pay and conditions for teachers in England and Wales. It submitted them to the Secretary of State who had powers to accept them, and implement them by Order of the House of Commons, or to reject them. The establishment of the IAC was a distinctive break with previous practice in the school sector, arising from special circumstances, and initially the government announced that it would be restoring limited national negotiating rights for classroom teachers and heads. In April 1991, however, the government decided to set up a permanent teachers' pay review body, supported by five out of the six teachers unions, and it dropped its plans for restoring collective bargaining machinery for teachers.

Another HRM innovation in the public services, since the early 1980s, is the growth of interest in management development schemes. In essence, management development seeks to integrate the managerial training needs of the employing organisation with those of individual and potential managers. It has three main purposes. These are: to develop, consolidate and use effectively the skills and experience of managerial staff in performing their existing job tasks; to identify future managerial talent and to develop those who have it; and to help managers develop their potential. Management development programmes have been running in local government and the NHS for many years. They have expanded in these sectors and been extended into the civil service and education more recently. Such programmes are now directed at continuous self-development rather than merely being aimed at acquiring qualifications and attending training courses.

The Fraser Report, for example, published in 1983, established a framework for management development in the civil service. It required each department to produce written policies on career management and management training, including one on postings for younger staff and for specialists. Departments were also asked to improve and extend their succession plans. The Report initiated a study of managerial competencies, against which performance could be measured. It suggested a minimum of five days' training for all principals under 35 years of age. A senior management development programme was established in September 1985. This covers individual study, self-development, experiential learning and external courses. One of its features is the responsibility placed on individuals for assessing themselves against the list of competencies needed for effective performance. The Eland Report in 1985 discussed the development needs of specialists and administrators, revealing a deficiency of staff with the right skills to reach principal level. In addition, a top management development programme was introduced from 1985. It brings together top managers with high potential from both the private and the public sectors. Civil servants have also been seconded to the industrial and commercial sectors. As Tyson (1987, pp. 68–9) concludes: 'A theme throughout has been to give responsibility for his or her own learning to the individual manager, which is consistent both with the notion of devolved accountability and with the ideas of continuous development'.

Changes in Collective Bargaining and the Role of Trade Unions

Collective bargaining in the public services has typically taken place in national Whitley councils, supplemented by district level and workplace joint consultative machinery. In addition to the former nationalised industries, such as gas and electricity, public service Whitleyism is particularly associated with the civil service, local government and the NHS. Public service Whitleyism has traditionally operated on broadly common principles (Farnham, 1978). The first is that each national joint council determines its own representative arrangements between employers and recognised unions. Second, the detailed work of Whitley bodies is normally carried out by working parties or subcommittees of the joint committees. Third, decisions within the joint machinery are normally taken by a majority of each side voting separately. The purpose of this is to prevent the stronger side outvoting the weaker one and compelling it to adopt a decision to which it is opposed. Arbitration arrangements are often built into Whitley arrangements to prevent disputes between the parties when there has been a failure to agree. Fourth, there are institutional links between national, intermediate and local Whitley machinery.

One of the implications of public service Whitleyism is that trade union recognition has not normally been a problem amongst public employers. They have generally recognised public service unions for bargaining and consultative purposes. Yet, as we have seen above, pay bargaining rights were taken away from school teachers, nurses and midwives and the professions allied to medicine in the 1980s. This was a distinct departure from normal public service practice. Moreover, amongst civil servants, negotiating rights were removed from the civil service unions at the General Communications Headquarters (GCHQ) at Cheltenham in 1984. This was on the decision of the then Foreign Secretary, Geoffrey Howe, who announced that independent trade unions at GCHQ threatened national security and would be banned. As a result of a sustained campaign by civil service management, most of the 5000 staff at GCHQ left their unions. Staff who stayed in their unions incurred financial penalties, were denied certain pay rises and allowances and failed to obtain promotion and training. Despite governmental statements that dismissal would not be an appropriate penalty, 14 union members refusing to give up their union membership were dismissed between November 1988 and March 1989.

In 1990–91, the Conservative government signalled its intentions to encourage the development of decentralized pay bargaining, as opposed to national bargaining, in parts of the public services. This was especially the case in the NHS and education. For governments like the Thatcher and Major ones, committed to free market ideas and the enterprise culture, national pay bargaining is regarded as an inefficient interference with the workings of the market mechanism. Decentralised bargaining, in contrast, offers the possibilities of flexible employer responses to local labour market conditions, including lower labour costs, and it dissipates union bargaining power. As the Secretary of State for Health said to the Social Services Committee of the House of Commons in 1989: 'I do not like centralised pay bargaining. I do not like national pay bargaining. I do not think it is good for management and staff' (House of Commons Social Services Committee 1989, p. xxv). Fatchett (1990, p. 258) argues that while the unions appear to have rejected decentralised bargaining, they 'might be forced, or be persuaded by their members, to consider developing a pattern bargaining model', against a background of skill shortages and with the potential for enhancing real wages.

In the new NHS, directly managed units determine their own staffing structures and employ their own staff, though consultants agree their contracts with the regional health authorities. Pay and other terms and conditions of employment of staff are subject to PRB or national Whitley council agreements or departmental determination. With the establishment of NHS trusts, run by their own boards of directors and directly accountable to the Secretary of State, each trust was able to employ its own staff, including consultants, and set its own staffing structure and staffing levels. Staff transferring to trust employment retain their existing terms and conditions of service when they transfer. But trusts and staff can negotiate changes in terms and conditions of employment at any time after the transfer. As the Department of Health states (DoH, 1990, pp. 21–4, 36–7):

> Trusts are free to set the terms and conditions of service for their new staff they employ. They can take account of, but are not bound by, national agreements . . . The Transfer of Undertakings Regulations provide for the transfer of collective agreements, including those covering trade union recognition, and the new employer should recognise any independent trade union which was recognised by the former employer.

It is for the Trust itself to consider whether it wishes to seek changes in existing recognition arrangements after the transfer . . . [However] collective agreements are not legally enforceable unless they form an express term of the contract of employment. There may be a legitimate expectation that unions will be consulted about any proposal to terminate a collective agreement. Until that expectation is displaced they will be entitled to be consulted.

Clearly, such statements presage a different mode of decentralised, or even non-unionised, ER environment in NHS trusts. Here, it seems, the right to manage and employment flexibility are likely to take priority over notions of model or good employment practices in the public services. It also seems an open invitation for trust employers to establish new forms of ER, on a 'greenfield site' model. Indeed, one of the first NHS trusts to break away from national terms and conditions was the Northumbria ambulance service. It was reported in March 1991 that it had bypassed the ambulance unions and had offered its emergency crews a pay rise of 21 per cent. The offer did not apply to ambulance personnel employed on non-emergency duties and was conditional on the crews agreeing to work 12 hour shifts and forgo routine overtime pay (Brindle, 1991a, p. 8).

Another change in collective bargaining practice in the 1980s was the shift from 'pay comparability' in the public services to 'employer affordability'. In the civil service, for example, the former pay research system, which was abolished in 1981, aimed to ensure that the pay of most civil servants was broadly comparable with that of those doing similar jobs in the private sector. Employers and unions were allowed considerable input into the process and this 'was backed up by an arbitration agreement allowing unilateral access to [it] subject . . . to parliamentary approval and, in practice, to government's retention of the right to refuse access "on grounds of policy"' (Blackwell and Lloyd, 1989, p. 71). Since then, ability of the employer to pay, and so called market forces criteria, have dominated pay bargaining in the civil service. Indeed, as indicated earlier, in April 1989, the Treasury signed new but separate flexible pay agreements with the civil service unions. One was with the union representing executive and office support grades, the other with the union representing clerical and office grades. 'As a result flexible pay arrangements now cover almost all non-industrial Civil Servants' (HM Treasury, 1989, p. 4).

In local government, similar employer strategies have developed, with increasing emphasis being placed on ability to pay in response to both manual and white-collar union wage claims. As Kessler (1989, p. 179) notes: 'in a period of cash constraints the ability to pay has become the key criterion in pay determination, overshadowing any broader conceptions of comparability'. One consequence has been that both these groups have experienced falls in real wages and in wages relative to other groups in recent years. Another has been the increasing sensitivity of employer representatives to 'local authority concerns about the outdated parts of the national machinery and its failure to accommodate their specific needs'. Finally, faced with the need to absorb nationally-agreed changes in terms and conditions in their own authorities, within governmental determined financial constraints and controls, local government employers adopted 'a range of strategies primarily related to manual rather than white collar workers.'

One of the most profound changes in the public services over the last several years has been the introduction of 'compulsory competitive tendering' and 'contracting out' of certain public services. These requirements have had particular effects on collective bargaining and the role of trade unions. It is claimed in the civil service, for example, that contracting out, which has chiefly been concentrated in low pay areas such as cleaning, catering and security work, has had a very damaging impact on terms and conditions of employment. Indeed, the Treasury reported that most of the savings from contracting out are because contractors offer poorer conditions of employment. The Treasury went on to recommend intensifying the drive to contract work out, as well as using it as a form of leverage to bring about reductions of in-house costs.

In local government, too, there are similar examples where terms and conditions of employment have been seriously affected by the requirements of compulsory competitive tendering. Even where in-house bids are successful, and basic national pay rates retained, overtime premia have been removed and standard rates are paid for evening and weekend work. Attendance allowances are used and pay bonuses are not awarded where workers go sick or absent. Further, in some cases, weekly hours of work have been increased, sometimes to as high as 45 hours per week, with Saturday mornings being contractually required. Under these new contracts of employment, employees often have standard holiday entitlements of some 20 days per year, with no extra days being provided as allowed under national agreements. Whilst national agreements do not require sickness certificates for the first three days of sickness, under some new local contracts, there is no sick pay for the first day's sickness. Attendance allowances have been lost for each day's sickness and a doctor's certificate is needed for any absences due to sickness. Finally, with only 20 days sick leave allowed in any 12 month period, these types of new contracts compare very unfavourably with those determined by national agreements for other local authority workers.

Evidence from the NHS indicates that competitive tendering for ancillary services has significantly increased the role of market forces in influencing locally determined employment conditions. It has also provided opportunities for increased managerial control over pay and work. Two NHS case studies by Sheaff (1987, pp. 103–4) show that there was a shift towards local bargaining over issues which would have previously been determined nationally. Though some managers were cautious about this, others welcomed it, reflecting as it did a shift in relative bargaining power in their favour. In Sheaff's view, 'competitive tendering has pushed the initiative in favour of management-desired change, and unions have appeared to acquiesce to many of the proposals.' According to Mailly and his colleagues (1989, pp. 137–8), most NHS managers have not relished putting services out to tender and they have involved staff, both indirectly and directly, in dealing with the problems arising from it. They have also 'had an underlying preference for their existing workforce and have been able to ameliorate, to a degree, government policy in this area'. Mailly (1986, p. 14) asserts that competitive tendering draws attention to the inherent conflict of interest between staff and management over labour costs. This arises from 'management's need to keep labour costs as low as possible, and [the] employees' wish to better or maintain their terms and conditions of employment'. As one manager commenting on the effect of competitive tendering on management-staff relations said, employee 'loyalty has gone to the wall'.

Conclusion

It is clear from the above analysis that there has been a significant shift in personnel management and industrial relations values and practices in the public services since 1979. These changes are epitomised in the increased use of the terms human resources management and employee relations in the public services, terms which originated in the private sector. Public service employers can no longer universally claim to be model or good practice employers, setting an example for other employers to follow. They, like their private sector counterparts, are now far more likely to be concerned with efficient human resource utilisation, effective employee performance, flexible working arrangements and widening pay and benefits differentials amongst employee groups. Again, like some leading private sector employers, more public service employers appear to be adopting: more sophisticated and systematic recruitment practices; staff appraisal procedures; performance-related and individualised reward systems; structured management and staff development programmes; direct communications between managers and their subordinates; and decentralised negotiating and consultative arrangements with staff unions. Most of these practices have been adapted from the private sector and have been influenced by the ideas of management consultants, management theorists and management practitioners in North America. To what extent public service employers have been successful in achieving their personnel policy objectives in adopting HRM and ER practices is too early to say.

The social costs of adopting sometimes assertive HRM and ER strategies by public service employers have not been insignificant. Throughout the 1980s, there were a series of often bitter industrial conflicts between almost every public service employer, their staff and the trade unions. In 1981, for example, one million working days were lost in the civil service alone. There was a pay dispute in the NHS in 1982 and a long dispute in local government in 1983. In 1984, the Civil and Public Services Association and the Department of Health and Social Security were in dispute at the department's computer centre in Newcastle, with a number of local disputes arising from the contracting out of NHS ancillary work. For two years running, there were difficult disputes between English and Welsh schoolteachers and their LEA employers in 1985–6. There was also a protracted national dispute between ambulance personnel and the Department of Health in 1989. One of the most obvious features of this series of disputes was the failure of the employers to allow any of these confrontations to be settled by arbitration. This was in line with the government's view that it was the responsibility of the parties themselves to determine the outcome of negotiations and disputes, not with the help of ministers or independent third parties.

From the unions' viewpoint, though some of them have been involved in many of the changes occurring throughout the 1980s and early 1990s, there is rising concern among them that HRM and ER practices threaten their normal negotiating and representative roles. The prospect of decentralised bargaining, for example, challenges the traditional bases of industry-wide union power and internal union solidarity. There is anxiety that members will be detached from their unions by proactive managerial policies emphasising personal contracts of employment, attractive individualised reward packages and direct communications between management and staff. There is also the prospect of union derecognition in certain cases. Peter Kemp, second permanent secretary at the Cabinet Office, is reported as saying about union membership in the 'Next Steps' agencies: 'Provided unions continue to be truly representative of the staff in agencies, then we will continue to do business with them. If not, not' (Corby 1991, p. 42). It is Reed's and Ellis's view (1987, p. 191) that the civil service unions believe that good personnel management depends on the sum total of an employer's policies affecting the work-force. But 'when the workforce is battered and demoralised, neither the disciplines of management accounting nor the endeavours of personnel managers can undo the damage'.

Underlying these developments in HRM and ER practices are attempts to impose a series of new attitudinal and cultural changes in the public services, led by governmental and managerial initiatives influenced by private sector ideas. In the civil service the language is characterised by phrases such as 'performance indicators', 'management matters' and 'service delivery'. In local government, there are references to 'contracting-in' and 'contracting-out', 'quality assurance' and 'care plans'. The NHS is increasingly focusing on the ideas of 'purchasers and providers', 'internal markets' and 'running budgets'. In schools, concepts such as 'attainment targets and testing', 'parental choice' and 'devolved budgeting' are now commonplace. Even in the police services, we note the use of such terms as 'policing by objectives', 'customer awareness' and 'quality management systems'. This managerialist terminology is bringing about sea changes in organisational cultures in the public services and the ways in which managers and subordinates go about satisfying 'customer' and 'client' needs.

The introduction of 'new' HRM and ER practices, and their underlying values and ideologies, are subsets of the 'new managerialism' in the 'new' public services. These new practices are characterized by the use of: systematic HRM techniques of personnel management; individualised employer-employee relationships; widening internal pay relativities; decentralised and fractional collective bargaining; and flexible patterns of employment. Public service and private sector employment practices, in short, are increasingly converging, but with the private sector providing the dominant model to be followed.

Part III

Case Studies

6

The Civil Service

SYLVIA HORTON

Significant changes in the managing of the civil service have taken place since 1979. There are differences of opinion whether these changes can be described as managerial incrementalism or as a managerial revolution, but there is no doubt that they have had a major impact on the organisational culture of the civil service. Though some of these changes have their origins in the proposals of the Fulton Report (1968), or even earlier, the impetus for the reforms which took place during the 1980s, and are continuing, was the election of the first Thatcher government in May 1979. Committed to a range of policies designed to reduce state activity, curb public expenditure, remove the inefficiency of state bureaucracy and deprivilegise the civil service, this government and those elected in 1983, 1987 and 1992 embarked on a programme of structural, cultural and managerial change.

Their programmes involved redefining the role of the civil service, evolving it from an administrative to a managerialist culture and putting in place new management structures and processes. These were made possible by introducing advanced, computerised information systems and were facilitated by new personnel policies. Businessmen (*sic*) were co-opted and recruited to introduce private sector approaches to economy, efficiency and effectiveness (the three 'Es') which have dominated thinking on the civil service since the 1980s. This chapter analyses the innovations made during this period and assesses the extent to which they were incremental, reformist or radical. It also speculates about future developments in management in the civil service in the 1990s.

The Fulton Legacy

The civil service grew in size from 53,000 in 1871, to 318,000 in 1922 to over 680,000 by 1950. At the time of the Fulton inquiry, in 1968, it is estimated that there were some 709,000 civil servants in post. By this time the civil service was recruiting a wide range of specialist staff. This had been in response to changing public policy, wars and the advent of the social service state. As the role of the state was extended from a limited range of activities in the mid-nineteenth century to the Welfare State of the post-war settlement, the management of the civil service, and all other parts of the public sector, became more complex and politicised. By the 1970s the state was using economic resources at an ever-increasing rate and still not satisfying a constantly-rising demand for public services.

There had been many inquiries into the civil service since its creation in 1870 and it had been upheld as a model bureaucracy by successive Royal Commissions. The first challenges to its organisation and culture came in the 1950s and 1960s and were related to its use and control of resources. The Plowden Report was a milestone in the history of management in the civil service. First, it provided the most comprehensive definition of management which subsumed all the activities identified with managers and managing (Plowden, 1961, pp. 16–19). These included:

> The preparation of material on which decisions are taken; the technical efficiency with which large operations of administration are carried out; the cost consciousness of staff at all levels; the provision of special skills and services (scientific, statistical, accountancy, O & M, etc.) for handling particular problems, and the awareness and effectiveness with which these are used; the training and selection of men and women for posts at each level of responsibility. These are the real substance of management, and it is upon them that the effective control of expenditure and value for money must in the last resort depend.

Second, the Report acknowledged the difficulty of prescribing managerial practices for the civil service as a whole because of its diversity. It saw the responsibility for managerial efficiency resting with each department and stated that:

> it is becoming increasingly necessary for the Permanent Secretary to devote a considerable amount of personal time and attention to problems of

management. . . . to ensure that approved policies are carried out economically and that his Department is staffed as efficiently as possible.

These responsibilities 'seem to us no less important than his responsibilities for advising the Minister on major issues of policy'. Third, Plowden saw the role of the Treasury as developing management services and assuming responsibility for efficiency and economy in management. Finally, it emphasised 'the advantage of seizing every opportunity for interchange of ideas and experience with people in commerce and industry'.

From that time onwards the term 'management' had entered into the vocabulary of the civil service. There followed a lengthy debate, both inside and outside of government, about the difference between public administration and management (see Chapter 2). This led to a questioning of the way in which the service was run and in particular of the role of senior officials in the higher levels of the civil service (Thomas, 1959; Fabian Society, 1964; Chapman, 1963). Blamed for both poor policy advice and inefficient management, they increasingly became the focus of demands for reform. The Labour government under Harold Wilson appointed the Fulton Committee in 1966 to examine the service and its report marks a watershed in the development of public service management.

Fulton established within Whitehall thinking the idea that civil servants were and should be managers. The report argued that although public administration was distinct from private administration, the managerial problem was the same. It defined management (Fulton, 1968, p. 50) as: 'being responsible for organization, directing staff, planning the progress of work, setting standards of attainment and measuring results, reviewing procedures and quantifying different courses of action'. Fulton found that too few civil servants saw their role in those terms. In particular, senior officials still perceived themselves as policy advisers to ministers above them, rather than as managers of organisations below them. They therefore failed to carry out their managerial functions with the result that the service was in many instances badly organised and inefficiently run.

Fulton went on to say that managers must design organisations so that they are appropriate to the functions they perform. In the case of the civil service, its functions could be divided into four types: executive activities, administrative work of a non-executive character, day-to-day work on the internal organisation and personnel, and the formulation and review of policy. Each type of activity called for a different type of structure and different methods of control. Executive operations and administrative tasks could be hived off to autonomous public bodies or made the responsibility of accountable management units within departments. Their performance could be assessed and their efficiency measured by setting predetermined criteria and objectives. The policy function should also be separately structured with policy and planning research units reporting directly to the minister. Measuring the efficiency of these units was more problematic, however. The Report proceeded to make proposals for a new central management capability, the development of personnel management and the use of modern management techniques.

The Report was given high agenda status by the Labour government which accepted most of its 158 proposals. Some of the major structural changes were introduced quickly such as the creation of a Civil Service Department (CSD) and a Civil Service College. Others followed after negotiations with the trade unions in the Whitley Committees. The 1400 separate classes which existed in 1968 were gradually integrated into a simpler arrangement of six major categories and the hierarchical barriers were removed to provide an open structure within groups. By 1973 a limited open structure at the top of the service allowed for top positions to be filled by either generalists or specialists.

Further structural reforms occurred during the Heath government from 1970–74. These included hiving off areas of work to separate agencies and the creation of accountable management units within departments. These executive units, however, continued to be financed from votes approved by Parliament and remained subject to close internal and Treasury control. The passage of the Trading Funds Act 1973 enabled certain agencies performing commercial activities to move to trading accounts, including the Royal Mint and Royal Ordnance Factories. In general, however, financial management remained highly centralised within the Public Expenditure Survey (PES) system, set up after Plowden in 1961. Experiments with Management by Objectives were tried and by 1974 ten departments and over 40 units were involved. A comprehensive programme of management reviews was carried out and management services divisions were set up in all but the smallest departments.

The Heath government was less interested in financial and operational management than with policy planning and improving systems for developing policy analysis. It believed that government was overloaded and lacked a policy framework within which new policies and programmes could be formulated. It created the Central Policy Review Staff (CPRS) as a central capability unit and introduced Policy Analysis Reviews (PARs) in 1970. These were based on a management idea, popular in the United States during the 1960s, known as Planned Programme Budgeting (PPB). PPB was designed to facilitate a rational approach to strategic management and policy-making. Departments were required to strengthen their planning machinery and create planning units. Between 1971 and 1973 two cycles of PARs were carried out.

In 1973 the momentum for reform of strategic management came to an end but a great deal of change had taken place. Seventy per cent of all staff were in a new structure, the recruitment systems had been overhauled and changed, the service was recruiting more graduates and more people from industry. Management training was available throughout the service for specialists and administrators, although its content and scope was still limited. Personnel management had begun to feature more prominently, computerised personnel information systems had been installed and job appraisal reviews had been introduced.

With the election of the Labour government in 1974, reform of the civil service dropped from the political agenda. The Labour government was not interested in management reform and it was also wary of planning because of the experiences of the 1960s. Although the CPRS and PARs survived, they tended to be in form only. The rise and fall of these two experiments with strategic planning and review have been well documented by Gray and Jenkins (1982, 1983, 1986). The one area of management which concerned the Labour government was financial management. Faced with rapidly-rising public expenditure, high levels of inflation and a weak currency, it was forced by the International Monetary Fund to adopt a monetarist approach to economic policy, to abandon Keynesian demand management and to cut government spending. In 1974 it introduced cash limits on local government grants and these were gradually extended to other areas of government spending which were not demand led. The preoccupation of the Treasury with refining PES during this period is significant in understanding the Treasury's support for the Financial Management Initiative (FMI) in the 1980s.

The Expenditure Committee of the House of Commons sought to restart the Fulton programme in 1977 but with limited success. It was convinced that the civil service could be better managed but not without further changes in its organisation. It recommended the transfer of responsibility for efficiency from the CSD to the Treasury and the introduction of accountable units in all areas of executive work and, where possible, administrative work. It argued that accountable units should be scaled down to a size enabling officers in charge to know what was going on. Only then could heads of units be held properly accountable. The Committee felt that there had been too little progress in introducing management accounting, partly because of the failure to recruit sufficient accountants, only 68 more in 1977 than in 1967. There had also been a limited role assigned to them. Among the Committee's many suggestions were that departments should be charged for common services and tendering should be introduced. It noted a serious resistance to any form of comparison with the private sector. Whilst it felt there were some areas of the civil service where the political element predominated and outside comparisons were pointless, it felt that comparisons should be the normal practice. The Committee also urged that productivity indices and performance related pay should be introduced (House of Commons Expenditure Committee, 1977).

It is clear that the issue of management in the civil service has been on the political agenda since 1960. Innovations, adaptations, reviews and reforms litter the subsequent 20 years. However, in spite of the many structural and procedural changes, the impact of these on the culture of the service appeared to have been limited. Left to reform itself the civil service had adopted a pragmatic, incrementalist approach. This left intact a service dominated by an administrative élite which still saw itself as serving ministers above rather than managing large organisations below. It was still a public bureaucracy with long hierarchies, detailed financial and accounting procedures and excessive record-keeping. The emphasis was on regularity, following correct procedures and avoiding errors. Very few civil servants had responsibility for budgets and those that did lacked a detailed breakdown of costs. There was no systematic attempt to assess the outputs of the various programmes for which the departments were responsible. Civil servants were in the main still centrally recruited and subject to highly-standardised pay structures and career progression. Individual managers had no power to hire and fire, promote staff or withhold salary increases. Manpower and cash control was regulated from above and recorded below. The ethos of the organisation was one of service rather than of business. The civil service was still essentially a system of public administration rather than public management. The changes that had taken place since Fulton had not penetrated the financial management of resources, although the PES system was continually being refined. The top administrative élite still saw their role as guardians of the constitution.

It was this system that the Conservative government elected in 1979 was determined to change. It is clear in retrospect that it had no blueprint but only a number of vague goals. These were to roll back the frontiers of the state, reduce the size of the civil service, cut public expenditure and increase the efficiency of public bureaucracies. Underlying these aims were a number of assumptions and ideological beliefs which influenced the decisions that the government subsequently took. These were, first, a conviction that the market was a better way of allocating resources and distributing wealth than was state provision. Second, the government believed that private organisations were more efficiently managed than public bodies and that they should therefore be a model for changing state bureaucracies. Third, it believed that the civil service needed to be deprivilegised and the power of public sector trade unions curbed. Finally, government asserted that the culture of the civil service had to be changed to an enterprise culture, if value for money was to be achieved in the 'business' of government.

The New Managerialism in the Civil Service

The post-1979 managerial emphasis was not new but it was different. The Conservative government had learnt some lessons from the earlier failed attempts at reform. Initially it laid less emphasis on structural solutions in favour of procedural changes and the use of managerial tools and techniques to make civil servants more conscious of resources and performance. It also recognised that in order to change the way in which civil servants behave it was necessary to change the culture. Two stages can be identified in the period 1979 to the early 1990s. The first was the development of a new system of financial management designed to cut costs and increase productivity. The second was the establishment of a management culture and a new approach to managing people. These overlap in time and are interdependent but broadly cover the periods 1979–85 and 1986 onwards.

In 1979 there were 742,000 civil servants costing over £7 billion pounds. From the outset the first Thatcher government saw them as an adversary, a privileged class which exploited its monopoly position and a feather bedded and oversized group which had no incentive to look for economy, efficiency and value for money. The Prime Minister stated that the government was determined to improve civil service performance by scaling it down in size, eliminating waste, making civil servants efficient and cost-conscious and increasing productivity and value for money.

There does not appear to have been a planned approach to reform, although a strategy of sorts has been identified by Fry (1984). First, there was an attempt to reduce overstaffing. Second, there was an assault on waste and a search for increased efficiency. Third, there was a commitment to creating a financial management system which would provide information to top management, including ministers, and within which managers at every level would be held accountable. On assuming office, the government immediately put a freeze on all appointments and requested a 3 per cent reduction on staff expenditure. Within three months it had set targets for a reduction in size from 742,000 in 1979 to 642,000 by 1982. New targets were set each year with a figure of 490,000 set for 1988. By 1990 the service had been reduced by 20 per cent. This reduction was achieved by a combination of natural wastage, non-replacement of staff, hiving off and contracting out. A review of staff deployment was enforced, leading to an increase in productivity.

Immediately after the 1979 Election, Margaret Thatcher appointed Derek Rayner from Marks and Spencer as a part-time efficiency adviser to head a small efficiency unit located in the Prime Ministers' Office. His tasks were twofold. The first was to bring about real and immediate improvements in efficiency and the way that civil servants did their jobs. The second was to raise the status of management in the civil service so that senior civil servants regarded management as a central part of their role, thereby changing the culture of Whitehall from an administrative to a managerialist one.

The method adopted for achieving these twin objectives was the Rayner scrutiny. As Chapter 4 demonstrates, scrutinies were meant to bring immediate short-term financial improvements but were also devices for persuading senior officials to accept the responsibility for efficiency and managerial issues. The Rayner Unit promoted the scrutinies but did not conduct them. It set down guidelines on the timing and procedures to be adopted but left departments to choose the subjects on the grounds that ministers and their officials were best equipped to examine the use of resources for which they were responsible. Between 1979 and 1985 about 300 scrutinies were carried out. After that investigations became incorporated into the normal processes of departments.

Rayner imported business management practices from the private sector but he understood the need to overcome entrenched departmentalism, realising that reform has to be an internal process. If there was not internal support and commitment from the top, both political and official, it would fail. But it also needed support from below. He began on a small scale involving lower level staff in a bottom-up process of discovery, reflection, learning and change. There is some dispute about the amount of money that was saved as a result of the scrutinies. There was also criticism within the civil service that they were often rushed and ill thought out or chosen by departments because of their low priority. Even if this was true, they served the purpose that Rayner had intended. He had seen them as setting the climate for reinforcing more general management change. Through the scrutinies he had gained support and agreement that efficiency and value for money were the concerns of top officials. This paved the way for the FMI which became the main vehicle for improving both strategic and resource management.

Two Rayner scrutinies provided the sources of FMI. The Bradley Report (1980) proposed a ministerial information system (MINIS) which became the prototype for top management systems in all government departments. The Joubert Report (Joubert and Derwent, 1981), which led to the creation of 150 cost centres in the Department of the Environment, provided a second prototype for management accounting systems throughout the service. Six interdepartmental reviews, co-ordinated by the Efficiency Unit, into running costs, personnel management, budgeting, competitive tendering, purchasing and accommodation were also important in the new approach to management.

If scrutinies had become the 'touchstone of the whole process of reform', it was FMI that was its heart and foundation. FMI was 'designed to improve the allocation, management and control of resources throughout central government' (Collins, 1987). The outline of FMI first appeared in a White Paper (Cmnd 8616, 1982) in response to the Treasury and Civil Service Committee's report on efficiency and effectiveness in the service (Treasury and Civil Service Committee, 1982). FMI was not as novel as is sometimes suggested. It was in part the natural outcome of developments in the PES system and the extension of cash limits, both of which pointed to the need for a more decentralised and cost-conscious system. FMI was a call for more responsibility to be delegated to lower level managers who would have more financial autonomy. It was also a call for more flexibility in financial methods. Managers at all levels were required to develop not only 'a clear view of objectives and performance but also a well defined responsibility for making the best use of their resources including a critical scrutiny of output and value for money' (Cmnd 8616, Appendix 3). In addition, all departments were expected to establish management-accounting systems which would be incorporated into the existing PES system and their estimates and appropriations accounts cycles. Departments were also called upon to examine the way they managed all aspects of their programmes and to work out the best pattern of managerial responsibility, financial accounting and control.

Though all departments were left to formulate their own plans, there were certain common features which emerged including a top management system for ministers and senior managers (see Chapters 3 and 4). An early report on progress in financial management was cautious, however, about the achievement of decentralisation and delegation (Cmnd 9058, 1983). It pointed out that whilst some progress was evident in some departments, in others senior officials were not enthusiastic. Also central control over manpower ceilings and pay scales severely constrained the authority delegated to budget holders. In 1987 the Public Accounts Committee found that progress had been so slow as to threaten the success of FMI. The problem was, as Gray and Jenkins (1986) point out, that the private sector criteria of managerial efficiency, upon which FMI was based, were in conflict with public administration ideas of ministerial responsibility and parliamentary scrutiny and Treasury control; accountability in Whitehall is not the same as that of the management accountant.

Whilst change was slow on the budgetary side, more progress had been made in introducing performance measurements. By 1987 some 1800 measures were in use 'as a tool for measuring value for money not only in Whitehall but also in outside agencies . . . implementing departmental programmes' (Greenwood and Wilson, 1989, p. 132). However, it had proved easier to measure substantive service outputs than the quality and effectiveness of advice. Generally inputs were the main type of measure although some departments had used intermediate output measures such as the number of cases dealt with or the number of visits made. A range of performance measures was also used including product ratios and unit costs. It was proving more difficult to assess the quality of output. In some areas such as the Department of Social Security, the same performance indicators were being used in 1985 as in 1975 and they still reflected the traditional administrative culture of promptness, accuracy, clearance time and avoidance of error in payment.

In 1985, a report on policy work and FMI recommended that all policy divisions within departments should take responsibility for all the stages of the policy process regardless of who carried it out (Cabinet Office, 1985). Every new policy proposal had to be accompanied by a plan of how its effectiveness would be assessed and measured. This provided for a managerial approach to the work of the policy divisions to match that applied to the executive units and the line activities. From 1985 Performance Review Reports were grafted on to MINIS in the Department of the Environment. This good practice was disseminated by the Treasury. Further developments in performance indicators came with the transfer of the Exchequer and Audit Department into the National Audit Office with responsibility for identifying unsatisfactory performance. The performance being sought, however, was economic performance and value for money. As Pollitt (1986) states, what was being measured was predominantly inputs and process activity. Performance indicators were also being used as an instrument of management control and as a cost cutting exercise.

It was obvious by the third Conservative government led by Margaret Thatcher, in 1987, that its ideas on the management of the public services had started to crystallise. Presented with another five years in which to carry out its policies of reform, it started from a review of where they were and what were the next steps to take. The Prime Minister's Efficiency Unit under Robin Ibbs, successor to Derek Rayner who left in 1983, had undertaken an extensive study of the progress in management reforms. The Ibbs Report stated that whilst considerable progress had been made there were major institutional, administrative, political and attitudinal obstacles to better management and efficiency that still remained (Jenkins *et al.*, 1988). Ibbs said that although FMI and MINIS had led to better financial control there was still too little emphasis on the management of the delivery of services and too much control from the centre. In particular the Report felt that the range and scale of the services provided by the departments was such that they needed to be managed more flexibly and much closer to the point of delivery. Many civil service managers wanted to see further change to give more room and flexibility for the exercise of personal responsibility.

The Report recommended that as far as possible executive functions of government, as distinct from policy advice, should be carried out by agencies. These should be headed by chief executives responsible for day-to-day operations and managed within a framework of policy, objectives and resources set down by the responsible department and in consultation with the Treasury. The main thrust of the Report was that the civil service was too complex and multifunctional to be run as a single entity. Each function or activity should be seen as separate, operating in its own market, with its own clients and customers and its own operational needs. In those areas which were commercial and where money passed between the supplier and the receiver then financial targets should be set to assess efficiency. In other, non-commercial, areas, such as the prison service, it was still possible to have clear targets against which performance could be measured and costs and benefits assessed. The message of the Report was that the scope for any further improvements in management was limited unless there was a major structural change. Echoing the Fulton Report of 20 years earlier, work needed to be hived off. There was a need to balance autonomy, freedom and flexibility with control but a clear 'framework document' could achieve this.

The government responded enthusiastically appointing Peter Kemp, Second Permanent Secretary in the Cabinet Office, as project manager in charge of a Next Steps Unit. By April 1992, 72 agencies had been set up involving over 290,000 civil servants, approximately 50 per cent of the total. Peter Kemp predicted that eventually 80 per cent of the staff in central government would be working in agencies leaving the remaining 20 per cent in small central departments, primarily involved with policy work.

Robin Butler, head of the civil service, in his Redcliffe-Maud speech in 1990, praised the Next Steps initiative and said that it was giving the civil service a new image and breaking up the old system. Civil servants were rediscovering the values of public service, there were better customer and client relationships, more openness, new people were coming into the service and recruitment was better. There was clear improvement in management as the framework documents provided for a clarification of objectives and targets and performance indicators. Although every agency was different, the process of drawing up and enforcing and monitoring the 'contract' was the same. Civil servants within the agencies had more scope for personal initiative, they were empowered to do things and the emphasis was on creativity and new ideas. The management of resources was their responsibility. They now had genuine accountability and were rewarded with more responsive pay and performance bonuses.

Clearly the relationships between the Treasury and the departments and agencies are still evolving and the picture drawn by Robin Butler does not apply in every case. Price Waterhouse (1990), the management consultants, found that with the first agencies there was a tendency for the parent departments to still see the agencies as part of the departmental structure, although all framework documents stated that the day-to-day management should rest with the agency executive. A report by the Efficiency Unit in May 1991 confirmed that the relationships between the agencies and their departments had not always been successful, despite the clarity of the framework documents and the corporate planning process (Cabinet Office, Efficiency Unit, 1991). Chief executives were not always given a free hand and objectives were not always achieved because of policy changes or unforeseen changes in the operational environments of the agencies and departments. The Report called for 'each agency to have a handful of robust and meaningful top level output targets which measure financial performance, efficiency and quality of customer service'. They should then be allowed to operate with a minimum of interference.

Relationships between agencies and departments depend on how far the chief executives are directly responsible to the minister or to the permanent secretary internally and to the Public Accounts Committee and the select committees of the House of Commons externally. It is early days yet but the Next Steps initiative has started the breakup of the unitary civil service created in 1920. Although this appears to be conducive to more effective management, it may, in fact, create a federal structure which is difficult to co-ordinate and control either by the central machinery of the civil service or by Parliament. The movement towards a more managerialist civil service may end up with one or several civil services that are far less controllable.

Personnel Management and Industrial Relations

The importance of personnel management was first highlighted in the Fulton Report. This criticised the lack of career planning, insufficient motivation, little reward for initiative and absence of clear accountabilities in the function. It recommended a higher status for personnel work. There were many changes in the 1970s. The civil service was already in advance of the private sector in many areas of personnel policy and in the use of personnel techniques. It had also built up 'a considerable body of expertise in the welfare field and had specialists in occupational health, occupational psychology, industrial psychology as well as statistics' (Storey, 1989). Further changes were required, however, if the civil service was to adapt to the reforms imposed by the government in the 1980s.

Since 1979 there have been further significant and radical changes in both personnel management and industrial relations. A series of reviews into the structure of the civil service, its recruitment and the role of personnel management, during the first Thatcher government, led to a shedding of posts at the higher levels within departments, more flexible systems of entry into the service and a new approach to the management of people. The Cassels Report (1983), which was a Rayner scrutiny, examined all aspects of personnel work including the roles of line managers and personnel specialists as a means of 'raising motivation as well as securing maximum possible cost effectiveness'. It found that there were still significant differences between the civil service and outside organisations where line managers had much more responsibility and authority for personnel decisions and where individuals took more responsibility for their own careers. The role of personnel in private companies was more to provide advice and support to line managers and to monitor compliance with company policies than to undertake the activities associated with employee resourcing. The private sector model clearly influenced the report which recommended more delegation to line managers on the one hand, and a more professional personnel service on the other. It made specific recommendations on recruitment, probation, staff appraisal, career development, promotion and for dealing with poor performance. Major changes were subsequently introduced in all these areas. From 1983 recruitment of all clerical and equivalent posts became the responsibility of individual departments and this was extended to include some executive posts in 1990. Departments now advertise, use job centres and delegate responsibility for interviewing to line managers. Many of the new agencies have full responsibility for recruitment and selection subject to their framework documents. All departments now operate annual appraisals or annual staff reports for non-industrial staff. This was initially seen as part of FMI and as the successor to Management by Objectives introduced in the 1970s. Its scope, however, was much wider, with appraisal being concerned with performance relating to prior targets and objectives set at the previous appraisal as well as rewards and development. In October 1990 the Cabinet Office reassessed staff appraisal, proposing that it should be known as 'personal review' and should consist of two elements: performance review and potential review. It was required that each departmental system should be linked with performance pay and that procedures should identify poor performers (*Management Matters*, February 1992). Departments can design their own systems but in general they are expected to operate 'joint appraisal' procedures. Performance-related pay was introduced in 1986 and now covers almost all staff, excluding the most senior grades. Other policies following on from Cassels have been in the areas of career development and succession planning. A review of promotion procedures, undertaken primarily to save time and money, has led to an emphasis on self development and personal initiative in seeking promotion. The changes in management procedures which characterised the period up to 1987 required that civil servants not only accepted them but also were capable of operating them. Initially there was far more investment in information technology than in people. But training was given priority after 1982, both to provide people with skills and to act as a vehicle for transmitting a new culture. In 1982 the Office of Management and Personnel introduced a senior finance course for all Senior Principal Finance Officers. Three other major initiatives in the area of management development and training followed the introduction of FMI. A six-week Top Management Programme was introduced in 1985 as a prerequisite for all grade three civil servants involved in strategic management. This involves managers from both the public and the private sectors studying together and developing skills in designing corporate strategies appropriate to their organisational environments. A Senior Management Development Programme was launched in September 1985 designed for principals and above. This is a modular programme which seeks to combine on the job and off the job training. Finally, a

Management Development Programme for junior staff was designed to identify managerial talent and to introduce a management succession programme. It was a feature of all these programmes that they were formulated with the involvement of outside consultants from the private sector (see also Chapter 5).

There clearly have been many changes in personnel policies over the last decade. Personnel management, or human resources management as it is sometimes described, is now recognised as an important functional area of management, but with much more delegation to line managers. Staff are now more obviously managed with the personal review interview acting as an instrument of control. The performance criteria set down in appraisals have enabled the managerial emphasis on cost, output and efficiency to become internalised throughout the service. Equally the major expansion in management training has provided another avenue through which to bring about behavioural and cultural change. If civil servants responsible for resources did not think of themselves as managers previously, they do now. To reinforce the point, there is an in-house publication distributed throughout the service entitled *Management Matters.*

Linked to the developments in personnel management have been changes in industrial relations. Throughout the period of the post-war settlement, industrial relations in the civil service had been relatively stable. The Whitley system established after the First World War had provided the framework within which widespread collective bargaining took place. Union membership was high even at the top management levels of the service and disputes were rare. Pay was determined for top civil servants through a pay review body and for all other grades through collective bargaining. The civil service sought to set an example to the private sector as a model employer and operated on the principle of pay comparability (see Chapter 5). It soon became clear that civil service industrial relations would take on a different emphasis when the Conservatives came into office in 1979, if only because their proposals for trade union reform were likely to impact on one of the most highly-unionised sectors of the economy. In addition, government was the employer seeking to set an example for other employers to follow.

The first confrontation came in 1981 when the government abolished the Civil Service Pay Research Unit and the Standing Commission on Pay Comparability, chaired by Hugh Clegg. A 21-week strike was eventually called off and the government had won one of its first battles with the trade unions. It proceeded to abolish the CSD, which it saw as sympathetic to the strike, and to abandon the Priestley principle of civil service pay comparability. This was replaced by the principle of 'what the government could afford to pay' or 'what it had to pay'. This clearly opened the way for a more market approach to pay determination.

The next confrontation came when the government unilaterally derecognised trade unions at the General Communications Head-quarters (GCHQ), Cheltenham, in 1984. It was no secret that the government disliked trade unions and its industrial relations legislation was clearly seeking to weaken or tame them. It was not easy, however, to get rid of them in the civil service, in the short term at least, and GCHQ was the only area where they were banned. Yet there was nothing to stop the government from seeking to break up national collective bargaining which, it argued, was costly and rigid. It introduced premia payments, for example, for staff that were difficult to recruit or retain. In all Next Steps agencies, existing collective bargaining arrangements with the trade unions continued to apply initially but were subject to review and development in the future. It is perhaps significant that to date none have chosen to derecognise trade unions but some have negotiated their own pay structures and other terms and conditions such as Her Majesty's Stationery Office. All these developments reveal that the government's priority has been to keep staff costs down and to persuade individual civil servants that a more individualized approach to employee relations is to their advantage The Rayner scrutinies and FMI were both vehicles for changing the culture of the civil service but it was changes in personnel management practices, too, which were aimed at facilitating the required changes in employee behaviour. New personnel procedures such as appraisal, performance and development reviews, combined with the introduction of performance indicators and financial targets, are now the context within which individual efficiency is measured or assessed. Management training and management development give a high profile to the role of management within the service and are aimed at socialising all civil servants into a new perception of their role.

Conclusion

The civil service has proved itself to be capable of adaptation and adjustment throughout a century of dynamic social, economic and political restructuring. It has responded to changes in the role of government, new technology and knowledge, growth in population, urbanisation and an increasingly complex economy. New personnel, structures, processes and techniques have been introduced and the service has expanded to meet the demands made upon it by successive governments. With hindsight it appears that the process has been incremental, piecemeal and pragmatic. The sources of change can always be traced back to an earlier period and the policy fits the disjointed incrementalism model (Lindblom, 1959). A seamless web straddles the decades. This is most clearly illustrated in the area of financial management where the first initiative for change in the post-war period came from the Select Committee on Estimates in 1957. This was followed by the Plowden Report (1961) and the introduction of PES in the same year. The PES system emerged throughout the 1960s but gave rise to criticisms and demands for reform in the 1970s. The seeds of FMI were already sown and growing in Treasury circles before the Thatcher governments' 'efficiency initiative' provided the opportunity for it to germinate.

Not only has the method of change been incremental and pragmatic, it has also been reformist, designed to tackle problems on an *ad hoc* basis and to lead to improvements. Where improvements have not occurred or unanticipated consequences of change have produced problems, a new reactive response has ensued. Also fashions have changed along with governments. For example, the fashion for planning was short-lived with the Wilson government of 1964 to 1970; and the fashion for super departments and economies of scale waxed and waned with the Heath government of 1970 to 1974. The pragmatic approach was instrumental and practical, a continuous process of experimentation, review and adaptation. However, the changes that occurred up to 1979 were consistent with and in accord with the administrative culture of the civil service. They did not challenge the shared values, norms and beliefs about the roles and responsibilities of officials within the organisation. In particular they left in tact the élite culture of the higher civil service.

The changes, which occurred during the 1980s, although traceable to earlier initiatives, appear more radical and more far-reaching than any since the Northcote Trevellyan reforms of 1854. The latter transformed the civil service from a system of patronage and nepotism into a modern bureaucracy. There has been a comparable ideological attack on the administrative culture of the service since the late 1970s and an attempt to change that culture into a managerial one. This is more compatible with Conservative governments' ideas of an enabling state rather than the Welfare State, which the government inherited in 1979. Changing the culture was necessary if civil servants were to accept and internalize the behaviour that the new managerialism called for. Civil servants were required to see themselves as public officials and public service managers rather than as civil servants and public administrators. Whether the cultural frame of reference has changed is difficult to assess although there is some evidence to suggest that it has (Richards, 1987b).

Cultural change in organisations is a product of organisational development. The principal means for effecting cultural change are: structural reorganisations; recruiting new people and changing the mix of staff; training and educating people into new skills and attitudes; changing the internal language of an organisation; creating a new image of an organisation; and communicating that image throughout the enterprise. Finally, rewards need to be linked to the new behaviour to reinforce it, with penalties being imposed for resisting change. All these methods have been used in the civil service since 1979.

The 1980s was a period of radical organisational development in the civil service. Managerialism in the sense of a preoccupation with the economical, efficient and effective use of resources to achieve predetermined goals and objectives is now anchored as part of the mission of all civil servants. Managerialism in the sense of a clear structure of responsibility and accountability, with individuals having to answer personally for their own performance, use of budgets and meeting predetermined targets, has penetrated down to the first levels of supervisory management in most areas. There is greater decentralisation and devolution of budgets, clearer line management accountabilities and an efficiency ethos is pervasive.

Metcalfe and Richards (1987b) suggested that it was an impoverished concept of management that was adopted in the civil service in the early 1980s because it was inward looking and top down. Management in this model is seen as an executive function concerned with carrying out predetermined objectives and policies and meeting predetermined performance criteria. It disregards the role of management in managing the interface of the organisation with its environment and with adapting policies and structures to environmental change. Certainly the early and mid-1980s was a period when the government was narrowly preoccupied with financial management and the emphasis was on economy and cost consciousness. It focused on setting up structures and procedures for financial control and introducing the business language of the accountant into the civil service. Cost centres, input/output budgeting and value for money became the media of communication.

By the late 1980s, however, there were signs of a shift from emphasising the input side of the resource equation towards the output side. Next Steps was seen as a means for ensuring that governmental services were more responsive to their customers and that managerial decisions would be taken nearer to the point of delivery. Management education and training were directed towards total quality management, customer satisfaction and market research. It now looked less like the outdated scientific/classical model of production management to which Metcalfe and Richards had referred earlier. It was now more like that of the Peters and Waterman model, drawing on the 'in search of excellence' literature, outlined in Chapter 2. Both models of management, however, were borrowed from private sector thinking.

The level of management which had received the least emphasis throughout the 1980s was that of strategic management. Unlike in the 1970s when structural and procedural changes were concentrated at the top level of the civil service, and on ways of improving strategic planning and decisions, such as through PAR and CPRS, the 1980s focused on operational and tactical management. This was in part because the civil service was seen as being inefficient and ineffective in translating policies into practice. It was also because the government made a distinction between policy and implementation. The former was seen to be the role of the politicians, aided by their advisers and external think tanks. The latter was seen to be the role of the civil service. MINIS and Policy Reviews were intended to provide top management with the information about what was being done, why and how much it was costing. This was to enable ministers as strategic managers to keep more control over expenditure in general and to prioritise when decisions on resources had to be made.

Although top management systems provided a strategic capability within each department, it depended on the willingness of ministers to use them. Not all ministers had the interest in management for which Michael Heseltine was known. Even when some attempts at strategic planning were made, the time span tended to be short and generally linked to the PES system. Strategic management or corporate strategy requires environmental analysis, value analysis and internal resources analysis. This enables options to be generated, evaluated and selected. There is a noticeable absence of either a central co-ordinating structure, designed to carry out such planning, or a research role in the civil service currently. As Metcalfe and Richards (1987b) point out, such a concept of creative management challenges the constitutional theory of the divide between politics and administration. It also challenges traditional forms of public accountability, ministerial responsibility, and the anonymity and impartiality of civil servants.

Without changes in these constitutional and political institutions, the scope for really fundamental, radical and permanent change in the role of the civil service is destined to be limited. Christopher Hood and George Jones, in a memorandum to the Treasury and Civil Service Select Committee in 1990, identified four possible medium-term scenarios following the Next Steps initiative. The first was 'a new stable but substantively different type of public management' in which real autonomy would be given to upper- and middle-line managers, but within a unitary civil service with a single public service employer.The second was of a transition to a more radical system which Hood and Jones called 'incorporatisation', that is, ' the unbundling of a formerly unitary organisation into units with separate identity and a degree of management autonomy'. Both these scenarios would require the abandonment or limiting of ministerial responsibility and changes in the system of public accountability.

The third scenario is that of a widespread but superficial adoption of the Next Steps initiative in which change would be confined to the adoption of a new 'management speak' language at middle levels without reaching the 'sharp end' of operations. There might be the appearance of change but substantive relationships and behaviour may remain the same. Finally, there is the possibility that the Next Steps could go the way of other reforms and be terminated or wither on the vine. This would depend on the strength of commitment and attitude of any future government. Hood and Jones opt for scenario three as the most probable if only because that has been the fate of administrative reforms in the past. However, in the past reforms have lacked the two ingredients which have characterised the changes since 1979. The first is the political clout given to the reforms by Margaret Thatcher during her 11 years as Prime Minister, and subsequently by John Major. The second is the concerted effort to change the culture of the civil service over the same period. By claiming that managerialism enhances the rationality of the system, those supporting it have increased the chance of it being accepted. Initially this focused on internal mechanisms, but Next Steps has once again opened up the question of what should be the relationship between politics and public management. It is this political context within which the management of the civil service takes place, and the long traditions of a 'neutral' civil service, which makes predictions about the future speculative.

What is evident is that the trends of the 1980s have continued into the 1990s. A new model civil service is likely to continue evolving along the lines first set down by the Fulton Report, institutionalised by the Rayner scrutinies and FMI and propelled by the Next Steps. The civil service of the 1990s is likely to be less monolithic and more federal in structure than it has been in the past. As more agencies are created and distributed around the country, small departments in Whitehall will focus on policy. Strategic management will fall to the core departments where, relieved of operational responsibilities, they will be able to build up a stronger capability and capacity for environmental search and scanning than has been the case previously. These core departments are likely to identify the issues needing to be addressed by the politicians and to assume a supervisory and control relationship with the constellation of satellite agencies for which they are responsible. It is likely that some Next Steps agencies will be privatised, but the creation of further agencies will continue. These will constitute part of a greatly-decentralised civil service, as the Treasury relinquishes detailed control. Control will be linked to predetermined performance criteria consisting of financial, procedural and output targets. The absence of a market will be compensated for by clear objectives, rewards and penalties.

The presently unified civil service is likely to be replaced by a more fragmented employment structure. Career patterns will become more varied as agencies provide different career opportunities and there is mobility between the public and the private sectors, agencies and the central departments. Working patterns will also become more flexible with the emergence of a two tier structure of core and peripheral workers.

It will always remain the case, however, that political organisations such as the civil service, unlike their private sector counterparts, have multiple goals and objectives and multiple demands made upon them by people who are not solely consumers of services but also citizens and taxpayers. Managing and governing society is an infinitely more difficult task than managing a private sector market-based enterprise.

Governments have to be accountable, not only for the efficient use of resources but also for the exercise of public power. It is ultimately a political decision what is left to politics and what is left to markets. That decision is never irreversible and reflects the changing political, economic and social environment.

Further change in the civil service is now certain, given the return to office of a fourth consecutive Conservative government in April 1992. New legislation has been introduced requiring most civil service activities to be opened to tender in competition with the private sector. The creation of further agencies has been accelerated although the main architect of the Next Steps – Sir Peter Kemp – was dismissed in July 1992. The creation of a new Office of Public Service and Science responsible for the civil service, open government and the Citizen's Charter suggests the new areas of policy emphasis which will mark the mid-1990s. It is clear than an increasingly privatised service will emerge as the entrepreneurial spirit is spurred on by both tight budgets and claimed consumer-orientated policies. In retrospect the 1980s are likely to be seen as a watershed in the evolution of a new-style civil service smaller, more politicised and characterised by public management rather than by public administration.

7

Local Government

HOWARD ELCOCK

This chapter examines the long-standing concerns of managers in local authorities, above all with the tendency of local authorities to fragment into a series of largely autonomous departments which are not subject to corporate control in terms of policy and the management of resource allocation – or where control in terms of these activities is weak. After examining how local government and those involved in it responded to this besetting problem during the 1970s, we explore the impact of new demands in the 1980s and 1990s, especially for reduced expenditure, exposure to competition and greater responsiveness to citizens' needs and requirements. We then consider the changes that resulted from the ending of the post-war social welfare consensus, including demands for local government services to be both reduced and exposed to market competition. These have resulted in a considerable change and a reduction in the scope of local authority powers and functions. We also examine the changes which were inspired by the 'New Urban Left' in the early 1980s (Gyford, 1984; Hampton, 1991). These changes were intended to increase citizens' contact with and participation in local authority decision-making and service provision – especially those citizens who are members of minority groups who have traditionally not participated and have become alienated from public authorities. However, the long spell of Conservative government after 1979 pushed this second set of reforms increasingly into the background.

Management in Local Government

The development of management in local authorities before 1979 chiefly involved strengthening corporate control and co-ordination. By the same token, management changes were mainly concerned with reducing the fragmentation of local authorities into a series of largely autonomous committees and departments responsible for providing the services for which the authority has responsibility. The development of corporate management was the result of two trends in the management of local authorities from the late 1950s onwards.

The first trend was an increasing concern that the departmental fragmentation which characterised the traditional local authority was a recipe for poor co-ordination of policies and service provision, together with the inefficient use of resources (Greenwood and Stewart, 1974; Elcock, 1986a). In order to improve co-ordination and encourage the coherent central management of local authorities' resources, most authorities now have some or all of the main features of corporate management, as a result of the combined persuasive efforts of management consultants, academics and official reports since the late 1960s (Maud Report, 1967; Bains Report, 1972; Greenwood and Stewart, 1974). These features include:

- A policy and resources committee with responsibility for developing authority-wide policies. However, many of them have become fora for bargaining among the chairpersons of the authority's committees and, in any case, most of the real decisions are usually taken in party group or group executive meetings before the actual committee meets.
- The policy and resources committee usually having subcommittees which are responsible to it for the management of the authority's resources: money, personnel and land. Many authorities also have performance review subcommittees concerned with monitoring efficiency.
- The appointment of a relatively small number of programme or service committees, at least compared with the local authorities of the 1950s and 1960s. Each of these committees has quite a wide span of control and may be responsible for controlling more than one department.
- Most local authorities now having a chief executive officer, although a few have not appointed one or have dismissed their

chief executives (Haynes, 1980). Government has not implemented the Widdicombe Committee's recommendation that all local authorities should be required by law to appoint a chief executive (Widdicombe, 1986). Also, an increasing number of chief executives have departmental responsibilities, contrary to the recommendations of the Bains Report (Bains Report, 1972). Recent research has indicated a trend towards strengthening the chief executive, often by giving him or her overall control of the central administration and finance departments, where authorities need to develop strategic plans for community government (Isaac-Henry and Painter, 1991; Norton, 1991).

● One of the chief executive's main responsibilities being to convene a management team of chief officers to discuss authority-wide or cross-departmental issues and to give advice to the policy and resources committee. Usually all chief officers are management team members but some may be reluctant participants in meetings which may have few items on their agendas which affect their departments (Elcock, 1986a). One authority has disbanded its management team so that chief officers can concentrate on the effective delivery of their services (Isaac-Henry and Painter, 1991).

● Relatively few departments with wide remits – a trend which began with the creation of generic social services departments, as recommended by the Seebohm Report (1968) which merged the former children's, welfare and public health departments into generic social services departments. Equally, leisure services departments now commonly manage libraries, theatres, concert halls, parks and gardens, which would formerly have been managed by separate departments.

The second trend which changed local authority management in the 1960s and 1970s was the increasing acceptance of what Greenwood and Stewart (1974) call a 'governmental' role by local authorities. Whereas local authorities traditionally regarded themselves as being responsible simply for the discharge of the functions allotted them by Parliament, they now commonly accept that they have a wider responsibility for the prosperity and well-being of the communities and areas they serve. Local authorities are multi-service organisations which are controlled by democratically-elected councillors: the only elected representatives Britain has apart from MPs. They nowadays frequently take a relatively wide view of their responsibilities. One consequence is that they need an increasing range of contacts with other organisations, both public and private. In consequence, the 'inter-corporate dimension' has become increasingly important for local authority councillors and their senior officers (Friend, Power and Yewlett, 1977). As pointed out in Chapter 3, this is particularly important for the strategic management of the authority because its strategic plans will affect and are affected by the activities of other organisations.

The emergence of the governmental local authority has brought a number of changes in the management of local government. One has been the emergence of new offices and new professions, of which the chief executive officer is only the most senior and visible. One aspect of the 'governmental' role has been the development of local economic development policies, which are designed and implemented by economic development officers (Shaw, 1987). Some of these new professionals are to be found in the central policy units and research units that many local authorities have established, again partly because of the demands of the 'governmental' role for new policies and a wider range of information (Norris, 1989). One of the existing local government professions, that of town and country planning, has seen its role greatly expanded by the development of the governmental local authority and by the introduction of Structure and Local Plans under the Town and Country Planning Acts of 1968 and 1971. Planners and other local authority officers have had to acquire skills in communication, negotiation and co-ordination which Friend and his colleagues describe as 'reticulist', with individuals, a department (for instance, a planning department) or an authority developing a reticulist role (Friend, Power and Yewlett, 1977; see Chapter 3 above). Further, council leaders have increasingly felt the need to employ political advisers. This trend aroused concern that some local authorities were appointing political partisans to posts which should be filled by politically neutral local authority officers, although the Widdicombe Committee found few indications of actual or potential impropriety (Widdicombe, 1986).

One other consequence of the development of corporate management and the governmental local authority is that the management structures of local authorities now vary considerably – much more than they did before 1970. Committee and departmental structures, the existence and role of the offices of leader of the council and chief executive and of central planning units, together with the use made of researchers, differ widely from one authority to another, even where the authorities are near neighbours (Elcock, Fenwick and Harrop, 1988; Greenwood *et al.*, 1978; Norris, 1989; Isaac-Henry and Painter, 1991).

In practice, however, in the period up till 1979 local authorities in general continued to provide services on the basis of the 'bureaucratic paternalism' (Hoggett and Hambleton, 1987) which characterised the post-war settlement, despite increasing signs of public disillusion with public services which appeared to be provided by insensitive, monolithic bureaucracies in conformity with rigid and apparently unnecessary rules (Crewe, 1982; Parkinson, 1987a). This public disillusion came to a head during the wave of public service strikes which occurred in late 1978 and early 1979 which became known as the 'Winter of Discontent'. Criticisms of public services were increasingly heard and were a contributory factor in the election to office in 1979 of the Conservative Party, then under the leadership of Margaret Thatcher.

Managing Local Government under the Conservatives

The new government was innately hostile to public sector organisations in general and the local authorities in particular. Margaret Thatcher and her colleagues – in common with many citizens – saw them as being large, unresponsive bureaucracies which needed to be converted into leaner, fitter organisations, in particular by exposing them to market competition and by transferring some or all of their functions to the private sector. A number of new management themes began to emerge. These included:

● An emphasis on the achievement of the 'three Es' – economy, efficiency and effectiveness. Improvement in these respects has been encouraged since 1982 by the work of the Audit Commission. This government-appointed body supervises the auditing of local authority accounts, either by the district audit service or by private auditors. It also publishes handbooks of 'good management practice' which inform local authorities of one another's management innovations, either in general or in particular services. It publishes league tables which give an indication of local authorities' relative efficiency. Its remit also extends to Regional and District Health Authorities.

● The need to regard the authority's clients as customers whose wishes and needs must be considered in the process of providing public services for them (Fenwick and Harrop, 1988; Hague, 1989).

● The establishment of market conditions, through transferring services or assets to private ownership, encouraging competitive tendering for services or creating internal markets.

The Thatcher governments also attacked what they saw as over-mighty professions, again striking a chord with a public which had become increasingly sceptical of the professionals' wisdom and competence (Norris, 1982). One local government profession in particular, that of town and country planning, faced an attack on its legitimacy, especially when Nicholas Ridley was Secretary of State for the Environment. Decisions have been transferred from local authorities to the central government in order that they can be devolved and be determined by market forces. Public participation in planning decisions has been reduced as a matter of policy (Thornley, 1990).

Linked to the reduction in the size and importance of the public sector has been a reduction in the powers and influence of the trade union movement, which became a major target of public hostility after the 'Winter of Discontent'. The results discussed, in Chapter 5, have included a series of Acts of Parliament regulating trade unions and industrial relations, as well as more confrontational industrial relations policies by some local authorities (Laffin, 1989).

The changes which constituted the strategy of Margaret Thatcher and her ministers for local government have been of three main kinds, all of which have had major consequences for local authority management. They are financial control, structural change and changes in how services are delivered.

Budgeting in Hard Times

The first, increasing financial control and financial stringency, has been implemented through reductions in the grants the government gives to local authorities. This has been accompanied by changes in the system by which grants are allocated to local authorities. The grant allocated to a particular authority is now based on a central estimate of its spending needs. The changes were followed by the introduction of rate-capping in 1984, then the community charge and uniform business rate in 1989 and 1990, all of which increased the pressure on local government. This pressure caused local authorities to make significant changes in their financial management and budgetary procedures.

The traditional local authority budget was demand-led, with the service departments and committees preparing their estimates which were then aggregated and usually had to be reduced in order to keep rate levies within reasonable bounds. Since the onset of financial stringency in 1976 by the Labour-government, central policy-makers in local authorities have increasingly prepared guidance as to the amount of resources likely to be available, before the committees prepare their estimates (Greenwood *et al.*, 1978). In the 1980s many local authorities developed 'standstill' strategies, under which, if a service department and committee wished to propose a new service or project, it had to abandon or reduce an existing activity to pay for it because no growth, in real terms, was available (Elcock, Jordan and Midwinter, 1989). In practice, however, this is a recipe for the gradual growth of spending because the cuts offered by spending departments are never sufficient to 'pay for' the new growth items inserted in the estimates. Local authorities have also been obliged to scrutinise the efficiency of their services more thoroughly and have been assisted in doing this by the Audit Commission.

Second, local authorities have had to be increasingly ingenious in finding ways to reduce the resources they spend, while not having to make cuts in their services or dismiss staff. They developed a wide range of measures to buy time, raise revenue or cut costs, some of which go under the collective title of 'creative accountancy' (Parkinson, 1986). They also include increasing income charges, making more use of voluntary organisations, freezing capital projects and seeking private tenderers or voluntary agencies which can provide services at a cost lower than the authority itself can provide them. There are 'ladders' of escalating measures which finally end with service cuts and redundancies (Wolman, 1984; Elcock, 1987). Many local authorities used such measures to stave off cuts in the hope that a government more sympathetic than the Conservatives were to local government would win office. After the 1987 General Election, their hopes of the cavalry riding over the hill to the rescue receded (Elcock, Fenwick and Harrop, 1988).

Third, control over the preparation of budgets became increasingly centralised in the hands of small, informal groups consisting of three or four leading members of the council, working with a similar small number of the authority's most senior officers. Such groups would include the leader of the council and probably his or her deputy, the chairperson of the finance subcommittee, an opposition councillor, together with the chief executive and the treasurer. In these small groups, the usual divisions of roles between members and officers, as well as cross-party divisions would virtually disappear (Greenwood, 1983; Elcock, Jordan and Midwinter, 1989). These groups would take responsibility for preparing resource guidelines, such as the promulgation of a 'standstill' strategy towards the beginning of the budgetary process. During the process they would monitor the preparation of estimates, interview the committee chairpersons and departmental chief officers to secure reductions in proposed spending. This is a role which Greenwood (1987) calls the 'Spanish Inquisition' (Greenwood, 1983). Towards the end of the budgetary cycle, the same or a similar small group might have to act as a 'sweat shop', demanding further reductions in order to match proposed spending with the resources known to be available, after the government announced its support grant settlement for the year (Game, 1987).

The result of these processes was that many local authorities developed budgetary strategies for meeting the government's demands for spending cuts. Midwinter (1988a) offers a threefold classification of such strategies, on the basis of a series of studies of local authority budgets throughout the United Kingdom. Most authorities follow compliance strategies, accepting the government's demands for lower spending, however, reluctantly. Others engage in shadow-boxing, using creative accountancy and other methods to avoid having to make cuts or increase local taxes to unacceptable levels, while staying more or less within the confines of the government's policies and grant allocations. A few authorities tries to confront the government with 'brinkmanship' strategies, proclaiming that they would not reduce their work-forces or cut their services and in effect daring the government to do its worst. Some councillors, however, went beyond the law and engaged in illegal actions, such as delaying to set a budget, as a result of which they were surcharged and disqualified from holding public office (Parkinson, 1985, 1987b).

Structural Change

The second major set of changes that have affected local authority management came about when the government abolished the Greater

London Council (GLC) and the six metropolitan county councils in April 1986. This removed a major capacity for strategic planning from England's large cities. The GLC and the metropolitan county councils had also been able to co-ordinate the policies and activities of the metropolitan district councils in their counties, notable instances being the radical public transport policies pursued in South Yorkshire and Tyne and Wear. The abolished authorities had also been in the forefront of the development of local economic strategies and the establishment of local economic development agencies, which did, however, survive their creators' abolition. The fragmentation of policy-making and service provision in the metropolitan areas is now producing poorly co-ordinated plans and policies, deteriorating services and a weakening of democratic accountability. This arises because those services which are still provided on a county-wide basis are overseen by joint boards of councillors nominated by the district councils. Others are provided by the district councils individually, so that the former county-wide co-ordination of policies and service provision has been largely lost.

Delivering Services

The third thrust of the Conservative government's assault on local government, changes in service delivery, gained pace rapidly over the 1980s. It began with the provisions of the Local Government, Planning and Land Act 1980, which compels local authorities to sell council houses at substantial discounts to sitting tenants. The Act also empowered local authorities, if they wished, to put their services out to competitive tender. A few authorities took up this opportunity. Southend and Wandsworth Councils, for example, both put their refuse collection services out to tender and awarded the contracts to private firms (Mallabar, 1991). Most local authorities, however, chose to continue to provide services themselves, although there was a trend towards more contracting out over the decade.

In 1989, competitive tendering was made compulsory and is being introduced for an increasingly wide range of local authority services. The services which local authorities are having to put out to competitive tender include:

- refuse collection
- cleaning of buildings and other cleaning, including street cleaning and litter collection

- catering, including staff canteens and catering in schools and welfare establishments
- ground maintenance
- repair and maintenance of vehicles (Mallabar, 1991; J. Painter, 1991).

Further items have been added to this list since 1989. These include street lighting and the management of sports and leisure facilities. In 1992, legislation was introduced into Parliament to extend compulsory competitive tendering to professional and technical services, such as legal and financial services and engineering. In the case of professional and technical services, local authorities will be able to make a judgement as to whether or not the lowest tenderer is capable of providing the expertise and competences required and if not, accept a higher tender where they are assured that the appropriate expertise and competencies are available. Manual services are excluded from this provision. Here the lowest tender must win.

The government's intention was, therefore, that a very wide range of local authority services, and the people who provide them, would be exposed to competition. If the tender from the authority's staff was undercut by a private company, the latter had to be given the contract except in very exceptional circumstances. However, so far about three-quarters of the contracts issued have been won by the local authorities' own staff. As a result, the government introduced further legislation designed to make it easier for private firms to submit tenders, to remove an obligation for tenders to include redundancy costs and to introduce tougher guidelines on tender evaluation to prevent favouritism of the in-house bid. Furthermore, the government warned 20 local authorities that their direct service organisations had failed to meet their statutory obligation as regards the rate of return they must earn (*Municipal Journal*, 11 October 1991). In November 1991 four authorities were ordered to close their direct service organisations because they had made losses in the financial year 1989–90 (*Municipal Journal*, 28 November 1991). It would seem likely, therefore, that more tenders will in future be won by private firms.

Other related reforms have included removing the former polytechnics and colleges of higher education and the further education and sixth form colleges from local authority control, as well as the introduction of the local management of schools. The consequences of these policies for local authorities are discussed in Chapter 9.

The general thrust of these reforms has been either to expose local authority services to market forces or to simulate such exposure to internal markets. Managers are encouraged to save money, render their organisations more efficient and look carefully at whether they are achieving their financial objectives as effectively and efficiently as possible. This has been achieved either by exposing internal services to external competition or by devolving responsibility for provision to managers or groups of managers, such as boards of governors of schools. Also, individuals have to take more responsibility on themselves once they have bought their council houses, as they are responsible for their upkeep.

Changes are also under way in the social services, where the introduction and extension of community care for the elderly, the mentally ill and handicapped and the disabled must be carried out as far as possible by the local authority buying services from the private or voluntary sectors. For example, social services departments are expected to purchase places in privately-run residential homes, rather than providing such homes themselves. Indeed, they have been encouraged and put under pressure by the government to sell residential homes to private owners. At the same time, there is serious concern about whether local authorities have sufficient resources to inspect private residential homes and ensure that adequate standards of care are being maintained in them, as they are required to do by law. Full implementation of community care was also delayed for two years until April 1993 to hold down poll tax bills. A leaked Department of Health memorandum in March 1992 warned that 'difficult aspects of the community care reforms will take much longer than the 1993 deadline to implement' (Cervi, 1992).

The New Urban Left

Although the dominant force for change in the management of local government since 1979 has been the Conservative governments, a second set of demands for management change has come from the Left. As a result of massive Labour gains in the local elections of the early 1980s, a new generation of councillors came to office with new policies and new attitudes to a local authority's work. Gyford (1984) calls this movement the 'New Urban Left'. These new councillors were very aware that public disillusionment with and alienation from the public services was one reason why their party had lost office nationally in 1979. They also had to accept that Labour was unlikely to win national power again for some time. They therefore sought changes which would both improve the quality of local authority services and test out policies which could then be implemented with greater confidence when Labour did manage to win a General Election.

The New Urban Left embarked on three main reforms in the local authorities they controlled. The first was to develop local economic strategies along the lines of the Alternative Economic Strategy which the national Labour Party designed in the early 1980s. Associated with such strategies was the creation and strengthening of local authority economic development agencies, of which the best known were the Greater London Enterprise Board (GLEB) and the West Midlands Enterprise Board. These boards were responsible for supplying risk capital for local industries, providing 'nursery' workshops and factories to enable small businesses to get established and trying to attract major outside industrial investments to the local authority's area. The impact of this innovation on local authority management was relatively marginal but it did give local authorities additional experience of running autonomous agencies at arms length, which was to become important as competitive tendering developed. Also, we have already noted the rapid establishment and expansion of the profession of local economic development officer in this period. The increasing emphasis on economic development also strengthened the governmental orientation of local authorities because they needed to establish extensive networks of communication with business firms and organisations in order to assist the development of local industries and commercial services (King and Pierre, 1990; Hampton, 1991).

The second major innovation undertaken by the New Urban Left, but not confined to them, was the internal decentralisation of local authority service provision. In the 1970s there had been a series of experiments with area management initiatives which had been funded by the Department of the Environment. Under these arrangements, local offices were established by local authorities in particular wards, areas or estates, especially deprived areas. The activities of these area management offices are guided by area committees which include ward councillors and local community leaders (Harrop *et al.*, 1978). When Labour won control of Walsall Metropolitan Borough Council in 1980, it began the implementation of a decentralisation scheme under which 33 neighbourhood offices were to be established so that services could be provided from points close to the authority's clients. They could easily contact council staff about their needs and problems. The scheme proved so popular that when an alliance of Conservatives and Liberals won control of the council two years later, they dared not reverse the neighbourhood office programme, although the programme was not completed (Wintour, 1983; Seabrook, 1984).

During the 1980s a great many local authorities experimented with decentralisation schemes which were of three types:

- **Departmental decentralisation**, under which a single service department devolves its service provision and many of its staff to neighbourhood offices or teams. Social services and housing departments have been especially active in decentralisation at this level.
- **Corporate decentralisation**, under which several departments combine to staff a multidisciplinary neighbourhood office. This provides a version of corporate management 'from below', as street-level staff collaborate to meet their clients' needs and improve conditions in the localities covered by their offices.
- **Political decentralisation**, where the neighbourhood offices are advised by committees consisting of ward councillors, community leaders, local clergy and others. Those authorities which have progressed furthest along this route, such as Islington, are especially keen to stimulate participation in local affairs by those groups which commonly are excluded or exclude themselves from such participation. these include women, racial minorities and the disabled.

Decentralisation programmes have radical implications for local authority management, because they entail giving considerable discretion to relatively junior staff in neighbourhood offices, thus weakening the control functions of middle management. Middle managers have sometimes resisted decentralisation for this reason. Furthermore, an extensive training programme is needed both to prepare neighbourhood staff for their new roles and to reorientate middle managers in order to ensure that they do not seek to control excessively the activities of the staff in the neighbourhood offices (Elcock, 1986b, 1988). This training must therefore be concerned chiefly with changing the organisation's culture.

Another source of resistance has been trade unions, notably the National and Local Government Officers Association (NALGO), whose members are wary of changes which entail alterations in their members' location and conditions of employment. Many local government staff would prefer not to have extensive face to face contact with the public: one NALGO branch regarded neighbourhood offices as places where people would be 'noisy and nosey'. A decentralisation project in Hackney was blocked by union opposition and there was considerable resistance in Tower Hamlets, where decentralisation was introduced by a Liberal-controlled council. Another radical change entailed by political decentralisation is that committee and other procedures need to be altered in order to make it easier for members of minority or disadvantaged groups to take part in meetings or enter discussions with councillors and council staff.

This leads to the last main feature of the New Urban Left's programme for local government: positive discrimination to assist disadvantaged groups to take their full place and play their full roles in society (Lansley *et al.*, 1989). One aspect of this policy aroused much vicious criticism, especially in the tabloid press: the making of local authority grants to minority groups, including organisations working with racial and ethnic minorities, women and gay people. However, more important in managerial terms was the attempt to involve the members of these and other minorities more in discussions and decision-making in the local authority and the local community, often as part of a decentralisation initiative. Local authorities controlled by the New Urban Left were also especially anxious to recruit women, gays and members of racial minorities to their staffs, in order to establish their credentials as equal opportunities employers. Recruitment practices therefore had to be changed to encourage such people to apply and to ensure that they are not discriminated against during the selection process (Lansley *et al.*, 1989; Hampton, 1991).

Local authorities which became involved in the support of such groups also engaged extensively in monitoring their own practices and those of others. Equal opportunities officers and units were appointed and given a mission to reduce gender and racial discrimination, together with the attitudes and vocabulary fostering it. Frequently, these policies were executed to the accompaniment of unfavourable tabloid publicity. The combination of the arrival of the New Urban Left, coupled with the passage of anti-discrimination legislation in the gender and race fields, gave rise to the development of yet another new profession, that of equal opportunities officer. It has also generated further demands for training in gender and racial awareness, self-assertiveness and related subjects. Sometimes, the development and enforcement of anti-discrimination policies have given rise to disputes between local authorities and individual members of their staffs, such as the McGoldrick case in Brent, where a headteacher was disciplined by a Labour-controlled local authority for making an allegedly racist remark.

Increasingly severe financial constraints, however, have inhibited the development of such programmes as decentralisation initiatives and anti-discrimination programmes, since they cost significant sums of money to implement. Also, the defeat of the campaigns mounted against rate-capping and the abolition of the GLC caused much of the heart to go out of the New Urban Left. Several of its leaders have now moved from their local authority posts to the House of Commons (Hampton, 1991).

Managing the Enabling Authority: 1987 Onwards

The consequence of all these changes and new pressures from both right and left has been a major reorientation of management in local government. Management is simply not concerned with the same issues and problems as it was ten years ago. The changes which have come about are commonly labelled 'the enabling local authority' but this phrase has been used by different people to denote very different sets of developments. The phrase itself has become so ambiguous as to be meaningless.

The New Right and the New Urban Left have both introduced a stream of innovations into local government which have major implications for its management. These have been extensively examined by Stewart (1986). Many of his ideas have been worked out by him and collaborators in the Local Government Training Board (LGTB) (now Management Board) (LGMB) (Clarke and Stewart, 1988; Barratt and Downs, 1988; Brooke, 1989) and the Institute for Local Government Studies. The agenda for change encompassed under the phrase, 'the enabling local authority', can be classified under two headings: market-based solutions and collectivist solutions (Hoggett and Hambleton, 1987). Because the Conservatives were in power for so long after 1979, it is market-based solutions which predominated. One of the most radical market-based solutions was compulsory competitive tendering. This has forced local authority managers to revise their methods radically, especially in the management of their direct labour organisations.

The responses of local authorities and their managers to the advent of compulsory competitive tendering (CCT) has been of several kinds. Probably the most common has been the establishment of a Direct Service Organisation (DSO) to tender on behalf of the authority's own staff for the contracts offered by a particular department or the authority as a whole. The 1988 Local Government Act requires that the roles of tenderer and client must be clearly separate where a DSO is tendering for its own authority's work. DSOs can also tender for work in other local authorities. The extent to which a local authority may favour its own DSO when considering tenders, as well as the ability to require private sector tenders to take account of redundancy costs in their tenders, was to be reduced by further legislation in 1992.

Some DSOs have now become free-standing companies linked to the local authority. A more radical step is the management buy-out, whereby some staff retire from their local authority posts and set up as a supplier which sells the relevant services to the local authority. However, there have been cases of malpractice here. For instance, several senior officers of West Wiltshire District Council who had been involved in preparing computer software for the authority took early retirement and set up a software company. This was highly successful in selling high quality software not only to West Wiltshire but also to many other local authorities. However, it became apparent that the former officers were profiting from work done for West Wiltshire District Council, which therefore belonged to it. The result was the initiation of criminal proceedings by the police.

Within these DSOs, trade union restrictive practices have commonly been removed or reduced and employment levels and wages have been cut, in order to try and ensure that the DSO's tender is successful. The overriding objective for managers and unions has been to keep work 'in-house' and they have worked together to achieve this, albeit not always harmoniously (Laffin, 1989). However, the alternative is to risk losing the tender to a private contractor, with consequent redundancies and at best the partial re-employment of the redundant local authority workers by the successful tenderer, at lower wages and with worse conditions of service (IPM-IDS, 1986). In the first round of competitive tendering, about three-quarters of 'in-house' tenders were successful, although in Conservative-controlled authorities the proportion of contracts let to the private sector was considerably higher (J. Painter, 1991). As noted earlier, the government took steps in 1992 to encourage more private firms to submit tenders and so make it easier for them to win competitions against DSO tenders. Tenders must also be accepted from firms in other European Community countries under the terms of the Single European Act. The impact of this will be felt after the single market is completed in 1993.

Where services are to be contracted out, care has to be taken to prepare an appropriate specification for the work to be done, and after the tender has been awarded the contractor's work needs to be monitored to ensure that the service is provided to a satisfactory standard. The preparation and monitoring of tenders therefore provides extra work for lawyers, administrators and accountants – the very bureaucrats whose numbers Conservative governments were determined to reduce. However, these white-collar services are soon themselves to be exposed to compulsory tendering.

A problem which has arisen on several occasions, especially in catering, is that very few private contractors are interested or able to undertake the very large volumes of work involved in, for example, catering for schools or welfare establishments. Furthermore, once a contract is let and substantial assets, such as a fleet of vehicles, have been handed over to a private contractor, it may become very difficult for the local authority to move to another contractor when next the contract falls due to be put out to tender. The process of letting contracts can, therefore, be fraught with difficulties.

In education, as pointed out in Chapter 9, relatively few schools have so far taken advantage of the opportunity to remove themselves from local authority control altogether and be directly funded by central government. But the pressure and inducements for them to do so are increasing. Similarly, although many council houses have now been sold and the government is trying to persuade remaining tenants to change their landlord from the local authority to a housing association, a housing action trust or private ownership, so far there has been only limited response. These are areas where changes are likely to increase in the future.

In some ways the most radical of all the market-based solutions are contained in the provisions of the NHS and Community Care Act 1990. This, as stated above, is being implemented by stages in order to limit the impact of its provisions on local taxation levels. The local authority is to divest itself as far as possible of the ownership of assets and the provision of services and is instead to become a planner and purchaser of services. At a strategic level local authorities are required to develop community care plans, having assessed community care needs, set local priorities and service objectives and developed local plans for the delivery of services in consultation with health authorities, housing authorities, voluntary bodies and private providers of care. Here, therefore, the local authority needs to develop a series of partnership relationships not only with private providers of care, and voluntary agencies, but also with district health authorities, health trusts and general practitioners. Local authority social services departments will commission services specifying the needs to be met and setting in place a system permitting 'bids' from potential voluntary or private sector providers. Contracts will specify not only quantity and costs but also quality. The social services department will need to spend much time developing relationships with these partners. However, at the same time, those same departments are required to check by inspection that the standards of care they provide are satisfactory.

The ideal local authority, then, for the supporters of market-based solutions, is one that meets once a year to review and let or re-let tenders for the provision of its services. It then leaves the successful tenderers to provide the services for which the local authority is responsible. However, in practice local authorities continue themselves to be large providers of services and must in any case monitor contractors to ensure that the services they provide are satisfactory. The problems inherent in competitive tendering became apparent when Wandsworth Borough Council, which had tendered out residential care for its old people to a private contractor, discovered that the meal portions served at the privately-run old people's homes had been reduced to starvation levels in order to protect the company's profit margins. The contractor concerned was discharged. There have been other cases, both in local government and the National Health Service, where contractors have had to be discharged for failing to comply with the terms of their contracts.

One development which market-based and collectivist solutions have in common is an increasing concern with the client as consumer – as an individual rather than as a member of a wider community. Hence, concern with consumers may entail allowing discretion to service departments and service providers, which in turn produces relatively weak management at the organisation's centre (Isaac-Henry and Painter, 1991). We need to bear in mind, however, that in applying consumer reforms to local authority services we are dealing not with customers in the commercial sense but with citizens. Citizens have rights which they expect to be able to enforce and votes, which give them the ultimate sanction, if they do not like the way a local authority is run, of voting the councillors who control it out of office. Citizen's rights are being augmented and publicised through the publication of *The Citizen's Charter* and related *Charters* covering particular public services.

The reforms which are intended to make local authorities more accessible and responsive to consumers have varied from the cosmetic to carrying out extensive consumer research (Fenwick and Harrop, 1989). Some have involved such radical changes as carrying out internal decentralisation schemes. Programmes of consumer reform include, at the less significant end, innovations like a new letterhead or the introduction of jingles to entertain callers waiting on the telephone. Others entail improving the accessibility of the authority and its staff to consumers. Some authorities, for instance Manchester and Leicester City Councils, provide complaints or information centres where citizens can go to seek advice or register complaints (Mallabar, 1991). One chief executive of a relatively small shire district council in the North-East of England announced that for one hour each week, he could be telephoned directly by anyone who wished to complain or make a point about his authority's services. He claims to have enjoyed the experience (Elcock, Fenwick and Harrop, 1988).

A third dimension of consumerism in local government is the conduct of consumer research, to discover how far citizens are aware of what services the local authority provides, how much they use them and what their opinion of them is. Finally, local authorities may hold public meetings and encourage citizens to participate in the taking of decisions which affect them. Great efforts were put into increasing opportunities for participation in planning decisions after the publication of the Skeffington Report in 1969, but these opportunities have now been reduced in the interest of securing quick decisions in favour of developers. Beyond such consumerist reforms, the main collectivist approach has been to develop decentralisation initiatives.

Various combinations of market-based and collectivist proposals have been brought together under the general heading of the 'public service orientation', a term which was originally devised by John

Stewart (1986). Public service orientations are encouraging three main kinds of management change for the future. The first is that councillors should give 'directions' to the authority's staff, rather than being involved in the detailed administration of the authority's services (Barratt and Downs, 1988). Like previous attempts to prise councillors' hands off the minutiae of local government (Maud Report, 1967; Bains Report, 1972), this proposal seems destined to founder on councillors' beliefs that the energetic pursuit of their electors' cases will win them extra votes at the next elections. However, the proposal is now couched in terms of councillors establishing a new, more consumer-oriented organisational culture, as well as in involving them in strategic planning processes which do not interest most of them. Councillors may therefore have an important role to play in changing the authority's culture.

A second trend is towards strengthening the role of the 'street-level bureaucrats' (Lipsky, 1980): the relatively junior members of local authority staffs who have direct contact with members of the public. Decentralisation initiatives, community fora, participation exercises and general efforts to improve the accessibility of staff and services for citizens, all force local authority staff to have more frequent contacts and to relate more sympathetically with members of the public. Clients must also be offered more choice, through real or simulated markets. At another level, headteachers now have greater autonomy, together with their boards of governors, to decide local issues concerning individual schools, including their spending priorities.

Decentralisation and devolution of powers also increase the area of discretion which must be available to the street-level bureaucrats so that they can respond effectively to the needs, problems and wishes with which their customers present them, thus in turn weakening the supervisory roles of middle managers and senior staff. This process of rendering the middle managers redundant is being accelerated by the introduction of information and communications technologies in decentralised offices. Information is available both to street-level bureaucrats and their clients at the touch of a button, instead of having to be supplied by staff at headquarters. The result can be the 'polo effect': the creation of an organisation with a hole at the centre (Booth and Pitt, 1984).

Third, the notion is gaining ground that local authorities would be more coherent organisations if they were controlled by general managers. The LGMB is increasingly advocating the appointment by local authorities of general managers whose remit would be, in collaboration with councillors, to change the organisation's culture (Brooke, 1989). A consultation paper produced by the Department of the Environment (1991a) under Michael Heseltine put forward a number of options for the internal management of local authorities. These included a council manager, a directly-elected executive and a directly-elected mayor. This had been preceded by two further consultation documents on *A New Tax for Local Government* (DoE, Welsh and Scottish Office, 1991) and on *The Structure of Local Government in England* (DoE, 1991b). Greenwood (1992) states that after the turmoil and vicissitudes experienced by local government in the 1980s, 'the 1990s seem unlikely to provide a time for reflection and settling down'. The management of change is likely to be ongoing.

Conclusion

Although the 'new management' of local government is still evolving, some aspects are already clear:

• power is being transferred from the centre to decentralised offices closer to the consumer and power is being exercised increasingly by those who deliver the service – whether they are local authority employees or private sector workers;
• local authorities are trying to become more responsive to the community, aiming to provide differentiated services relevant to a diverse set of needs;
• local authorities are working increasingly closely with a wide range of agencies in the private and commercial and voluntary sectors and a new style of interagency networking, co-operation and collaboration is becoming the norm;
• the enabling role of local government is calling for new skills, new structures and new attitudes;
• local authority managers are producing mission statements and business plans, costing services, drawing up contracts, establishing quality assurance systems and developing customer awareness. These are now central to management agenda.

Local government is undergoing radical change as a consequence of a sustained attack by central government with the objectives of increasing choice, efficiency and accountability. The movement to the mixed economy of service provision is producing a decline in the number and range of services actually supplied by local authorities and an increase in their planning and purchasing role. They have had to develop the capability of identifying community needs and for monitoring and controlling service provision by contractors who may be inside or outside the authority. The market-based aspects of their new enabling role are at present in the ascendant because the Conservative governments have enforced the policy, through legislation and put consistent pressure on local authorities to reduce costs. Pressure has also come from the Audit Commission to reform management practices and to develop performance indicators. *The Citizen's Charter* (Prime Minister's Office, 1991) is aimed at creating further changes in service delivery and the strengthening of customer rights. In particular, consumers will be able to see whether the services they receive match up to targets set in the *Charter* and related documents.

As to the future, changes in local government are planned by the Conservative government, elected in April 1992. Their election manifesto confirmed their commitment to further reforms in the structure, finance and accountability of local government. These included looking 'at ways in which the internal management of local authorities might become more effective' (Conservative Party Manifesto, 1992). The community charge will be replaced by a new Council Tax in April 1993 and the principles of *The Citizen's Charter* will be extended to the local authority sector. This will require the publication of more information to enable local people to judge the efficiency of their councils in providing services. The drive towards consumerism and more flexible, responsive and accessible local authorities is set to continue. CCT will be extended to internal professional services and performance indicators and league tables will be emphasised. Enabling councils will be more limited in their range of responsibilities as a result of hiving off, either to the private sector or to independent agencies. For those services remaining in local government, tensions will arise from the collective choices made by the elected representatives, the need to provide value for money, the need to be responsive to consumer expectations and the values of local government professionals. These will continue to colour the managing of local government for the foreseeable future.

8

The National Health Service

GRAHAM MOON and IAN KENDALL

The establishment of a National Health Service (NHS) without service-user charges and with the twin goals of minimising inequalities in health and maximising access to health care is understandably associated with the socialist aspirations of the immediate post-war Labour government. However, it has long been argued that a key motivating factor was the less ideological, more technical goal of an efficiently managed health care system (Eckstein, 1958). Although the terminology may have changed, there is therefore a case for seeing a consistency in discussions concerning the management of health services in Britain.

This chapter takes as its start point the establishment of the NHS in 1948. It examines the development of administrative and clinical management within the service over the 'consensus' years preceding the recommendation of the Griffiths Report (DHSS, 1983) that the NHS should shift to a general management model. The Griffiths Report is reviewed and its impact assessed. Attention then turns to the implications of more recent NHS reforms for the management of the service.

The Consensus Years

The socialist notion that centralisation and nationalisation were to be a means to greater efficiency might find a sceptical audience today. At the time of the creation of the NHS, however, it was an idea clearly rooted in two sets of experiences. First, there was the lengthy period in which a combination of local authorities and voluntary institutions had been the key arbiters of the availability of health care resources. The result was a geographical distribution of services which depended on 'the wealth of each area, the political initiative of different local authorities, the donations of the living and the legacies of the dead' (Abel-Smith, 1990, p. 11). The outcome for the hospitals was a collection of independently-managed institutions providing an arbitrary patchwork quilt of services of varying degrees of efficacy, separated and enclosed by financial, legal, medical, residential and occupational barriers. The second experience was of the changes induced by the exigencies of total war. These included a degree of effective planning and a considerable input of much needed investment associated with the establishment of the Emergency Medical Service. Both experiences indicated a case for a centrally planned national health service.

The operational details of how the new NHS was to be managed proved to be controversial. Representatives of the medical profession successfully sought to minimise lay control over their activities. This was most obviously achieved by the eventual tripartite administrative structure of the service, the relative autonomy of the teaching hospitals, the proscribed role for local government and the independent status of General Practitioners (GPs). In management terms this structure meant that there emerged at least three different forms of management. The self-employed general practitioners were virtually beyond management in any formal sense, although they maintained a strong professional consensus and were often extremely effective at managing their own workload and what amounted to their own small businesses. Community and public health services were, until the 1974 reorganisation, to be managed in a manner similar to other profession-based departments in county councils and county boroughs, with the added complication that some of these services could be controlled and managed by district as opposed to county councils. Their chief officers (Medical Officers of Health) also had a special status: their appointment and dismissal required the approval of the relevant central government ministry (Ministry of Health to 1968, then the Department of Health and Social Security – DHSS) and their remit included the publication of an annual report that could, and often did, contain some scathing criticisms of their own employers. Within the hospital sector there emerged a further tradition of tripartite management based on doctors, nurses and administrators and resulting in a form of shared managerial responsibility predicated on a perceived need and demand for considerable professional autonomy – especially for the hospital consultants.

These traditions of professional autonomy were challenged as early as 1954 when the Bradbeer Committee concluded that efficient hospital administration necessitated one officer charged with ensuring that policies were carried out. This view was echoed in 1966 by the Farquharson-Lang Report for the Scottish Home and Health Department, in which the call was for chief executive posts to be filled by either lay or medically-qualified administrators. The following year the first 'Cogwheel' Report (Ministry of Health, 1967) sought to reconcile clinical autonomy and managerialist goals, recommending the organisation of hospital medical work in a manner that anticipated a later theme of encouraging clinicians to take on managerial responsibilities. The Salmon Report (1966) on nurse management attempted a similar task.

The 1960s and early 1970s have been characterised as 'the heyday of technocratic politics in the NHS' with an emphasis on efficiency and rationality in the use of resources (Klein, 1983, p. 64). This emphasis saw the 1964–70 Labour government anxious to unify the tripartite structure of the NHS. This, it was hoped, would resolve the problems of planning and administration identified with an arrangement that funded and managed hospital services separately from both community health services and the GPs. The first important changes concerned the payment and organisation of GPs. The 'Doctors' Charter' of 1966 substantially reduced the role of capitation payments to GPs; other changes encouraged GPs to work together in group practices, employ support staff and improve premises. When allied to increasing government capital expenditure on the NHS, the Charter provoked a boom in health centre construction. From 30 in 1965, the numbers of health centres in England and Wales rose to 523 by 1973. A second set of changes related to the Health Services and Public Health Act (1968). This enabled local authorities to arrange cross-boundary visiting by their community nursing staff and, thus, removed an important obstacle to the establishment of primary health care teams. By 1972, 70 per cent of health visitors and 68 per cent of home nurses were working in association with GPs. Without major organisational restructuring, these two developments achieved a significant change in the management environment of general practice.

Over the same period, first Labour and then the Conservative governments also advocated major organisational changes. Green

Papers in 1968 and 1970 presented proposals for unifying the separate NHS administrations and also paid some attention to managerial issues. The first Green Paper advocated a smaller number of strongly staffed management authorities as the basis for a unified NHS in which the Chief Administrative Officer and Chief Medical Officer would be key personnel. The second Green Paper appeared to take the idea a stage further, identifying the Chief Administrative Medical Officer as a key management figure, who would have a major responsibility for the general co-ordination of planning and the use of services. The second Green Paper also made it clear that the NHS would be reorganised outside of local government, thus taking all aspects of the service away from any managerial changes to be implemented in association with local government reorganisation.

The need to foster NHS/local government collaboration was also recognised and accommodated by proposing organisational changes that would see the major tier of NHS management covering geographical areas equivalent to that part of local government which was managing the personal social services. The final outcome of this principle was a set of area health authorities (AHAs) compatible with the post-1974 county councils. This, unfortunately, was incompatible with the operational and strategic needs of health service management and so additional tiers of management both above (Regional Health Authorities) and below (District Management Teams) were also created.

The Conservative government's 1971 Consultative Document on NHS reorganisation placed even more emphasis on effective management. A 'sound management structure' at all levels and 'effective management' were identified as crucial to the success of the reorganised service with the corporatist implication that the new health authorities might employ chief executives in the manner advocated by Bradbeer and Farquharson-Lang. However, the 1972 White Paper made no mention of 'Chief Executives' and instead stated that 'to allow for the exercise of professional discretion in their work, professional people are most suitably managed by members of their own profession' (DHSS, 1972a, p. 57). At regional, area and district levels, there would be teams of officers including doctors, nurses and administrators responsible for ensuring that plans and activities were co-ordinated at each level. It was clearly stated that the District Management Team (DMT) would be a 'consensus group': all decisions made would have to be unanimous.

These proposals reflected ideas developed in a management study commissioned by the Secretary of State and undertaken by management consultants accustomed to working in the private sector. They were subsequently published in the 'Grey Book' (DHSS, 1972b). The organisational and management changes were implemented in 1974 and have been characterised as something of a triumph for then current notions of 'management' (Hayward and Alaszewski, 1980). The 1974 reorganisation is another stage in the tussle for control of the NHS in which some key professionals had again maintained a considerable degree of autonomy. The 'Grey Book' expressed some significant reservations on conventional managerial approaches in one respect: the usual managerial hierarchies were seen as inappropriate for hospital consultants and general practitioners. The latter retained a distinctive organisational position, with resources flowing directly through Family Practitioner Committees (FPCs), and continued their self-employed, independent status. Second, the emphasis in health policy shifted rapidly to community care but advocates of this shift saw little rationality in the reorganisation. The respective outcomes of the parallel health, local government and personal social services reorganisation, completed between 1971 and 1974, left the effective delivery of co-ordinated community health and social services in the hands of separate organisations with little financial incentive to work together, and whose most convenient point of organizational contact, for example, at county council and area health authority levels, had more obvious political than managerial rationale. In summary, the related aims of organisational and managerial rationalisation had proved elusive. Furthermore the critical reaction to the 1974 reorganization provided a rationale for further government action.

The relationship to central government was the first area to be considered. The Three Chairmen's Report (DHSS, 1976) into the working of the NHS in relation to Regional Health Authorities (RHAs) recommended a restructuring of the DHSS in order to bring together the functions of determining policy, allocating resources, setting objectives and monitoring performance. A central office was to act as the main management organisation within the DHSS. A subsequent DHSS/RHA steering group endorsed these suggestions, but a management review within the DHSS concluded that there was insufficient evidence to show that gains from the proposed changes would justify the cost.

At the end of the 1970s the Royal Commission on the NHS (HMSO, 1979) lent its support to criticisms of the DHSS and also to the widely-held view that there should be only one management tier below the regional level in England and Wales. The latter view was endorsed in the publication of the 1979 Consultative Paper *Patients First* and, in April 1982, the new District Health Authorities (DHAs) replaced the AHAs and removed the necessity for separate District Management Teams. The new DHAs typically served areas smaller than those of county councils (social services departments) and larger than those of district councils (housing departments). This further exacerbated problems regarding the joint planning of community care (see Audit Commission, 1986, pp. 49–60), as did leaving the administration of GP services in the hands of the Family Practitioner Committees at the otherwise defunct AHA level.

Patients First drew a distinction between structural change and changes in management arrangements; these did not have to be handled together and to the same timetable. However, the structural changes (DHAs for AHAs) were seen as needing to be complemented by changes in management arrangements and the new DHAs were to be asked to undertake a review of these arrangements for the areas they served. This review was not intended to be a further element in a corporatist strategy designed to lead to the possibility of appointing Chief Executives responsible for all DHA staff but, nevertheless, it was rejected by the government as being incompatible with the professional independence required by many NHS staff. Instead the government reiterated its commitment to the appointment of a consensus forming team of equals to co-ordinate DHAs' activities.

General Management

After 1982 the DHAs were initially required to organise their hospital and other services in consensus management units. The Unit Management Teams (UMTs) were intended to comprise an administrator, a nursing officer and a medical representative, although the pattern that emerged often departed from this particular model. The outcome of the process took one of two forms. In a few situations units were set up which were geographical in basis. More generally the units were service-based and reflected the hospital/community division of the

NHS. Larger hospitals tended to be units in their own right as did, within the community sector, mental health, learning difficulties and primary care services. These units were still coping with the impact of the 1982 reorganisation, and some DHAs were still in the process of appointing staff to their UMTs, when the Secretary of State announced the establishment of an independent NHS management inquiry.

The recommendations of the NHS Management Inquiry Team (MIT), published in October 1983, represented a break with the tradition of shared managerial responsibility that had received the Conservative government's seal of approval only a few years earlier. Following the MIT's observation that there was a 'lack of clearly-defined general management function throughout the NHS' (DHSS, 1983, p. 11), there was a recommendation for the establishment of a single general manager acting as a chief executive and final decision-taker for the decisions previously delegated to consensus teams. This commitment to general management was to be extended above and below the level of health authorities. As well as a District General Manager for each DHA, there would be a general manager for every unit of management within the DHA. As well as a Regional General Manager for each RHA, there would be a small management board at the centre, the Chair of which would have the general management function at national level. This NHS Management Board would be full-time and 'multi-professional'. The Chair (the NHS General Manager) would 'need to have considerable experience and skill in effecting change in a large, service-orientated organization' (DHSS, 1983, p. 4). The Management Board would be accountable to a Health Services Supervisory Board (HSSB) chaired by the Secretary of State and responsible for the determination of the purposes, objectives and direction of the NHS, the approval of the overall budget, resource allocation, and strategic decisions. The MIT's commitment to the appointment of general managers regardless of discipline appeared to mark a significant move away from the 1972 White Paper and Grey Book principles that some NHS professionals should be exempted from managerial hierarchies and others should be managed by their fellow professionals. It instigated the notion that health care is a business in which managers should manage efficiently using management skills.

The MIT recommendations came to be known as the Griffiths Report (after the team's chairman) and, given their apparently radical nature, were the subject of considerable professional and political comment. Criticisms could be said to focus on both the process through which the proposals were formulated and implemented and the nature of the proposals themselves (Carrier and Kendall, 1986, pp. 206–13). Regarding the former, the Report attracted criticism for its lack of detail and research base, whilst the government was criticised for its lack of consultation and the speed with which it implemented the proposals. The recommendations for the DHSS were accepted by the government 19 days after their formal receipt, whilst the Secretary of State's letter to the health authorities, anticipating that they would be setting the Griffiths' proposals in train by 1 April 1984, went out on 8 February 1984, four weeks before the Social Services Committee's report on the proposals and almost three months before the House of Commons debated the Griffiths Report. The substantive points made by the Social Services Committee, and in the House of Commons debate, mirrored concerns expressed in the professional journals. These included reservations about the presumed similarities between the NHS and business management, the implications for political accountability, the more managerial and less representative health authorities and the abandonment of teamwork and consensus management.

There was an implicit assumption in the work of the MIT concerning the superiority of private sector management. The new general managers, it was suggested, would bring efficiency-oriented skills from non-NHS settings to bear on the service. There was therefore a further implication: that people with experience outside the NHS, particularly people with experience in the private sector, would be attracted to the new District (DGM) and Unit General Manager (UGM) posts and even to the lower tier service and locality manager posts. This was not to be. General management posts were largely filled by internal appointments. Of the exceptions, a number attracted applicants from the armed forces, several of whom later resigned claiming they found the culture of the NHS incomprehensible. However, the culture of the NHS changed perceptibly following the introduction of general management, even if the personnel changed little. Two issues merit specific mention. First, the one-time administrators were quick to embrace a managerial culture with an emphasis on objective setting, performance measurement and business planning. Private sector management methods were not introduced by imports from the private sector but by converts from within the NHS. The establishment and development of a comprehensive management training system was central to this sea change. The general management training scheme (GMTS) in its successive formats and Institute of Health Service Management (IHSM) courses introduced an awareness of management issues and skills at many levels within the service.

Second, general management challenged the role of the clinical professional in the operational and strategic management of the NHS. Medical and, to a much lesser extent, nursing personnel had previously played a substantial role in service administration through the provisions of the Cogwheel (Ministry of Health, 1967) and Salmon Reports. Indeed many had been, *de facto*, in charge of substantial areas. Following the Griffiths Report, although a few clinical professionals entered general management, the role of the professions was generally reduced. In a service centred on professional care provision, this was problematic. Furthermore, GPs were largely unaffected by recommendations which had, rather obviously, been framed in terms of the perceived management needs of large district general hospitals. This raised questions about the ability of the new NHS general managers to manage, given their lack of control of the major generators of NHS workload. None the less, one of the key tasks of the new general managers was to involve (hospital) clinicians in management. This was largely done through a continuation of the Cogwheel approach with lead consultants being identified in each service sector to provide a clinical input to management decision making.

Following the Griffiths Report, a management ethos was therefore introduced relatively quickly into the NHS's hospital and community services, although not into primary care. On to a tradition of public service were grafted such originally private sector concepts as cost improvement programmes whereby efficiency savings were exhaustively sought in all elements of the operation of the service. Managers were also encouraged to develop local measures and participate in national initiatives to combat issues such as waiting lists and to look to the private sector when buying services. Some also sold NHS services to the developing private hospital sector. Most importantly there was an increasing focus on the need for and use of management information in the planning, monitoring and evaluation of service provision. There was a growing emphasis on performance indicators (PIs) and, following the Korner Reviews (NHS/DHSS, 1982–5) which defined a standardised minimum dataset to be produced by each health authority, the Resource Management Initiative (RMI) was developed seeking to facilitate the costing and quantification of activity and expenditure within the service and to contribute to more informed decision-making. Along with this information explosion went a growing investment in computer technology and a requirement for personnel with appropriate skills.

A final measure of the impact of general management was the way in which it rapidly filtered down the NHS. General management, at least in its initial conceptualisation, was intended to revitalise the service through a focus on working methods and was, inevitably, concerned with internal issues. The mid to latter 1980s saw this concern change. Following an earlier lead in local government, locality management emerged in the NHS. In a few authorities, notably Exeter, the locality movement became a corner-stone of general management development. The more outward-looking locality approach fitted many of the concerns of Thatcherite public policy. It was less monolithic: a locality manager would be responsible for a small community, and would work within that community rather than at a distant district office and might well be deemed to be 'closer' to local needs. For many of the relatively large DHAs, locality management became an effective way to relate more efficiently to their population. The utility of locality management was further enhanced by the provisions of the Cumberlege Report (DHSS, 1986) in which it was proposed that community nursing services should be delivered, and by extension managed, on a neighbourhood basis. The joint impact of Cumberlege and the locality management movement was such that, by the end of the 1980s and early 1990s, most authorities had in place a subdistrict set of divisions with general managers charged with the day-to-day running of local services and the promotion of consumer input to health care planning.

On the negative side, if the largely unjustified forebodings of clinicians are excluded, the consequences of the introduction of general management were mainly felt by other agencies. As indicated above, general management was introduced only to the hospital and community services of the NHS. It bypassed the family practitioner services where the old system of clinical autonomy and consensus administrators remained. The Family Practitioner Services were thus excluded from the disciplines of general management and the structural separation of the two services became compounded by a difference in management cultures. Such a clash also affected relations with other welfare agencies. The joint finance frameworks set up in 1976 to facilitate interagency work between health and other, mainly social services, agencies, although relatively effective, saw an often counter-

productive meeting of corporate, administrative and general management approaches.

By the late 1980s general management pervaded all levels of the
NHS. However, despite expectations as to the effect of 'management
discipline', there were recurrent crises, particularly in the hospital
service, stemming from the incompatibility of finite resources and an
infinite demand for health care. By early 1988 these problems had
escalated to the point where a fundamental review of the NHS was
announced (Kendall and Moon, 1990). The then Prime Minister played
a strong role in this review and, in a parallel development, attention
was also focused on to the future role, function and management of
community care services. The two reviews, *Working for Patients* and
Caring for People (DoH, 1989a, 1989b), formed the basis for the NHS
and Community Care Act 1990.

The central plank of the 1990 Act was the concept of the internal
market. Essentially this involved the separation of the purchasing and
providing functions of the NHS. The unitary health service, in which a
health authority both planned care and provided it through hospital or
community services, was seen as inappropriate in a market economy.
Cartels could too easily flourish in which inefficient hospitals would be
sustained by captive markets unable to use any other service. The
solution was the functional separation of *purchasing* – buying health
services to satisfy local needs – from *providing* – the day-to-day
business of delivering that care. Purchasing agencies, holding a budget
to ensure the health of a defined population, identifying health needs,
planning ways to satisfy them and ensuring the quality of the service,
were to develop contracts with the providers who would, in turn,
invoice the purchaser for care provided. General Practice, as the point-
of-entry to the NHS, assumed a pivotal role.

This concept of the internal market was largely welcomed by existing
managers within the NHS. Their professional organisation, the
Institute of Health Services Management, was among the few bodies
outside the government which supported the changes. The support of
the managers was essentially an outcome of the recognition that the
reforms gave to the centrality of both strategic and operational
management. Perceived obstacles to effective management were
removed: clinical excellence was to become a marketable commodity
rather than an excuse for over-spending and health authorities were to
be slimmed down and converted from (purportedly) representative
bodies into small management boards, modelled on the private sector

company board and comprising executive and non-executive members. The non-executive members were to be selected by the Regional Health Authority (RHA), or in the case of non-executive RHA members, by the Secretary of State for Health, for the skills they could bring to the job. Often these skills were those of business.

The Managerial Tasks

The reformed NHS was established on 1 April 1991. On that date the internal market became operational, although it had earlier been generally recognised that a fully-developed system would take some time to evolve. Certain elements of the reforms, notably those relating to the role of local health authorities as lead agencies – quasi-purchasers – for community care, were officially delayed. General managers had a relatively short time to prepare for the new environment but undertook extensive development work, with some districts being selected as Locality Projects to move further and faster with the reforms.

Those managers charged with establishing the purchasing function faced a major change of role. Many were originally attracted to the NHS by the notion of running a service providing health care. Now they found themselves separated from the provider function. Effective purchasing required strategic and operational management skills very different from those required, for example, to run a hospital. First, the concern has shifted from people receiving care from a particular service to the broader health needs of all the residents of an area. The health needs of the local population have had to be assessed on an annual basis. Following a recommendation that purchasing should initially be on a steady state basis, the services which historically satisfied the needs were then pinpointed and costed. Second, annual contracts with the larger providers have had to be drawn up detailing, in addition to methods of payment and monitoring mechanisms, requirements for information provision and quality assurance. The legal/accounting, epidemiological, planning and quality assurance skills required for these tasks indicate the membership of the typical purchasing team. Teamwork has clearly been central to the development of the role, and the formulation of the annual Health Investment Plans by which purchasers are supposed to indicate their strategies for buying health care for their population.

Management in the provider units, in contrast to the purchasing agencies, exhibits some elements of continuity with the pre-April 1991 situation. The operational management of health care provision has retained its concerns with containing the costs of medical technology and chemotherapy, ensuring staff recruitment and retention, and promoting efficiency through the maximisation of throughput with due regard to quality. It is on the strategic level that changes have taken place, with hospital performance and quality indicators assuming a key importance in the contracting process. Annual business plans and prospectuses have been produced down to the level of hospital and community specialities outlining the services provided and the relevant performance statistics.

With the majority of providers initially operating as directly managed units within a district health authority with a steady-state purchasing policy, most provider managers have secured a major contract with their erstwhile partners in the local purchasing team and minor contracts with other purchasers reflecting historic patterns of use of their services. However, as purchasing moves away from the steady state, business planning is likely to become increasingly important with providers marketing their services to different purchasers. The securing of contracts is therefore essential to the economic survival of a provider unit. Inefficient providers with poor performance or poor quality services could, at least theoretically, go out of business. For the managers of those provider units which were formally separated from district health authorities as NHS trusts with semi-independent status within the NHS, these pressures are particularly real. As early as late April 1991, two trusts announced that they were cutting back their work-force in a purported effort to achieve efficiency requirements.

In the pre-reform NHS, the sphere of influence of general management had been drawn relatively tightly around the hospital and community services. The 1990 Act changed this situation and, through the application of the internal market, significantly extended the sway of general management. The family practitioner services were re-incorporated into the mainstream of the NHS under the control of Family Health Service Authorities (FHSAs) with general managers. The reactive administrative approach of the earlier Family Practitioner Committees was abandoned, the managers were appointed, para-doxically largely from the ranks of the former administrators, and the FHSAs sought to present themselves as purchasers of primary health care from independent contractor family doctors and dentists, pharmacists and opticians. For the FHSA general managers this shift was not easy. They faced highly-independent providers, were often poorly resourced, and had little experience of general management. Despite these shortcomings, the more innovative FHSA managers were able to develop strong partnerships with DHA purchasing agencies and lead social services purchasers, effectively laying the base for comprehensive health and social care purchasing. At the same time, primary care providers (GPs) began to develop much closer working relationships with community health services, raising the possibility of a more effectively integrated care management system.

A second consequence of the reforms concerns the nature of 'management'. In the NHS hospital and community services at the start of the 1990s there had been a short but comprehensive experience of general management. Management culture, if such it could be called, was very different in the primary and social care sectors. However, as social service departments develop their lead agency role, and take on the characteristics of purchasers, the gap between the management cultures of the health and social care sectors could diminish. Furthermore, the integration of primary care into the internal market could bring a greater mutual appreciation of the management tasks involved in general practice and hospital/community care provision. The concept of the internal market therefore increasingly facilitates the emergence of a common, management-oriented approach to health care delivery. Agencies, with traditionally very different working methods, were able to come together to manage jointly the purchase and provision of services.

In a formal sense, clinical professionals lost out in the NHS reforms. Outside the trusts and FHSAs there was no requirement for a clinician to sit on a management board. Much of the opposition of clinicians to the reforms centred on this neglect. In practice, few health authorities, purchasing agencies or provider units were so confident in the omnipotence of general management that they felt able to function without any clinician input. Moreover, some clinicians actively sought involvement either directly as service managers or indirectly through clinical directorates or medical/nursing advisory committees. In the area of primary care, some of the larger general practices became fund-holders, appointed practice business managers and gained the right to purchase some care directly from providers rather than via a DHA purchasing agency. Limited early evidence suggested that this innovation, giving GPs direct experience of major management responsibility, was a success and indicated one potential future development track for the internal market (Glennester, Matsaganis and Owens, 1992). GPs additionally found their views being canvassed as purchasers, and providers sought to take on board the demands of the primary care sector. The reforms also significantly increased the role of clinicians in other ways. First, the purchasing managers need advice on the health care needs of their district populations. Skills in this area are the traditional preserve of public health doctors and district directors of public health often find themselves playing a direct management role in purchasing. Second, the contracting process is effectively dependent on clinical advice concerning appropriate treatment protocols and care standards. Third, medical and nursing audit – professionally-led assessments of the effectiveness of care – provide key elements in the often otherwise rhetorical commitment to quality assurance and, latterly, total quality management.

For the general managers, information on treatments, where they take place, to whom they are given, where those people come from, how long they wait, how long they occupy a bed and how much their treatment costs forms the basis of service specifications and contract monitoring within the internal market. To manage this information requires skills and technology. In neither area is the NHS developing from a position of any great strength. The recruitment and retention of information and information technology staff has been difficult and the technological infrastructure has been bedevilled by a lack of standardisation. The immediate consequences of the reforms have been an increased demand for more sophisticated systems, the rapid extension of the resource management initiative to facilitate detailed costing of activities, a strong commitment to networked systems linking GPs, social services, hospital and community services, and an emphasis on information interpretation skills. Post-reform managers' skills in information interpretation are, however, merely one area for management training and development. The previously somewhat academic accent in the general management training scheme and the courses of the Institute of Health Services Management are being replaced by strongly skills-oriented packages. In the management development field the advent of the reforms has also led to a significant penetration by expensive private-sector management consultants into the NHS market. Most of the major consultancy firms now have substantial NHS divisions offering courses and software to assist the general manager. In perhaps the most interesting example of the infiltration of private sector ideas into the NHS, several such management consultancies have sprung up within the NHS and, with the exception of some spectacular business failures, are now busily marketing their services.

Conclusion

Managing the NHS is a rapidly changing task. Although the consensus years represented a period of some stability for the service there were seldom times when the management of change was not an issue facing the service. Since the 1974 reorganisation, and particularly since the advent of general management, the pace of change has been incredible. Its direction has reflected changing political emphases with the ethos of the internal market currently in the ascendancy and requiring appropriate skills from managers. As the internal market is extended it is likely that the already apparent trend to amalgamate purchasing agencies into larger consortia will continue, perhaps linking with FHSAs and developing a substructure of locality purchasing groups to reflect local community needs. It is clear now, after the result of the April 1992 Election, that more hospitals will seek trust status and that more GP practices will become fund-holders. The 200 trusts in existence in April 1992 will be joined by the 156 health units that have applied to become trusts from April 1993. The 3000 GP fund-holders in April 1992 will be joined by another 2000 or so over the following year. The future of RHAs is under review. The Patients' Charter, which sets out clearly what is expected from the NHS, will provide new performance criteria for health service managers to achieve. All of these developments will enhance the role of general managers and general management throughout the NHS. Given the complexity of the non-clinical aspects of running the NHS in the new internal market, the manager is likely to loom large during the 1990s.

9

Education

MALCOLM McVICAR

The underlying theme of this chapter is that education policy has changed quite dramatically since the late 1970s in Britain and that these changes are leading to a transformation of the education system. This transformation is having a major impact on both the nature of the service and the way in which it is managed. It is generally agreed that the basic structure of the post-war state education system in Britain was laid down by the Education Act 1944. This Act essentially created a partnership between local education authorities (LEAs), central government and later the teaching profession (represented by the major teaching unions) in the provision of the service, a partnership which remained largely intact until the 1980s. This tripartite relationship was based to a large extent on a consensus of values about the role of education in modernising both the economy and the society and on the worth of education for its own sake. It was the essential 'good thing'. This consensus did not lead to a static educational system, since there were very significant developments in policy between 1944 and 1980, some of which resulted from the development of existing policies and some of which represented partisan approaches. For example, the gradual growth of higher education was the result of general social and economic developments which made a university education both more accessible and more overtly rewarding to those demanding it. The publication of the Robbins Report (Higher Education) in 1963 and its acceptance by the Conservative government must be interpreted as a bipartisan policy.

Often policy initiatives, which are now portrayed as deriving from one party against the wishes of the others, were also more bipartisan. A good example of this is the gradual development of comprehensive secondary education. Long before the 1964–70 Labour government adopted this as a national policy objective, many LEAs, both Conservative and Labour controlled, had moved in this direction because of the financial advantages, especially in rural areas. The policy did indeed become more closely identified with the Labour Party during the 1960s, and did eventually lead to some interparty conflict, but this has been overstated.

The post-war consensus therefore indicated a basic agreement about the role of education and about the need to move forward keeping the tripartite relationship largely intact. However, during the 1970s this approximate consensus began to break down. This breakdown may be attributed to a number of factors. As the economy continued to suffer from major problems during the 1970s, some critics blamed the educational system for failing to produce young people with the value systems and skills needed by the labour market. There was a growing criticism of the alleged 'progressiveness' in education which was placing too much emphasis on individual development and child-centred learning and not supporting the 'traditional' functions which the service was meant to provide. This criticism found very strong voice in the 'great debate' launched by the Labour Prime Minister, James Callaghan, in 1976 (Salter and Tapper, 1981). To the criticisms from the centre can be added those of the far left, who believed that the education system merely served the needs of the dominant economic system, and those of the New Right, who felt it did not serve the economy enough. It was the critics from the right who were also particularly hostile to what they saw as the dominance of the LEA 'bureaucrats' and the professional power of the teachers in the provision of state education.

During the late 1970s the criticisms from the New Right did not form a clear, coherent policy agenda. Rather, they constituted a list of critical problems which a future Conservative government would need to address. These included:

- the allegedly-falling standards of basic literacy and numeracy;
- the creation of a culture which was hostile to the private sector, to wealth creation and to manufacturing industry;
- the abdication of responsibility by the Department of Education and Science (DES) to the LEAs and the teaching unions, constituting a prime example of corporatism in the public sector;
- gross inefficiency and wastage of public resources;

- in some LEAs, some schools and some college departments, a curriculum which had been strongly influenced by left-wing teachers;
- dissatisfied parents whose common-sense views on their children's education were denied by the closed ranks of the service providers.

The legislation of the 1980s was designed to deal with these problems and has heralded a very different structure, policy and managerial approach to education.

Management before 1979

The term 'management' was not much used in the context of the state education system before the 1980s. Clearly, in so far as any large, complex public service has to be organised and administered, with resources allocated, staff recruited and deployed and the service actually delivered, the functions of management had to be performed yet the term was not common. This reflects the underlying philosophy and approach to the provision of the education service. Largely as a result of the historical evolution of the English and Welsh educational systems, the roles of the partners in service provision had become complementary. The role of central government was to set the overall policy framework, to provide a large part of the necessary finance and then to leave LEAs, schools and colleges to administer the policy with a considerable degree of autonomy. The LEAs played a crucial role in service provision. They owned the buildings, employed the staff and determined the budgets. However, their powers were constrained by two major factors. The national collective agreements between central government, LEAs and the teacher unions determined a rigid framework for salaries and conditions of employment which gave little scope for local divergence. This codification of employment practice established a clear framework for human resource management within which the major role was *administration* rather than management.

The second major constraint was the tradition of autonomy of schools, colleges and their headteachers/principals. Headteachers were usually portrayed as first and foremost professional teachers who also had administrative duties concerned with running the institution. The degree of autonomy varied according to the specific function. For example, in terms of setting the school curriculum, with the exception of externally-set examinations, heads and their colleagues had almost complete independence. There was no national curriculum and no LEA curricula. Some LEAs certainly tried to assist in curriculum and professional development, mainly through the use of advisers or local inspectors, but the emphasis was strongly on advice and not instruction.

By contrast, heads had very little autonomy in finance. The buildings were provided, maintained and serviced by the LEAs. The staff were employed and paid for by the LEAs, with posts being allocated to schools according to a non-financed based formula. Heads had very little autonomy in personnel matters, where difficulties would trigger early LEA involvement and where the balance of power with the trade unions severely limited the scope of, for example, disciplinary processes or rewards systems.

Further and higher education colleges traditionally enjoyed greater independence but were still very much operating within LEA parameters. In the state education service only the universities and direct grant schools stood outside the local government framework. Even so, the universities also operated within the constraints set by the University Grants Commission and national pay agreements. Principals, like head teachers, did not describe themselves as managers. Had they done so it would have seemed strange to their staff and certainly few had received any overt management training. LEA officers were described either as administrators or as professionals, never as managers.

The traditional academic autonomy of schools and colleges was reflected in their relationship with the central government's inspectors. Her Majesty's Inspectors (HMIs) were introduced to provide a central government check on what free-standing institutions were doing with taxpayers' money. They themselves had developed their own degree of autonomy within the DES and portrayed themselves as independent professionals, often more in the role of advice and support than inspection. This general picture was to change over the course of the 1980s.

The Conservative Governments, 1979–92

There have been four major pieces of education legislation since 1979: the Acts of 1980, 1986, 1988 and 1992. It is argued here that until the Education Reform Act 1988, Conservative education policy could be described as incrementalist. It is not possible to identify a comprehensive, co-ordinated and planned blueprint for education policy available when the new government took office in 1979. Rather, policy was a mixture of individual decisions, shifts in resources and legislation, some of which were contradictory but all of which basically moved in the same direction (Knight, 1990). Although reached by incrementalist steps, this policy direction was radically different to the previous *status quo* and it reached a culmination point in the Education Reform Act 1988. There are a number of themes which have underpinned this policy development, forming the new context in which the system is being managed. These are outlined below and the new managerial context assessed.

Cuts in Public Expenditure

As we have seen in Chapter 1, until the late 1980s government policy was to cut public expenditure as part of its strategy of reducing the overall burden of taxation on the economy. Since it was committed to the expansion of some programmes, such as defence and law and order, and since some were too difficult politically to cut at that time, such as health, the burden of the cuts fell disproportionately on some of the social programmes. Public spending on education fell by 10 per cent in real terms between 1979 and 1986, although it rose again by 4 per cent in real terms from 1987 to 1989. Within these overall figures there were significant shifts amongst parts of the education programme, such as moving public resources to private schools and by reintroducing assisted places. Thus the impact of the expenditure policy on mainstream public education is greater than the figures suggest. The magnitude of these cuts has caused great problems for the state education system and forms part of the context in which it is managed.

Part of the impact of such expenditure cuts has been felt in the relationship between central and local government, which is addressed below. Part of it is reflected in the inevitable search for alternative sources of finance. This need to supplement mainstream funding has been used by successive governments to try to change the culture of the state educational system and to change the direction in which it faces. One of the potential sources of alternative income has been the business community. Although government has always overestimated the extent to which the private sector wanted or was able to contribute to the basic running costs of schools and colleges, the need to seek such funding and similar pressures has inevitably affected the orientation of the education service. Thus the specific requirement to add local business representatives to school governing bodies accompanied the encouragement to look to that community for financial aid and has contributed to the changed environment of the state system.

The government itself also provided additional sources of finance, but with clearly visible strings attached. At the beginning of the 1980s it was feared that the DES might be too slow to respond to the need to change direction in education policy, partly because it was too closely identified with the major educational pressure groups – the LEAs and the teaching unions. Thus a number of new initiatives were launched through other state agencies, especially the (then) Manpower Services Commission (MSC). Faced with a growing number of young unemployed, the government brought in a series of training programmes, such as the Youth Opportunities Programme and its successor, the Youth Training Scheme. These were highly contentious and were financed outside the main education budget. In time they became an important part of the overall provision of non-advanced further education. With the funding, however, went a clear concept of a contract to deliver specific services and a specific curriculum. This unquestionably weakened the power of the colleges and the teachers, bypassed the LEAs and strengthened the power of the MSC. Thus by a policy of reducing mainstream funding and offering supplementary finance tied to specific objectives, the government was trying to achieve major changes in the curriculum and approach of the state system.

Weakening Local Government

There cannot be many commentators who would oppose the assertion that since 1979 the power of local government in Britain has been considerably eroded. The culmination of a whole range of legislation, financial controls, taxation changes and so on have fundamentally altered the relationship between central and local government. Nowhere is this change more evident than in the role of local government in the education service. A dramatic example of this change was the abolition of the Inner London Education Authority and the dispersal of its education functions to the Inner London Boroughs as part of the 1988 Act (Stewart and Stoker, 1989; Stoker, 1991). Another example is the removal first in 1989/90 of the polytechnics and colleges of higher education and later (1992) the planned removal of colleges of further education from local authority control.

A further reduction in local education authority powers has been associated with claims for strengthening parent power, which was one of the major themes in the Conservative Party's Election Manifestos in 1979 and 1983. It was argued that the professional teachers and educational administrators had vested interests in maintaining the *status quo* and protecting their positions as providers. One way to reduce their influence – and especially their commitment to certain pedagogical philosophies – was to strengthen the power of the consumers of the service – or at least their parents. One way to improve 'choice', always a difficult concept in a state education system, was to help parents opt out of that system and into the private sector. In the Education (No. 2) Act 1980 the government introduced the Assisted Places Scheme designed to allow a relatively small number of parents who otherwise could not afford to send their children to private schools to do so. Lack of funding meant that the scheme has never made the impact which its advocates hoped for but this did little to weaken its contentiousness.

The government believed strongly in the superiority of the free market. However, it was fairly clear that within the state sector the normal forces of market competition could not operate. However, since these forces were believed to be the best way of allocating resources and of operationalising parental choice, they were to be approximated to. The assumption was that parents already had clear perceptions of the worth of schools in their areas but were prevented from sending their children to the schools of their choice by the LEAs. The authorities would be concerned with equalising enrolments, keeping as many schools as possible viable, and might even be antithetical to the institutional cultures of 'good' schools. By strengthening the power of parents to determine the schools to which their children went, 'good' schools would be rewarded with more enrolments and more resources and 'poor' schools would be punished. The movement away from such schools would result either in an abrupt change of direction or closure. Parental choice was strengthened in the 1980 and 1988 Acts and there are now strong pressures on schools to recruit in competition with others. This greater sensitivity to 'the market' is having an impact on the culture, organisation, curriculum and management of schools. It is also causing major problems for LEAs trying to provide a service across a whole area.

The introduction of City Technology Colleges (CTCs) in 1986 was an even more radical departure from existing education policy. CTCs were to be jointly funded by private industry, which would meet the foundation costs, and by the central government, which would meet their running costs. They were thus outside LEA provision. The autonomy of these schools and their whole ethos was meant to act as a catalyst for change and to reintroduce selective secondary education free of LEA control. Although less than 20 CTCs have been established, they are helping to shift the nature of the state system and they prepared some of the ground for the 1988 Act.

The move to decentralisation and autonomy was reinforced strongly in the 1988 Act. Schools were given the right to 'opt out' of local education authority control entirely and be funded directly from the DES, becoming grant maintained schools (GMS). Originally only offered to secondary schools, it is now open to all but the 'special schools'. This policy represented a fundamental shift in the provision of state education away from the concept of a local, integrated education service based on the principles of comprehensive education. Subject to certain procedures, it is now possible for a school to become directly-funded and to change the basis of its pupil selection and philosophy. With the government removing free-standing post-16 institutions from LEA control in the 1992 Act, further education and sixth-form colleges are becoming free-standing bodies, either financed directly from central government or through some regional state agency. This is further reducing the power of local government in the provision of educational services and will change the nature of the provision of education for 16- to 18-year-olds.

For those schools which do not choose to opt out, extensive devolved management is required under the 1988 Act. The introduction of the Local Management of Schools (LMS) transferred significant responsibilities from LEAs to schools. Schools now receive clear budgets, amounting to up to 85 per cent of their total expenditure. LEAs have introduced formula-funding for determining school budgets, in which at least 75 per cent of the resources are allocated on a pupil number basis. This weakened the discretion of LEAs in determining funding priorities, for example, by preventing the simple roll-forward of historic funding. The introduction of LMS has transformed the management role and responsibilities of heads and their senior colleagues that are very different from those they had before 1988.

Another aspect of the government's strategy has been to strengthen the governing bodies of schools and colleges, both to weaken the base of teacher and LEA power and as a way of enhancing parent power. Governing bodies in schools now have considerable responsibilities for determining some areas of the curriculum, for staff appointments and for discipline.

There are two policy developments in higher education referred to earlier which are pointers to similar developments in the rest of the system. The 1988 Act removed over 80 public sector higher education institutions from LEA or voluntary control and made them free-standing higher education corporations. These corporations are under the authority of new governing bodies on which 'independent' or private sector representatives are dominant, with each institution financed directly from the DES *via* a funding council. More radical than institutional autonomy was the introduction of competitive tendering for marginal finance. The concept of free market competition for the delivery of contracted educational services to the state is a long way removed from the concept of a planned integrated educational service. This movement has been strengthened further by shifting the balance of public funding for higher education from central government grant to student fees. Whereas these are still state funded, the move strengthens market forces in the sector. The new financial system in public sector higher education requires institutions to submit 'tenders' as part of a process in which price is the dominant factor. The effect of this system has been to reduce unit costs and increase numbers. The 1992 Further and Higher Education Act means that a similar system is being introduced into post-16 education, with most of that provision being removed from the LEA sector. Clearly, the role of local government in education has been diminished. If schools opt out in large numbers, then the government may decide to remove education from local authorities altogether. So far, by 1992 less than 300 schools had opted out so the short-term future of LEAs seems secure. However, they are likely to reduce in size as more services are devolved to schools and colleges, and procedures for opting out are eased.

Local Management of Schools (LMS)

The Education Reform Act 1988 accelerated the process of change which was already a feature of the management of schools by introducing LMS. LMS was seen by the government as a means of achieving a number of objectives. These were:

- to provide for flexibility so that schools could be more responsive to their local environment and consumer 'needs';
- to transfer control of educational provision from professional teachers to managers and boards of governors;
- to increase the accountability of schools for the way they use resources;
- to increase management efficiency in the education service by pin pointing responsibility for delivering educational services;
- to introduce an internal market in education.

The role of the LEA under the LMS scheme was initially to draw up schemes to delegate budgets to school governors in schools with 200 or more pupils. They determined a method of formula funding in accordance with a set of guidelines identified by Dixon (1991) and set out in Table 9.1. The formula consists of essential and discretionary elements but 75 per cent of the school's budget has to be devolved and allocated according to pupil numbers. By basing the formula primarily on weighted pupil numbers, according to age and subjects offered, it is thought that this encourages schools to compete for pupils and be responsive to parental demands. The LEA is responsible for revising and allocating budgets annually and for making adjustments as appropriate. Further responsibilities and functions of the LEA are:

- to assess overall educational needs within its area and to set down strategic goals and objectives within the framework of national policy;
- to supervise schools to ensure that the conditions and requirements of LMS schemes are met and to take action if they are not;
- to administer the 15 to 25 per cent of educational budgets which are not devolved to schools. This includes capital expenditure, specific grants and other school expenditure;
- to control the budgets of smaller schools not in the LMS scheme;
- to maintain a contingency fund to cover unforeseen costs;
- to advise and guide schools.

In addition, LEAs may provide services to LMS schools in purchasing, payroll administration and contract catering where

TABLE 9.1   *Categories of LEA expenditure under LMS*

*Must be allocated by formula to qualifying schools: 75 per cent
to be allocated according to pupil numbers weighted by age/subject*

Teaching staff costs
Non-teaching staff costs
Books, equipment and materials
Rates and rents
Routine maintenance costs
Examination expenses

*Discretionary exceptions which may constitute no more than 10 per
cent of a school budget*

Structural maintenance
Premises insurance
Statemented pupils
Educational psychologist
Educational welfare officer
Peripatetic teachers
Special staff costs
Library and museum services
School-specific contingencies
LEA initiatives
School meals
Early retirement and dismissal costs
Home to school transport
Inspectors/advisors costs
Central administration

Mandatory exceptions

Capital expenditure
Specific grants

Other school expenditure incurred by LEA

Costs of schools not covered by LMS including nursery schools and special
schools
Support services
Adult and youth provision
Careers service
Payments to other LEAs
Payments to non-maintained schools
Pensions increases to non-teaching staff

economies of scale can be achieved through centralised buying and co-ordination. Some of the most significant changes will be that LEAs will cease to generate educational data and information, unless specifically required for quality control or regional and national statistics. Schools will produce and control information which will inevitably change the balance of power within the school system.

The role of the school management under LMS is greatly enlarged. It assumes responsibility for staffing, the purchase of materials, furniture and equipment, cleaning, caretaking and building repairs. About 70 per cent of its budget goes to staffing and here it is constrained by national salary scales and the staffing needs of the national curriculum. However, it can choose to increase its administrative support and purchase computer assisted learning packages as an alternative to additional academic staff. It can trade off redecoration of classrooms for library books or leave a leaking roof or unfilled posts to avoid a budget overspend.

Schools may enter into agency arrangements with the LEA to benefit from central purchasing and competitive tendering contracts or go independent. The LEA remains the owner of all school premises and leases them to individual schools. But schools may spend money on capital projects, although this comes out of its revenue budget, unless the investment can be financed out of income generated from sources other than the LEA. Schools produce their own financial and personnel data and their own accounts. Government has encouraged LEAs to give schools their own bank accounts so that they can administer their own funds. It may be that in the near future schools will be held to account directly to the national audit, and local authority treasurers will cease to be responsible for maintaining their accounts. This would be near total autonomy.

The responsibility for managing schools now rests with a partnership between senior staff, in particular the headteacher, and the governors. The 1988 Act makes the governors responsible for the management of the school budget, but it is the headteacher who effectively manages the resources. How much real control the governors actually wield depends on their skills and abilities and those of the headteacher. In some situations the leadership might come from the chair of the governors – in others from the school head. The quality of school governors will need to improve if they are to perform their new tasks. However, it may prove difficult to obtain and retain suitable people when they realise the responsibilities attached to the unpaid, voluntary position. There is some evidence of resistance to the changed role amongst parental governors (Dixon, 1991).

Within the schools, new management structures are emerging, as the tasks of management increase. In some, bursars or administrators are being appointed to relieve headteachers of much of the work of management or to take on new tasks. In others, new managerial hierarchies are emerging with deputy headteachers specialising in finance or personnel issues, leaving the head to focus on policy issues and liaison with the LEA, governors and parents. Clearly teachers are likely to become increasingly distanced from the headteacher or managing director, although this will depend on the size of the school and on the style of management.

It is likely that considerable variation in the relationship between LMS schools and LEAs will emerge. There are a number of key issues which will have important consequences for that relationship. These are:

- the extent to which support services like legal services, payroll, accountancy are retained by LEAs or devolved to schools which may contract to other suppliers;
- the ability of schools to raise additional funds, for example, usage of premises outside school hours, and so pursue discretionary activities;
- the way in which LMS schools use their control of information to assert their independence and to develop direct links with bodies in the education network;
- the speed with which schools choose to 'opt out' of LMS and in to grant maintained status;
- the role which boards of governors choose to adopt and the relationship which develops between school managers and the governors.

Clearly, LMS raises a range of administrative, relational, financial and managerial issues for the school sector, those who work in it and those who use its services.

Institutional Management

The shift of managerial responsibility to schools and colleges has clearly placed major new demands on management teams, teaching staff and support staff. The School Management Task Force (SMTF), set up by the DES in 1989 to advise it on strategies for improving institutional management, identified a number of key characteristics of 'effective schools'. These were:

- good leadership offering a breadth of vision and the ability to motivate others;
- appropriate delegation with involvement in policy-making by staff other than the head;
- clearly-established and purposeful staffing structures;
- well-qualified staff with an appropriate blend of experience and expertise;
- clear aims and associated objectives applied with care and consistency;
- effective communications and clear systems of record-keeping and assessment;
- the means to identify and develop pupils' particular strengths, promoting high expectations by both teachers and pupils;
- a coherent curriculum which considers pupils' experience as a whole and demonstrates concern for their development within society;
- a positive ethos: an orderly yet relaxed atmosphere of work;
- a suitable working environment;
- skills of deploying and managing material resources;
- good relationships with parents, the local community and sources of external support;
- the capacity to manage change, to solve problems and to develop organically (DES, 1990).

To achieve 'effective' status, it is claimed that schools and colleges need competent, trained managers working in suitable organisational structures with the skills and resources needed to carry out their tasks. Although the SMTF denied that there was any crisis in institutional management, they certainly found that the existing situation was unsatisfactory. As stated earlier, before the 1980s the term 'management' was not commonly used in education. People became headteachers and deputies – the key leadership and administrative positions – with teaching qualifications and experience and not necessarily with any management training or management development programme. There was no comprehensive, co-ordinated approach to headteachers' training needs. This situation had been changing throughout the 1980s as central government provided more money for training at post professional level. The proportion of the central funding for staff development devoted to management training known as the Local Education Authority Training Grants Scheme was increased from £4 million in 1987–8 to £10 million in 1990–91, with probably about 20,000 teachers on management short courses. A number of LEAs have also collaborated to provide regionally-based consortia for management training. However, set in the context of about 27,000 state schools and 450,000 teachers the level of provision has been grossly inadequate.

The term 'management' is now commonly used in schools and colleges. Headteachers are increasingly identified as managers, with a growing differentiation between them and the teaching staff. Those schools which have opted out and left LEA control, and the City Technology Colleges, have already developed management systems to cope with their autonomy and the remainder of the state system is being forced down this path as a result of LMS. The training and support needs of senior staff are clearly to enable them to discharge their new responsibilities but they also need to be equipped with the ability to manage change, to manage a wider set of relationships, with governors, with staff within their schools, and to meet the demands of the community for greater accountability. The SMTF stressed the need for structured management development programmes to meet both the needs of individuals for planned career progression and those of the organisation for stable and effective management systems.

Change has had great impact on teaching staff as well as the new managers. The continuous changes throughout the 1980s, combined with resource constraints, caused a deterioration in industrial relations and a general lowering of morale amongst teachers. The teacher unions had been one of the partners in the old tripartite arrangement which dominated the governing of education in the 30 years after 1945. Nobody would give them that status now. In addition to simply being removed from the discussion of policy at governmental level, the teacher unions have suffered a series of reductions in their power base over the last ten years. In a number of industrial disputes in the mid-1980s the teachers failed to achieve any significant shift in government stance on pay awards, and this weakened their industrial relations position. In the Teachers' Pay and Conditions Act 1987, the government dismantled the existing collective bargaining machinery which had determined pay and conditions of employment and imposed new remuneration and employment conditions. To this abolition of national collective bargaining must be added the threat to move to locally-negotiated agreements, which would have serious repercussions on the teacher unions and the position of their members (see Chapter 5). This would be particularly difficult for unionised teachers in those schools which have opted out of LEA control and thus presumably would negotiate directly with their own staff. The DES is committed to introducing a staff appraisal system throughout the education service, possibly linking this to the rewards system. This is an extremely contentious issue and one which the new school managers will inherit. In addition to financial management skills they need to be trained also in personnel management.

Turning to further and higher education, we observe that heads of department and those above are now described explicitly as managers. The move to total institutional autonomy from LEAs in public sector higher education, enshrined in the 1988 Act, and the autonomy of most post-16 colleges, embodied in the 1992 Act, have changed the operation of those colleges. The collegial model has been replaced by a more hierarchical model in which the managerial roles of principals and directors, now called 'chief executives', deans and heads of department are clearly stated and incorporated into new contracts of employment and reward systems. These developments are leading to the erosion of the professional monopoly of senior posts. Until the late 1980s it would have been very exceptional for a senior post in the education service to be taken by anyone who had not been a teacher. Increasingly the recruitment process for such posts is stressing general management experience, irrespective of sector.

In further and higher education, institutions have needed to develop the full range of central services required by free-standing organisations, many of which were largely provided by LEAs before. Thus the personnel, finance, estates management and legal functions have been strengthened and senior management is responsible for what is, effectively, running a medium-sized business. The profit motive may be removed, but the need to achieve and maintain solvency is paramount. Most of these institutions have developed commercial units, indistinguishable from profit-oriented companies, to market their services and to generate independent sources of finance for the parent institution. In some of the colleges the culture has changed quite considerably, with managers – now clearly identified as such – using the language and techniques of the private sector and increasingly looking to be paid at similar levels.

The New Managerialism in Higher Education

Nowhere has the 'new managerialism' developed more than in public sector higher education. In 1979 this sector of education, which largely paralleled the universities, comprised the polytechnics, the colleges of higher education and the diversified teacher training colleges. It was concerned with higher education, like the 'old' universities, but it offered a wider range of courses, particularly in vocationally relevant subjects such as business studies or health care, a more flexible pattern of attendance modes and a larger percentage of sub-degree work than the universities. Most of the public sector institutions were under the control of local education authorities, although some, largely denominational colleges, were funded directly from the Department of Education and Science. The size of these institutions varied considerably from over 10,000 full-time equivalent students (FTEs) to less than 2000. The degree of autonomy which they enjoyed from their LEAs also varied widely. Under the Education Reform Act 1988 the 30 polytechnics and 50 other colleges of higher education became independent of their LEAs and free-standing Higher Education Corporations (HECs). They were to be financed directly from a new national body, the Polytechnics and Colleges Funding Council (PCFC), and were to be independent, legal organisations. In the run up to 'vesting' or 'independence' day, most of these colleges set up Foundation Committees, with a small number of governors, to plan for the new HECs. The scale of the planning which needed to be done becomes apparent when the items, which were previously the responsibility, at least in part, of the LEAs, now became the sole responsibility of the colleges.

New Management Functions

It may seem an easy task to identify the buildings and land which a college occupies and to effect a legal transfer of that from the LEA to the HEC. In many cases, the task was not so straightforward. Very often the original deeds were missing, making the establishment of a clear, legal title difficult. Some premises and land were occupied jointly by a higher education and a further education or other LEA college, making disentanglement and separation difficult. In some cases LEAs were very reluctant to transfer land which has a development potential and disputes had to be referred to an independent Educational Assets Board. Of course, the transfer of the buildings and estate did not signify the end of a process, merely the beginning. With the transfer of the assets went the responsibility for funding them, maintaining them and making sure they complied with the law, especially the Health and Safety requirements. Since LEAs had suffered from significant reductions in funding during the 1980s, most of the buildings transferred to the new corporations had a backlog of maintenance to make good. This was to add to the financial problems of the colleges. The transferred functions also required, in most cases, strengthened local management to carry them out. Even where policy decisions had been taken to contract out buildings services to LEAs or private contractors, these contracts had to be managed. Thus, most colleges had to make additional appointments in this area.

Before 1989 most colleges had only limited financial responsibilities, varying according to the degree of devolution permitted from the LEA. From 1 April 1989 they were to be completely free-standing organisations, responsible for all the financial functions of any other independent institution – or business – and capable of going bankrupt! Thus the colleges were required to develop and staff for a finance function which included the whole range of related tasks. A good example of a new task is cash-flow management. As parts of LEAs, colleges did not have to worry about managing the inwards and outwards flow of funds so that there was always a positive balance at the bank. As free-standing corporations they did have to worry. An additional responsibility, if successful at cash-flow management, was to invest any surplus balances wisely to earn maximum interest income. The financial side of the colleges' operations became more important on independence since the LEA was no longer there as a back-stop. Independence also meant providing a range of financial services previously provided by the LEA, including payroll, debt collection, internal and external audit and banking. Many colleges did not even have separate bank accounts under the LEA.

Colleges had normally relied upon their LEAs for legal services but now had to provide them 'in-house' or buy them on the normal commercial market. The range of advice needed varied from property, employers' liability, third party liability, students threatening legal action over exam results, and so on. Few colleges were large enough to be able to staff a central unit with the range of expertise required and thus entered into agency agreements with local solicitors.

LEAs had well-developed personnel management functions, since they were clearly major employers of large numbers of staff across a range of professions and groups. Staff in the pre-1989 LEA colleges were employed by the LEA, not by the college, and very often industrial relations were focused on the LEA-union interface, with college management to one side. This pattern of industrial relations clearly suited the teaching and support staff unions since it enabled them to deal with LEA-wide issues centrally. This weakened the power of college management. Incorporation meant that individual contracts of employment transferred from the LEA to the HEC, which now became the employer responsible for all personnel management and industrial relation matters. The responsibility for pay bargaining now rested with the corporations, which quickly formed the Polytechnic and Colleges Employers' Forum (PCEF), to act as a national negotiating body with the various trade unions. An early decision was taken to disentangle senior management (that is, heads of department and above) salaries and contracts out of any national forum and to make this an issue for local agreement on individual bases. Although the national forum existed, members of the PCEF were not bound to accept national recommendations but usually have done so. Personnel functions at college level therefore had to incorporate the whole range of responsibilities and services to be found in any business organisation.

The Impact on Management

By adding together all these additional functions with those already performed by college management for the core business activity, that is, providing educational programmes, it can be seen that there was a major increase in the roles and numbers of managers as those colleges moved to independence. Indeed, senior staff in colleges were now clearly identified as managers. The recognition of a managerial group and set of distinct functions has required a major cultural shift in colleges, a shift which is still underway. It has been strengthened by the continuing pace of change since incorporation. One example of this continuing development is in personnel management where the DES has been enthusiastic about colleges introducing formal systems of staff appraisal. In 1990–91 and 1991–2, part of the PCFC funding was withheld until such appraisal schemes were introduced. Similarly, senior staff have been placed on new contracts of employment which define much more closely their responsibilities, specify holiday entitlements and effectively introduce performance-related pay. Similar pressures are now being exerted on mainstream academic staff.

It is, however, in the area of finance and funding systems that the growth of the new managerialism is most obvious. Government policy in the 1990s is to expand higher education very considerably without a commensurate increase in funding. This leads inevitably to a lowering of the unit of resource. It is the responsibility of college management to deliver that expansion, financed in part by additional productivity gains and by supplementing state income from commercial activities. In order to supplement their state funding, colleges must draw in money from other sources. This may include recruiting overseas students, running full-cost recovery courses, providing consultancy and selling specialist services on the commercial market. Many of the larger colleges have formed limited companies to undertake these commercial activities, thus protecting the charitable status of the educational activities and covenanting profits back. The volume of activities of some of these companies exceeded £2 million in 1991–2. Naturally, as commercial companies they have to be run on normal business lines and usually have recruited specialist staff from the private sector to run them.

In addition to coping with new commercial responsibilities, college managements have also been required to engage in competitive tendering processes, activities previously alien to the public services. These processes have operated in two directions. First, many services such as catering, cleaning and security, which were previously provided in-house, are now offered to competitive contract. College management therefore moves to managing the contract and away from running the service. Second, and by far the most important, the new funding system introduced in 1989 compelled colleges to compete for part of their mainstream student funding. The objective of this element of the funding system was to encourage colleges to expand their recruitment and to drive down the unit of resource. In essence, the system guaranteed funding for a certain percentage of the previous year's enrolments, usually 95 per cent, in return for a percentage of that year's finance, usually between 90 and 95 per cent baseline. These tenders identified the price which the college charged PCFC for those students. The tendering process divided students into different subject areas and modes of attendance.

Clearly, unless colleges are prepared to run down their student numbers and finances progressively, they have to engage in this bidding process. As a competitive process in which price is acknowledged to be the primary factor, the tender bids will always be lower than the existing unit funding and to recover their previous year's state funding, colleges have to recruit additional students. College managements are thus engaged in a competitive process which involves great uncertainty and high risk with serious financial consequences for getting it wrong. This is a far cry from the pre-1989 tradition. The government is also introducing a range of sector-wide performance indicators (PIs) to assist them in the strategic management of the system. The national PIs are part of institutional management information systems used for operational managemen at college level. The new range of manage-ment tasks facing colleges has shown the inadequacy of existing information systems and most colleges are now engaged in developing the type of management and financial information systems found in large commercial organisations.

The range of tasks now to be performed by managers in colleges is very different from that of ten years ago. Although colleges are not private sector commercial, for-profit organisations, they often need to be managed as if they were and using private-sector techniques. This has placed an increasing strain on the existing senior staff, most of whom are untrained for these tasks and some of whom resent this change in their roles. The new 'managerialism' will affect post-16 education next, as this sector follows the path of higher education in 1993.

Conclusion

The changes described here are still underway and it is important not to reach premature conclusions. However, the direction of these changes is quite clear. What is also evident is that those running the education service have been doing so against a background of quite unprecedented change. Recent governments have used cuts in mainstream funding to reduce the autonomy of LEAs and institutions, which have been encouraged to look to the private sector for financial help and to specifically-targeted public funding. Governing bodies have been strengthened, with business more represented on them. It is claimed that the power of parents to select schools has been strengthened and schools now have to market themselves in order to survive. The cultural orientation of the schools is gradually changing. Vocationalism and instrumentalism are now more dominant than before. It is too early to assess the impact of the national curriculum, but it has clearly reduced the power of the teaching profession and the LEAs in determining what is taught.

Clearly the power of the countervailing groups within the old tripartite relationship has changed and that partnership is long dead. There has been a transfer of power from the intermediate level upwards to central government, and downwards to institutions. Although it is important not to overemphasise the speed with which something as large and complex as an education system can be transformed, it is now evident that such a transformation is under way. Nowhere are the consequences of those changes more apparent than in the developments in the management of the institutions. School and college heads/ principals are now becoming general managers with a range of responsibilities not dissimilar to those of comparably-sized private sector organisations. Increasingly the divisions between the two sectors are becoming blurred as private sector terminology and techniques are more widely adopted in education. Those becoming managers in the education service require training and support and may eventually need specialist qualifications before they can discharge their responsibilities. Although the provision of such assistance is increasing there remains a considerable shortfall.

Although state schools are still not-for-profit organisations, they are beginning to operate in an internal market. LEAs are becoming purchasers of education services and schools are the providers. There is an emerging mixed economy of schooling with private, grant-aided, LMS- and LEA-run schools. Competition is being encouraged through linking budgets to pupils. Schools are required to produce information on pupil achievement, in particular examination results. They are also required to produce information on performance ratings based on DES performance indicators. 'Poor' schools are likely to lose pupils to those with a good record. In this way, it is argued, schools will increase their efficiency and effectiveness whilst seeking to use their resources economically.

Within higher education, institutions have moved nearer to a market situation. They compete for students on price, length of courses and quality. They are becoming increasingly market-led, concerned with income generation and run as businesses. On one level they would appear to have become more efficient. Their productivity has risen significantly as they have increased their student population and reduced the unit cost of education. Staff student ratios have increased by over 50 per cent in the arts and social sciences. Participation rates have risen and the number of graduates has increased. New technology is transforming the processes of education and making possible distance learning and mixed modes of attendance. Academic staff are increasingly becoming managers of learning situations rather than professors of knowledge. 'Communiversities' or networks of higher education institutions are emerging on a local and regional basis extending opportunities for study to a larger, more segmented market and offering a wide choice to potential consumers. The market has entered education, which is increasingly seen as a consumption or investment good rather than a citizen right.

As this book goes to print still more changes are occurring. The polytechnics have been granted 'new university' status and the PCFC is being replaced by new funding councils for universities and the colleges. Further legislation is planned to accelerate the opting-out of schools and to introduce new bodies to fund opted-out schools and to manage poorly-run maintained schools; and the inspectorate is being privatised.

Clearly all these developments require considerable skills of management and flexible organisational structures to allow for the multiplicity and diversity of responses to the market and public policy to take place. There is, however, paradoxically, an even greater need for strategic management and planning to avoid inefficiency and waste. These can arise from unbridled competition on the one hand, or the emergence of restricted supplies on the other. Only central government, in effect, can perform this role.

10

The Police Service

FRANK LEISHMAN and STEPHEN P. SAVAGE

'Policing' and 'management' are not terms which sit easily together. The developments in managerial strategies which have occurred within police organisations in recent years have arisen against the backcloth of the difficulties, some would say insurmountable, of reconciling the activity of policing with the process of management. Arguably more than in any other area of the public services, the policing function presents specific dilemmas as far as attempts to introduce coherent managerial approaches is concerned. Whether these are the reflection of the inherent nature of the policing task, or of the ways in which policing, at least in its British form, has been traditionally organised, is an issue which this chapter considers as it progresses. At the very least, they involve features of policing which constitute a starting point for an evaluation and analysis of police management.

First, it is a widely-held view that policing activities are characterised by wide discretion at lower levels (Freeman 1981; Reiner, 1985). As a function both of the relative isolation of the patrolling officer, and of the breadth of scope of the laws which a police officer may in any particular context choose to enforce (or not), discretion is held to be an inevitable (and indeed desirable) feature of police work. The extent to which it is possible to reconcile such discretion with management strategies determined at other levels of the organisation thus becomes a central question. Second, and relatedly, it has been argued that a great deal of police-work is dictated, not by a planned process of objective setting and strategic decision-making, but rather by a reactive response to unpredictable demand (Waddington, 1986). According to this view, the sorts of 'rational' management approaches adopted in private sector organisations and other public service bodies cannot be imposed on police organisations. A third feature to address is the role of a rank structure within the police hierarchy. It is impossible to ignore the impact of rank on the nature of decision-making within police institutions. As will be argued below, the presence of a rank structure raises a number of issues in relation to the management training function and management development.

The structure of police management is very much dictated by the rank structure, many elements of which date back to the original framework of the police organisation established in the nineteenth century. Key policy decisions are in most cases made by the 'ACPO' ranks (the Association of Chief Police Officers): chief constable, deputy and assistant chief constable. Each of the latter normally has functional responsibility for one of the three central organisational tasks: personnel and training, administration and operations. In the Metropolitan Police Service (MPS), ACPO ranks have different designations, and extend a number of tiers down the hierarchy: commissioner, deputy commissioner, assistant commissioner, deputy assistant commissioner and commander. Policy committee within the MPS includes commissioner, deputy and assistant commissioners, together with senior civilian staff. Deputy assistant commissioners and commanders have, in addition to functional responsibilities, geographical command. The senior to middle tiers of police management include chief superintendents, who have responsibility either for police divisions or particular functional duties, and superintendents, who also may be responsible for particular functions, such as traffic, or a police subdivision. In recent years, attempts to devolve decision-making and budgets have paid particular attention to the role of subdivisional commanders.

The central tasks of middle management are undertaken by chief inspectors and inspectors, and the lowest level of management, with its primary task of supervision of constables, is that of sergeant. With the exception of a small number of posts, all middle and senior managers within the police organisation are police officers who have entered as constables and proceeded through the ranks. Although there have been significant shifts in the direction of the 'civilianisation' of certain management functions, in some cases at very senior level where, for example, some large forces have appointed civilians to the equivalent of assistant chief constable in charge of administration, it is still very much the case that police management is essentially a task for police ranks. We consider the consequences of this later in the discussion.

While the rank structure to a great extent welds police management to a framework which has survived for many years, the nature of police management has undergone substantial change since the early 1980s, very much in line with the experience of other public services discussed elsewhere in this book. However, not only has the police service felt the blast of government initiatives in public service management, which have imposed changes across the board of public services, it has also been the subject of pressures of its own which have made reforms of police management imperative.

Pressures for Change

Perceived deficiencies in police management began to accumulate in the early 1980s, and were reinforced further as the decade progressed. They added urgency to the emerging influence of central government policy on public management which was to dictate the direction in which managerial change was to go. In 1980 and 1981 many major cities in Britain experienced serious outbreaks of public disorder involving clashes between the police and (mainly black) youth. One such was in Brixton in April 1981, which led to an inquiry headed by Lord Scarman and ultimately to the Scarman Report, a document which quickly became a major source of influence on police reform during the 1980s. Among the many issues raised by Scarman, not all of which were linked directly to policing, were the nature and quality of supervision by middle-ranking officers over the lower ranks, the chain of command in operational decisions, and the adequacy of management training (Scarman, 1982, pp. 83–7). Scarman concluded that in each respect the Metropolitan Police were found wanting and proposed a number of reforms to rectify the deficiencies identified. It was difficult to ignore the extent to which similar conclusions could be reached about the police service as a whole, particularly in the light of the fact that Scarman's proposals were intended not just for the Metropolitan Police but for all forces.

Close on the heels of the Scarman Report was a research report by the Policy Studies Institute (PSI), again on the Metropolitan Police but similarly not just of parochial significance. At the invitation of the then

Commissioner, Sir David McNee, the PSI was employed to undertake a wide-ranging study of the 'relations between the Metropolitan Police and the community it serves' (Smith and Gray, 1985, p. 1). The publication of the full report in 1983 attracted widespread media attention and public debate because the conclusions reached by the PSI constituted in effect a wholesale critique of the police organisation and its personnel, although many senior officers within the MPS were less than convinced of the appropriateness of the conclusions reached. While the issue which was the focus of most concern was the relationship between the police and black people, more general problems were identified in the nature and structure of police management although, of course, police-public relations are in part themselves a function of the management system.

Criticism was directed at a number of attributes, many of which, it could be argued, are still to an extent a feature of contemporary policing. To begin with, the process by which officers were promoted to positions of middle management was found wanting. In what was described as 'the most fundamental weakness of the organisation of the Force' (Smith and Gray 1985, p. 591), the manner in which inspectors qualify for promotion, primarily on the basis of passing an examination which tests knowledge of law and regulations, was heavily criticised. Little attention was given, it was argued, to systematic assessment of performance or standards of conduct prior to promotion. One could have added that the examination bore little relation to the functional role which the examinee, if successful in both examination and promotion, would have to adopt. Steps are currently underway to enhance the promotion process in this direction with the introduction of the OSPRE system (the Objective Structured Performance Related Examination), which will replace the previous written examinations for promotion to sergeant and inspector with skills-based tests related to competencies identified as central to the job-tasks of those posts. The effectiveness of this reform will not be apparent until evaluations have been made, but the fact remains that for a considerable period of time the quality of police management will reflect the system of selection identified by the PSI.

Middle managers were also the subject of two other critical observations. On the one hand, it was argued that too little attention was being given to the career development of constables, through the use of sensitive and effective methods of performance assessment. On the other hand, the research concluded that managers exercised very little supervision over the lower ranks, and in so far as it existed it typically took a negative form, identifying when things have been done wrongly rather than encouraging officers for doing well. Again, one could argue that much of this 'management by sanction' still characterises police human resource management, despite a shift toward a more positive approach in recent years. The PSI (Smith and Gray, 1985, p. 594) made three further criticisms of the nature and structure of police management as a whole. First, its management style was described as 'authoritarian' and shaped largely on military lines. More recent evidence to this effect has been presented by the study of the Metropolitan Police 'A Force for Change', undertaken by management consultants Wolff Ohlins (1988). Both the latter and the PSI recommended the adoption of a more open and consultative approach to management of the organisation. Second, it was argued that much police work was 'aimless', based on 'waiting for things to happen', with little evidence of plans and objectives to underpin decision-making and resource allocation. Most certainly, as we point out shortly, this is one area in which management has moved significantly since the research by the PSI was undertaken. The final criticism concerned the paucity of management information on which plans could be made and activities evaluated, particularly at local level, a point reiterated more recently in the provincial study by Smith and Horton (1988).

The conclusions reached by the PSI gave impetus to a great deal of critical reflection over police management, both within the service and within the Home Office, which was already undertaking detailed analysis of police management systems under the auspices of the Financial Management Initiative (FMI). Many aspects of the PSI recommendations were to fit remarkably well with the thrust of the central document to emanate from the Home Office, Circular 114/1983 on manpower (HMSO, 1983), which examined effectiveness and efficiency in the police service. The combined effect of this document, an increasingly attentive Inspectorate of the police and close scrutiny by the Audit Commission was to put enormous pressure on the managerial framework of the police service. As if this were not enough, other incidents and events were to keep the pressure for reform very much on. Further outbreaks of public disorder in 1985 in Handsworth and Broadwater Farm kept the spotlight on the adequacy of police-public relations. The policing of the industrial dispute between the Times Newspaper Group and the print unions at

Wapping in 1986 was criticised in a subsequent report by the Northampton Police on the grounds that many Metropolitan officers acted as if they were 'out of control'. Also in 1986 the controversy over the inquiry into the alleged Royal Ulster Constabulary 'shoot to kill' strategy, during which John Stalker, Deputy Chief Constable of the Greater Manchester Police, was removed as head of the investigating team, directed attention at the most senior tiers of management and their conduct.

As the decade came to an end, two other events added to the catalogue. The disaster at Hillsborough in 1989, when 78 football supporters died, raised the question of the competencies of police managers, in this case at the level of superintendent, to undertake supervisory and managerial tasks requiring specialist knowledge and skills. In the same year, Geoffrey Dear, Chief Constable, disbanded the West Midlands Police serious crime squad, following evidence of detectives tampering with statements made by suspects. These events raised a host of questions about the police organisation, but one which ran throughout was to do with the capacity of police management to cope with the demands of, and policing in, contemporary Britain. It is within this context that the style, structure and processes of management have undergone change in recent years and will, no doubt, continue to do so in the years to come.

What has since transpired in the area of equal opportunities has ensured that pressure for change remains on the agenda. In the early 1990s the cases of Alison Halford in Merseyside and PC Singh in Nottinghamshire, the former under sex discrimination legislation and the latter under race relations legislation, have served to highlight questions not only of equal opportunities within the service, but also of the whole structure of selection and promotion from top to bottom in the organisation. As a consequence, the ripple effects of these actions may well reverberate throughout the police service in ways not limited to specific issues of equal opportunities, important as the latter are. Notwithstanding the possible impact of equal opportunities on the framework of police management in the future, there is little doubt that to date the major formative moment in regard to the latter was the release of Circular 114/1983, an event which added urgency to the pressures for change emerging within the policing system discussed above.

Towards 'Planned Policing'?

The release of Circular 114/1983 to all police forces in the country was the cornerstone of the redirections in police management which have taken place since the early 1980s. Its embodiment of the principles of the Financial Management Initiative are quite apparent:

> Her Majesty's Inspectors are now adopting in their inspections an approach which is more specifically directed towards ways in which chief officers . . . identify problems, set realistic objectives and clear priorities, keep those priorities and objectives under review, deploy manpower and other resources in accordance with them, and provide themselves with practical means of assessing the extent to which chief officers are achieving their objectives.

The Circular clearly pointed the way to new methods of managing resources in the police service, and on ways of setting and judging policing priorities (Collins 1985). What gave the Circular particular authority and influence was the attachment of its recommendations and proposals to the round of decisions on police establishments which determine the size of the police budget for individual forces. The use of the Circular to influence police decisions at senior levels is a reflection of the statutory position of the police in relation to central government (Weatheritt, 1986, pp. 99–104). Circulars are one of the means by which Home Secretaries can impose some sort of authority over chief officers in a situation in which the latter have operational independence and cannot be subject to directives from the Secretary of State. Where the Home Secretary has most potential to assert a policy shift or initiative is in relation to his statutory responsibility to ensure the 'efficiency' of the police, and in that regard a major instrument is the use, or threat, of financial penalties for non-compliance.

Circular 114/1983 did precisely this. Making it clear that after a period of substantial increases in public expenditure on the police service, it was to be the government's intention to curtail any further increases, it stated that any bids for additional funds by chief constables would be judged in relation to the ways in which each force indicates policy and sets objectives annually. A key role in guiding chief officers in what was for many forces new territory in management philosophy and approach has been played by Her Majesty's Inspectorates (HMIs). They are now adopting a far more assertive and demanding approach in their annual inspections than has traditionally been the case. Weatheritt (1986) cites one parliamentary description of their emerging role as acting 'just like bees fertilising flowers', providing information and advice on good policing practice as they move from force to force around the country. With the back up of possible unfavourable reports on force performance in the areas of police management now valued by the Home Office, and the potential therefore of financial penalties, a factor subsequently strengthened by Circulars 106/1988 and 81/1989 (HMSO, 1988–9), individual forces have been under almost irresistible pressure to move in the directions thus suggested.

In some police forces the early response to 114/1983, with its emphasis on rational management, objective setting, internal review and performance measurement, was the adoption of 'policing by objectives' (PBO), a variant of Management by Objectives (MBO). The central concepts of PBO were already mapped out in an influential American text on police management by Lubans and Edgar (1979). This was received enthusiastically by some of the new generation of senior police managers (Butler, 1984). What is more, concerted efforts were underway within the Metropolitan Police, under the stewardship of Sir Kenneth Newman, to develop a more systematic approach to planning and management at all levels within the force. Sir Kenneth's prior role as Commandant of the Police Staff College at Bramshill had already served to sow some of the seeds of a change in management style amongst many of the younger breed of senior managers. When the pressures for reform from 114/1983 arrived, the ideas and attitudes required for a shift in approach were already existent within the system. However, what was less clear was whether the management material necessary for such a major reorientation was available throughout the service and at appropriate levels within the management hierarchy. Subsequent studies of the implementation of PBO have highlighted this as one of the key problems experienced by forces across the country (Audit Commission Report, 1990). This is an issue to which we return later.

The essence of PBO was on a process whereby policing decisions would be based on a clear definition of objectives to be achieved and a reliable system for regularly measuring performance against them. Not all forces sought explicitly to implement PBO, and the term is now rarely used in descriptions of management systems – more common is some notion of 'planned policing' – but the central notions of objective setting and performance measurement are pretty much common currency in police management circles. The shift to this style of management, however, has not been an easy one, and early enthusiasm for its potential has given way to a growing realisation that the process is far more complicated than many charged with its implementation had thought. In addressing these issues we shall discuss police management under two constituent elements of planned policing: objective setting and performance measurement.

Setting Objectives

One has to appreciate the difficulties of reconciling policing as an activity with the concept of objective setting as a precondition for such activity. There are those for whom such a management philosophy is neither appropriate nor desirable within the policing context. This view is based on what are seen as unique characteristics of the policing function. First, policing is an inherently reactive task, responding to a wide range of unpredictable demands, and in that sense is primarily an 'open-ended' process (Bittner, 1970). To impose upon the organisation *a priori* aims and objectives is at best unrealistic and at worst damaging to the flexibility on which policing responses depend. Second, the police role is one which is associated with extensive discretion, particularly at lower levels in the hierarchy. The adoption of PBO or planned policing thus faces the almost insurmountable obstacle of a primarily self-directed work-force, whose members determine for themselves which of the many demands on their time the outside world makes to respond to and how.

This scenario has led some to question the whole wisdom of rational management approaches to objective setting in the world of police decision-making. Advocates of PBO on the other hand have questioned the view that policing is an activity essentially distinct from other areas of problem-solving and decision-making (Butler, 1984). Much of the research literature takes a less committed view, offering at most a cautious welcome for the PBO initiative, accepting that large areas of police work do involve at least the potential for a planned process of priority setting and goal definition, while reflecting that in practice more modest forms of purposive management are required (Horton, 1989; Weatheritt, 1986). The academic arguments notwithstanding, some form of planned policing through objective setting has emerged in most police forces.

It would be difficult to avoid the conclusion that early attempts at objective setting, and much that continues to operate, have been problematic. In its Report on performance measurement in the police service, the Audit Commission (1990) identified a number of weaknesses in the processes of objective setting as it had found them. First, many forces have relied on force-wide goals and objectives in place of more flexible and locally-based priorities. Typical examples of force goals are: 'To continue to reduce those levels of crime which cause concern to the public' and 'To reduce public apprehension about incidents affecting tranquillity'. The purpose of such statements is to provide policy direction for the whole force, but almost inevitably they are difficult to translate into particular policing functions and activities, and offer little more than general statements of intent or 'mission'.

Second, such 'top-down' approaches to objective setting fail to impress operational officers, who may be ignorant of the objectives set by their force. For example, research reported by the Operational Policing Review in 1990 found that less than one-fifth of officers surveyed were conscious of such objectives, even those set at subdivisional level. If they were aware of their existence, they were sceptical about their relevance to ground level policing. Furthermore, the Audit Commission identified 'a widespread feeling amongst operational officers that their superiors do not practise what they preach'. They do this by concentrating on objectives for junior levels of the hierarchy, rather than on those for its own levels of performance (Audit Commission Report, 1990). In place of force-wide goals and objectives, the Commission advocates a more locally-based and flexible approach to objective setting and problem solving, with more participation in the process both of junior ranks and the local community in arriving at priorities and approaches to policing the area. More active use, for example, of local opinion surveys to help in determining policing policies at ground level is to be encouraged. This is a strategy which is in fact very much in line with some of the earlier presentations of the PBO case (Butler 1984), although some commentators are less convinced of the benefits of public surveys in priority setting (Hough, 1989).

Performance Measurement

The most central problem identified by the Audit Commission with the processes of objective setting concerned the question of performance measurement. If arriving at *a priori* objectives for policing is difficult, the measurement of police performance is even more so. Objective setting without reliable and adequate measures of performance in relation to those objectives rather defeats the purpose of the exercise. Yet there are grounds for questioning the appropriateness of performance measurement to policing. Like objective setting itself there are those who consider it a generally futile if not dangerous pursuit. There are two primary arguments which underpin this view. First, much police work is not task-oriented but 'symbolic'. The police fulfil an essential role in 'providing a presence', in being what they are and not just in what they do. For example, the police response to a burglary cannot be assessed solely in terms of getting a 'result', by detecting the offender, indeed this is unlikely in most cases. The police in this instance can be fulfilling their role simply by seeming to take the matter seriously. This would appear to be as important, if not more so, than detection to the victim of the crime. Similarly, a police officer may be fulfilling a crucial role in deterring offenders through the basic act of patrolling on foot in a particular area, while not actually 'doing' something that could be measured as such. Management strategies tied to a concern for the immediately quantifiable would therefore be missing a major facet of the policing function: it is a question of what the police are, rather than simply what they do.

The second objection to performance measurement as a basis for management decisions is that the effectiveness of policing would tend to be measured against criteria over which the police have little or no control. The classic case is that of official crime statistics. Both the police and politicians have used the official data on crime rates as a basis for demanding increased resource levels for the service. Typically, increased crime figures have been taken as evidence of the need to increase manning levels and/or improve technical equipment and support. Alternatively, and more negatively, such increases have been taken as evidence that the resources made available have not been used effectively. The Conservative governments of the 1980s followed both paths at some time or other. An association is presumed to exist between officially recorded offences and police performance. The problems with this are many. First, recorded rates of crime bear little relationship to actual rates, as criminological research has established beyond doubt (Bottomley and Pease, 1986). The recording of an offence is the result of a complex range of factors and processes, with the effect that the official figures are indicators of only a fraction of those actually committed (Mayhew *et al.*, 1988). Second, although police activities have some impact on crime rates, that impact is, it would seem, fairly marginal. There are at least two reasons for this. On the one hand, while crime rates would undoubtedly soar if there was no police force at all, once one exists particular operations or changes in manning levels have little or no effect on crimes committed (Clarke and Hough, 1980). On the other hand, crime is the product of a host of potential factors outside of the control or influence of the police – such as social, cultural, economic and psychological influences – so that crime rates are perhaps more a measure of social circumstances than police effectiveness. To base management decisions at either force level or at some level lower down in the management hierarchy even in part on crime figures is therefore a dangerous game.

The same can also be said for a measure much closer to policing methods and activities, the clear-up rate. The rate of offences cleared up to offences recorded is more readily taken as an indicator of police performance than absolute crime rates (Kinsey, Lea and Young, 1986). As a tool for management it is, however, fraught with problems. To begin with, if crimes recorded are only a small percentage of actual crimes, to use the recorded rates as a basis for crimes cleared up, as if this would be a reliable measure of police effectiveness, is, to say the least, questionable. On the other hand, the extent to which those crimes cleared is an indicator of police effort and effectiveness is itself limited. This is because the detection rate is the function of a variety of processes, only some of which are even indirectly related to police activities. Much of the clear-up rate is a reflection on the public's willingness to identify suspects and provide other forms of information, which form the bulk of overall detections. This may reflect such factors as public confidence in the police, which is in part within the remit of the police themselves, but it may also reflect broader matters such as public attitudes to authority in general. A bizarre feature of police performance in this context is that a decline in the clear up rate may actually indicate an improvement of police effectiveness, because if public support for the police grows as a result of better police-community relations, the public may be more willing to report more offences. This may in turn have the effect of reducing the percentage, if not the absolute number, of detections. Other factors affecting the clear-up rate are variations in recording practices between forces, and the extent of offences taken into consideration by the courts on conviction, which, although they may be a reflection of police work, are not exactly a direct function of police effort.

What is an issue is whether these identified difficulties in attaching performance measurement to policing constitute an insurmountable barrier to management seeking an information base against which to assess the attainment of objectives as set. To the two main objections raised above, that much police work is 'symbolic' and thus non-measurable, and that those indicators traditionally available through officially recorded figures of offences and clear-ups are unreliable, the following points can be made. In so far as the symbolic work of the police is seen to have effects, there is no reason why such effects cannot in any way be measured. If we take the example given of the police response to burglary, if part of the outcome of that response is to give the victim the feeling that 'something is being done', even if the crime is not detected, then there are ways in which that outcome can be measured – for example, with victim satisfaction forms to elicit customer satisfaction. As we point out shortly, that is precisely the direction in which some police forces have gone in recent years in the pursuit of 'subjective' indicators of police performance. On the other hand, the accepted limitations of the traditional indicators of performance can to an extent be counterbalanced by more elaborate frameworks of indicators, which employ multiple variables. The HMI's sought to further this process by developing a 'Matrix of Indicators' to act as a starting point for their inspections, a format which most police forces have taken roughly as a template for their performance measurement. Typically they have been broken down into a number of central categories, such as force establishment and personnel information, incidents recorded, crimes recorded and detected, both force wide and per officer, arrests, traffic accidents, and so on. But within crime detection alone the matrix lists more than 70 measures of force performance.

There is no doubt that as a result of more sophisticated conceptions of performance measurement, police forces have made more of the information already at their disposal and have begun to develop new information systems to underpin the management process. They have also begun to develop more comprehensive views of what police performance overall can be about. One notable expression of this has been in the shift in recent years toward concern for 'quality' in policing processes, a shift apparent elsewhere in the public services and incorporated in the government's *Citizen's Charter* (Prime Minister's Office, 1991). This has been encouraged by the Audit Commission, which has criticised the tendency to concentrate on quantifiable measures at the expense of monitoring quality of policing. It is also reflected in a statement issued by the Association of Chief Police Officers in 1990, driven no doubt by concern that public satisfaction with the service has shown clear signs of deterioration. With its focus on 'professionalism', integrity and responsiveness to public preferences, it signals an attempt to regain lost public confidence by emphasising policing standards and not just quantifiable inputs and outputs. For police management to move beyond statements of intent to quality review and quality control has not been, and will not be, easy. For example, monitoring quality by means of the public survey has its pitfalls as well as its attractions. Similarly, the use of information on complaints against the police can act to understate the extent of 'customer dissatisfaction' with at least some individual officers, although closer analysis of the data might reveal useful indicators (Maguire and Corbett, 1989).

A culture of sensitivity to issues of performance measurement has begun therefore to emerge within the framework of planned policing. A shift from simple to more complex indicators of performance, and from the quantifiable or 'objective' measures, to the monitoring of quality, have typified the development of planned policing from its earlier approaches to its current status. Without adopting the absolute negativism of the arguments considered earlier, however, caution is required before arriving at the view that major advances have been made. Weatheritt (1989, p. 42), for example, has criticised the quality of the research and information gathering which have formed much of the basis of the evaluation of police work attached to performance measurement. With reference to police research, she states:

'that they are being pressed to do more of it perhaps speaks less to the value placed on achieving a genuine understanding of the difficulties of action in a complex setting than a need to demonstrate managerial competence consistent with certain political expectations.

In other words, much research and assessment takes the form of 'showing something works effectively' rather than genuine objective evaluation.

Value for Money

Notwithstanding these problems, it would be difficult to overstate the impact of the heightened emphasis on issues of effectiveness, efficiency and economy on the culture and actions of police management. 'Value for Money' now provides the framework for policing decisions at virtually every stage in the process. Above all, it has undermined the assumption that the police should commit maximum available resources in the blanket response to demands made on the service, and has led to attempts to prioritise such demands and allocate resources accordingly. Two initiatives illustrate the point, both of which emerged in the wake of efficiency/effectiveness drives. The first is 'graded response'. With the increase in telecommunications, and with the increased mobility of officers in vehicles, it has been acknowledged that the demands for a police response have increased substantially over the years. A number of forces have taken steps to determine an order of priority of calls for a response, and, in recognition of the limited resources available, not simply seek to respond to each and every call at the earliest possible opportunity. Graded response allows for an immediate response to emergencies, and a delayed response, or a different sort of response, such as a telephone call, to calls deemed less an emergency. The argument runs that this can be both a more efficient use of finite resources and a more effective use of police time in terms of a 'targeting' of certain calls.

A second example is 'crime screening'. This is designed to save time and to make efficient use of resources deployed for criminal investigation. A significant number of forces now operate an investigative policy which targets resources on crimes which are anticipated to be most likely to lead to detection, an approach based upon an assessment of 'solvability factors'. While serious crimes will continue, at least for the immediate future, to attract a substantial degree of investigative attention, it is thought that many lesser crimes can be prioritized in this way. The extent to which such initiatives succeed in enhancing effectiveness and efficiency is, however, a point of contention. According to the *Operational Policing Review* (Joint Consultative Commitee, 1990, Section 2), such gains as may be apparent in terms of short-term effectiveness may be at the expense of longer-term reductions in public satisfaction with the police. The dilemma facing the police is that police prioritisation of crimes and emergencies may not tally with public perceptions of their relative importance.

Another, and far more extensive, example of the pursuit of 'value for money' has been the development of 'civilianisation' within the service. Both Circular 114/83 and reports of the Audit Commission had stressed the need to identify tasks currently undertaken by police officers which could reasonably be handled by civilian staff, and if possible to transfer whole posts over in this fashion. Considerations of efficiency and economy – civilian staff operate on typically lower salary scales than do police officers – would seem uppermost in this respect. Home Office Circular 105/88 'Civilian Staff in the Police Service' (HMSO, 1988) has subsequently provided a guide to posts deemed suitable for civilianisation, and such guidance now features in HMI evaluations of individual forces. Administration is the primary area currently targeted for attention, and most forces have civilianised posts in such areas as personnel, finance, press and public relations, and subdivisional administration.

A number of semi-operational posts, such as photographers, counter assistants and even gaolers have also gone over to civilian status. Lower salary scales and the potential for freeing police staff for operational duties act as primary attractions in this process, although one must not ignore the possible enhancements in effectiveness and not just efficiency and economy. Civilian staff may well be better qualified to undertake the task than their police counterparts, though transfers of post may not necessarily reduce cost significantly. Civilianisation does, however, have its critics. The Operational Review pointed to higher civilian staff turnover, the lack of a proper career structure, and unionisation as areas which are problematic in what is termed the potential for 'over-civilianisation' in the current climate.

A further area in which value for money considerations are having effect is that of intra-organisational processes. Whilst attempts to separate purchaser agencies from provider units may not have advanced as far in police organisations as in other public service bodies, that process is very much under way. This has led to the introduction of agency status for the Forensic Science Service, and a similar destiny may await the National Identification Bureau, the Police National Computer, and various other departments. More generally, contracting out and competitive tendering have become commonplace in areas as disparate as catering and academic consultancy. Managers have also become increasingly aware of the income generation potential of police properties and units, with training schools and the courses they run very much the target of such considerations, a development encouraged by the Audit Commission Report (1990).

Training for Management

The cultural revolution which the value for money emphasis has encouraged raises many issues for the police service. These include the training of police managers and the placing of officers within the management structure. The fundamental fact of the British police service is that everyone has to start at the bottom, by undergoing initial constable, or 'probationer', training. This comprises a mixture of 'in-class' and operational tuition and experience, over a period of two years. In England and Wales, this basic probationer training is provided mainly by six District Training Centres, under the auspices of the Central Planning Unit (CPU) at Harrogate, paid for by contributions from each client force in proportion to the size of its establishment. The Metropolitan Police has remained independent of the CPU, and all their recruits undergo probationer training at their own Hendon Training Centre.

Traditionally, the emphasis and ideology of probationary police training have been allied to quasi-military discipline. Drill was very much a feature of the training programme, with training largely concerned with the rote learning of police law and procedure. Primarily in response to the Scarman Report, police training, initially in the MPS and since in the provincial areas, has in recent years undergone major transformations. The length of the training period has been extended and the content and delivery of training have shifted very much towards 'policing skills'. Practical policing role-play aims to equip recruits with an insight into how to handle real-life situations and, post-Scarman, the input on social and communication skills has been enhanced, some have argued to good effect (Bull and Horncastle, 1989). It will be some time, however, before recruits trained under the new regime will appear in managerial positions.

At first sight it might appear as if the police service occupies a singular position in the new public services as an organisation of egalitarian opportunity and a meritocracy in which every passing-out police constable could be said to have in his or her knapsack a chief constable's baton. It is undeniably true that, nowadays, all chief officers are drawn exclusively from the service's own ranks. That, however, only came about in the latter half of this century.

The first joint Commissioners of the Metropolitan Police were Sir Richard Mayne, a lawyer, and Sir Charles Rowan, an army colonel. From their appointment in 1829 to the end of the Second World War, the tradition was to choose successive Commissioners from the ranks of (mainly retired) senior officers in the armed forces. The selection in 1945 by the Home Secretary, Herbert Morrison, of a senior civil servant, Sir Harold Scott, to head the country's largest force can thus be seen as an important turning point in police professionalisation. By the time the Royal Commission on the Police reported in 1962, there were still a few retired army officers among the ranks of provincial chief constables and it was not until the 1980s that senior police officers were in place as directors of all police training establishments in Britain.

Against this background it is interesting to note the recurring concerns of politicians, academics and, indeed, the police themselves about how best to recruit, train and retain the managers they need. The debate seems to lurch backwards and forwards about whether, in fact, the apparently egalitarian entry point arrangement can provide the service with the managers it requires.

The earliest experiment in fast-tracking came in the 1930s when the then Commissioner of the Metropolitan Police, Lord Trenchard, created what was seen as a kind of police 'Sandhurst' at the Hendon Police College. Despite being responsible for producing some outstanding police leaders, the scheme did not survive long. As Stead (1985, p. 82) recounts, 'one reason for its unpopularity was that a proportion of entrants were selected on the basis of higher educational qualifications or competitive examination without prior police service'. Trenchard intended 'that eventually no one would reach the rank of inspector without passing through the college'. The resentment over injecting an 'officer élite' into an essentially artisan service has lingered long amongst the rank and file of the police and found new expression in the 1990s. This issue is addressed later.

Contemporary police management training in England and Wales, and for the most senior ranks in Scotland and Northern Ireland, is provided at the Police Staff College at Bramshill in Hampshire, where four key in-service management courses are conducted. These are:

- the Special Course – for high-flying sergeants;
- the Junior Command Course – for chief inspectors;
- the Intermediate Command Course – for subdivisional commanders;
- the Senior Command Course – for chief superintendents.

Since the 1980s Bramshill has also developed a carousel of short courses for middle managers, each with a more specific focus compared to the more general curricula of the command courses.

Bramshill has a virtual monopoly on higher police training. Indeed, attendance on a Senior Command Course is now a *sine qua non* for progression to ACPO rank (Reiner, 1991). Yet Bramshill is often characterised by critics and supporters alike as an institution with something of an identity crisis. As Plumridge (1985, p. 129) has asked, 'What is Bramshill to be – a staff college, the policeman's university, the centre of higher police training, a management and organisation development centre, or a resource centre?'. There are many unresolved questions about the role of the institution primarily associated with producing the managers the service needs. A great deal of self-examination has occurred over the last 30 years. In 1962 Bramshill became the location for the Special Course, set up at a time when graduate entrants to the service were few and for largely the same reasons that Trenchard had embarked on his enterprise. In its attempt to identify and develop potential leaders from among its own work-force, the original Special Course was an avenue for accelerated promotion to inspector rank. Like the Trenchard scheme before it, the Bramshill course with its residentially-based mix of academic, legal and police studies is credited with producing a number of outstanding senior managers.

For many, however, the fast track promise was never really fulfilled. By the mid-1980s, 'it was widely recognised that its format was outmoded and did little to enhance the performance and potential of its increasingly well-educated and sophisticated membership' (Mead, 1990, p. 407). As the number of graduates and more highly qualified recruits increased, a rethink took place . Consequently, the revamped Special Course now has a sandwich flavour, with a much greater emphasis on operational and organisational effectiveness. Unlike its forerunner, the current course does not offer automatic advancement to inspector on completion. While its Director has claimed positive signs for the short term, he has pointed out that it will be around the year 2000 before its first graduates achieve ACPO office.

The police service has, with a few exceptions, a propensity to train people after they have assumed the role and rank rather than to train them for it in advance. It is not unusual to hear of officers being promoted to front-line supervisory roles and middle management roles, without having received any job-specific training at all. One story, within the knowledge of one of the authors, concerns a sergeant with around 20 years service who was promoted to inspector in charge of the force's central charge office. An in-force arrangement of the time stipulated that, in the event of sickness, the charge office inspector would become acting chief inspector in the Force operations room. The newly-promoted inspector's first job was to be acting chief inspector on night shift and thus, effectively, the Force's chief officer. And he had not attended a course since basic training, nor passed an examination other than his police promotion exams! This is an extreme example, perhaps, but an illustration of what may happen when rank is allowed to dictate who does what management task.

Concern over the 'quality' of top management in today's service – and by extension the adequacy of the training and recruiting system to provide a sufficient yield – resurfaced in the 1990s when senior Conservatives, among them, it was said, the then Prime Minister Margaret Thatcher, complained that there were too many 'dead beats' at the highest levels of British police management. Favoured solutions voiced have included: a return to the practice of appointing senior military officers to senior levels in the force and/or an extension of the existing accelerated promotion scheme building on the Special Course to allow for the entry into the service of more mature candidates who have the skills and potential to progress rapidly up the hierarchy. A reluctance to appoint potential managers who have not done their time on the beat remains a stumbling block to reforms in this area.

Reflecting the climate of value for money which has been so influential in shaping the management of the new public services generally, the Chief Inspector of Constabulary, Sir John Woodcock, has stated that there will be no room for 'also-rans' at the top levels of police management. Changes in emphasis in police training at senior level would appear to be aiming at developing vision-builders and action-oriented leaders, but still very much from among the police's own ranks. The debate on how best to achieve the highest quality management material possible is one which seems to generate much more heat than light so far as the police service is concerned. Suggestions of more fast-tracking and 'transplants' of armed forces officers do not go down well with the police staff associations who remain wedded, by and large, to the need for single entry to the service, and to the notion that the broad base of police 'experience' is the best foundation for the multiplicity of managerial roles which the organisation exhibits.

Conclusion

Despite the changes which have taken place over the past decade or so, it would seem as if we have only witnessed the beginning of a process. The continuing pressure from central government, the critical evaluation of many aspects of the police by the Audit Commission, public concern over policing methods and priorities, and the police service's own expressed determination to pursue top to bottom improvements in the organisation, will all ensure that change is very much on the agenda. This may be accelerated with the growing clamour, seemingly with Home Office blessing, for reorganisation of the whole structure of the service towards 'regionalisation'. The amalgamation of existing forces into perhaps half as many combined units will inevitably require managerial reform, and the opportunity this will offer for an overhaul of management structure will be enthusiastically taken up by those seeking radical change.

It could be argued that a major obstacle to further advancement in managerial style and effectiveness, and ultimately to the enhancement of policing overall, is the combination of a quasi-military, rank-structured hierarchy, and single-entry point recruitment. These, of course, need not go hand in hand. The armed services, for example, operate on the basis of rank, but have dual-entrance points. Unfortunately, this model of an 'officer corps' has clouded much of the debate over possible changes to recruitment of police managers. A false opposition has been erected between *either* the continuation of single-entry *or* an 'officer class', in other words, a military analogy. Why not accept that the issue is not about 'officers' and the 'ranks' but about management and a work-force? Looked at in this way there would seem to be no insurmountable barrier to the recruitment of staff directly into positions of management, including to those holding ranks such as inspector, superintendent and so on. Such an apparently radical approach is in fact common to policing systems in Europe, Japan and elsewhere. In the Netherlands, for example, there are two points of entry, one for the post of constable, another for that of inspector. For the latter, entrants must undergo no less than four years of education and training if they are school-leavers, three if they are transferees from lower ranks (for whom a percentage of places are reserved), and two if they are university graduates. 'Practical experience' of patrol level policing, often the sticking point in the British context and the major objection to reform, is included as part of management training, along with study of management theory and skills, law, public administration, and other academic disciplines.

The adoption of a similar scheme, or even one with multiple entrance, could act as a major factor in facilitating further police management development in Britain. It could help establish training more explicitly on the basis of proven competencies; to precede the appointment of staff rather than to follow it. This is not to deny that the current system has thrown up many managers of the highest quality; the service has at all levels men and women of high calibre. The question is whether such people emerge despite, rather than because of the present structure of training and appointment.

There are other potential advantages of dual- or multi-point entry. First, it could act as a major factor in enhancing equal opportunities within the service. Arguably one of the reasons for the under-representation of women and members of ethnic minorities at management level is their reluctance to run the gauntlet of the single-entrance system, although this is an area deserving further research. The direct recruitment of women and black officers to middle management positions, possibly allied to a deliberate strategy of equal opportunities, could help increase representation not just at this level but, ultimately, at senior level. Second, it may help attract candidates from a wider pool of talent, some of whom may by deterred from joining under the present system. Third, and ironically, it might help enhance the position of police constables themselves, the backbone of the service. Under the present regime, there is the danger in them feeling that they are under-achievers because they remain at that rank, while others have proceeded further. The creation of dual-entrance might open up opportunities to create a reward structure for the rank and file of the service, which at present is locked into the rank-structure. The reality is that over 80 per cent of police officers remain at the rank of constable. Quality management means little without quality in those who are front-line providers of the service.

Notwithstanding these points, the future of police management depends on more than organisational developments, however radical they may be. Over and above questions about the ways in which the service can best go about its business, and the role of management in pursuing its objectives, is the wider issue of what the business of 'policing' really is or should be. There has traditionally been a dilemma between the 'law-enforcement' and 'service' roles of the police, which arguably dates back to the original objectives of the police set out in the early nineteenth century (Reiner, 1985). The tensions which have existed between these functions have inevitably been exacerbated with the social and political changes occurring since. Most commentators, inside and outside of the service, now seem to agree that a fundamental review of the police role, in the light of changing expectations of and demands on police organisations, is now required. Calls for a full Royal Commission on the police, going beyond the remit of the current Royal Commission on Criminal Justice, are now widespread. Perhaps only with the benefit of such a wholesale reconsideration of policing in contemporary Britain can police management be clear about their 'mission'.

Part IV

Conclusion

11

The New Public Service Managerialism: An Assessment

DAVID FARNHAM and SYLVIA HORTON

The aim of this final chapter is to review the nature, origins and impact of the new managerialism in the new public services and to point the way to the future. There is no doubt that the boundaries of state activity, the orientation of the public services and the ways in which they are managed are significantly different in the 1990s from what they were in 1979. It is also evident that these changes will continue. With the Conservatives being returned to office for a fourth consecutive term in April 1992, new managerial initiatives are planned and new organisational responses to public pressures are being proposed. As John Major (1989, p. 3) said, when Chief Secretary to the Treasury: 'the changes within our public services [over the last decade] amount to nothing less than a revolution in progress'. This has involved 'two radical changes. First, the change from volume to cash expenditure planning, and second the strong devolutionary push in financial management.' He described the system as one in which 'Ministers and senior managers concentrate on setting policy objectives and the resources needed to meet them; and the individuals who deliver the services use their ability and skills to tackle the problems.'

The new managerialism is the term that we have used in this book to describe the structural, organisational and managerial changes which have taken place in the public services in recent years. In essence, it incorporates the application of private sector management systems and managerial techniques into the public services. Some of the features of the new public service management include:

1. Adopting a rational approach to managing, which emphasises the role of strategic management in setting objectives and clarifying policy issues;
2. Changing organisational structures designed to separate policy from administration and creating executive units with delegated responsibility for service delivery, whether internally to other parts of the organisation or externally to the 'public';
3. Changing organisational structures which are designed to shorten hierarchies, devolving managerial responsibility for achieving set targets of performance and holding individual managers responsible for achieving them;
4. Measuring organisational achievement in terms of the criteria of economy, efficiency and effectiveness;
5. Developing performance indicators enabling comparisons and measures of achievement to be made and providing information upon which future decisions can be determined;
6. Developing active policies for changing the cultures of public organisations from ones dominated by traditional public service values to ones attuned to the market, business and entrepreneurial values of the 'new' public service model;
7. Implementing human resource management techniques aimed at weakening collectivist approaches and introducing individualist ones, including seeking to mobilise employee support and commitment to continual structural and organisational change;
8. Seeking to create flexible, responsive and learning public organisations; and
9. Developing a 'public service orientation' focusing on the public as clients, customers and citizens, with a move away from supply-led to demand-led services, no longer dominated by professional providers but responsive to the needs of those being served.

Managerialism also encompasses a set of ideas and values justifying a central role for managers and management within organisations and society. It is a challenge to both professionalism and syndicalism and has been opposed by both professionals and trade unionists, because it is seen as an attempt to weaken their power. As an ideology, managerialism has permeated the public services now for over ten years and there is some debate whether it is appropriate to the public domain and whether it has replaced more traditional organisational philosophies and cultures in the public services.

The origins of the new managerialism have been attributed to New Right ideology and the advent of the 'new politics' but its roots lie further back in classical scientific management theory and the ideas of Frederick Taylor and Henri Fayol. Many of the changes in management in the public services can be traced to the Fulton, Salmon, McKinsey, Maud and Bains Reports published in the 1960s and early 1970s. The wave of managerialism which swept through the public services in the 1980s, however, emerged out of the coincidence of particular economic, social and political circumstances which characterised the last quarter of the twentieth century.

First, there was the relatively slow rate of growth in the British economy from the mid-1960s. This meant that any continued expansion of the Welfare State could only be achieved by increased taxation and/or public sector borrowing. This had implications for private savings, investment and interest rates, which in turn had inflationary implications for the economy as a whole, thus affecting private willingness to save and invest. In these circumstances, a number of economic scenarios was possible. These included cutting real levels of public expenditure, redistributing existing public spending amongst different spending programmes and making more efficient use of existing public financial resources.

Second, on the social front two factors were of paramount importance. One was the rising expectations of an increasingly literate and demanding population who wanted more social provision by the state from the cradle to the grave. These were complemented by demands from professional public sector employees who pressed for more resources to be injected into the public services. The other social factor was the changing demographic structure, especially the ageing or 'greying' of the population. These, together with rising costs of provision, created a situation where social demands were beginning to exceed the economic resources available to provide for a continuing expansion of the Welfare State without some radical changes in the economic and social system, such as initiating large cutbacks in defence expenditure.

The third factor was a shift in political ideas about the role of the state and public policy which was linked to the economic and social contexts outlined above. The economic crisis of British capitalism and the overstretching of the Welfare State's resources, referred to by O'Connor (1973) as the 'fiscal crisis of the state', gave rise to theorists of the New Right challenging the orthodoxies associated with

Keynesian economic policy, Beveridge social policy and consensus politics. Public expenditure was no longer seen as desirable solely because it served 'good' purposes, whilst borrowing merely to sustain public expenditure was seen as an 'evil', since economic abundance was no longer assumed. Starks (1991, p. 10) describes what happened as a sea change. It represented 'a revulsion against excessive [public] expenditure and a new emphasis on thrift. The need for a healthy wealth-generating private sector as a pre-condition of non-inflationary public spending came into focus'.

These ideas were most coherently articulated in the writings of the New Right which captured the leadership of the Conservative Party when Margaret Thatcher succeeded Edward Heath in 1975. The New Right favoured economic liberalism, unregulated markets, free enterprise and a deregulated economy. The private sector was held up as a model of economic efficiency, business competitiveness, wealth-generating enterprise and rational approaches to management. It was contrasted with the wasteful, inefficient and monopoly-ridden public sector (Minford, 1984). Privatisation or the introduction of private sector management practices into the public sector were the remedies offered by the New Right to resolve the 'crisis of the state'.

There is no doubt that managerialism has had an impact throughout the public services and the wider public sector. The election of three Thatcher-led governments, determined to roll back the state and to expand the private sector, provided the political opportunities for experiments in privatising, marketising and managerialising the public services. This was a legacy inherited by John Major when he replaced Margaret Thatcher in 1990 but one to be reinforced by him after the fourth successive electoral victory of the Conservatives in April 1992.

The strategy of the Thatcher and Major governments has been incrementalist and implemented by a step by step approach, with a new political agenda being instituted, legitimated and acted upon since the early 1980s. It incorporates cutting global levels of public expenditure in real terms, redistributing expenditure amongst different spending programmes and making the remaining public services more cost effective and efficient. The latter is where the new managerialism has been applied. The new politics coincided with the popularisation and extension of new management ideas being promulgated in North America and being evangelistically disseminated through books, articles, conferences and the media. These ideas soon permeated British business language and from the early 1980s attracted attention amongst policy makers in both the private and public sectors. There were therefore some converts to the new managerialism, already in the public services, who responded very positively to the changes being introduced by government.

Through an extensive programme of privatisation, most of the public industries have been transferred to the private sector. John Major (1989) claims that by 1989 45 per cent of the public sector, as it was in 1979, had been returned to 'the disciplines of the market economy'. In addition, through policies of contracting out and compulsory competitive tendering (CCT), many activities, previously performed by civil servants, local government employees, NHS workers and other public officials, are now carried out by private firms. Although services such as catering, refuse collection, maintenance and management training are paid for out of public taxation, they are now, in many cases, provided by private 'for profit' organisations. The contours of the state have, through contracting out, extended into the private domain, blurring the dividing line between the two sectors still further. The contraction of the state, however, may be more apparent than real. Most areas of state activity inherited by the Conservative government in 1979 are not significantly different in 1992. The traditional security, judicial and welfare functions remain. There is still a NHS and a national educational system, which educates over 90 per cent of children between five and 16 and almost 100 per cent in further and higher education. Social security and income maintenance remain major planks of the 'Welfare State', even though that term is used less frequently today. The public sector still employs over five million people and accounts for 40 per cent of GDP.

It is within the public services that the impact of managerialism has been greatest. In essence, the orientation of the public services has changed. They were originally founded on the traditional principles of public administration and bureaucratic hierarchies, co-ordinated by generalist administrators or professional specialists and focusing on free services based on need, equity, fairness and altruism. They are now based, in part at least, on the principles of 'public business' and 'customer awareness', focusing on the instrumental objectives of economy, efficiency and effectiveness (the 3 Es), and the agency of professional management.

Since the essential feature of the new public sector managerialism is the introduction of private sector management systems, techniques and business language into the public services, it is, in a sense, a covert form of privatisation. The private sector model of management involves the use of economistic, rationalist and generic frames of reference. All public services are now perceived as businesses with mission statements identifying their goals and objectives, which can either be quantified or measured. They identify the markets that they are seeking to satisfy and the customers and clients that they serve. This is not always easy to do, for example, in areas like the police and prison services.

Sophisticated management and financial information systems have been or are in the process of being introduced and every organisation is committed to the three 'Es', and seeking value for money. Each major function or activity is clearly linked to a management structure where the tasks and accompanying budgets are delegated down to the operational level. Individual managers are responsible and held accountable for what is done and for the way that money is spent. Up to 1987, the managerial emphasis was on costs and controlling the inputs in an attempt to get public expenditure down. Since 1987, the emphasis has turned more to outputs, quality and the effectiveness of the services in meeting 'customer', 'consumer' or 'client' demands and expectations.

In the civil service, managerialism has challenged the traditional 'Whitehall' culture. This is based on an administrative philosophy which rejects the separation of politics and administration, sees administration as a fusion of science and ethics, and adopts a qualitative rather than a quantitative criterion of efficiency (Thomas, 1978). In addition to being reduced in overall size by over 20 per cent between 1979 and 1989, more than half of the remaining civil service has been hived off into separate agencies since 1988. These executive agencies have responsibility for achieving preset objectives and targets, with devolved budgets, which are set down by central policy departments. Whilst the degree of decentralisation varies, depending on the political salience and functions of the agency, it is claimed that their chief executives have the sort of control over their resources, including staff, that their private sector counterparts have. National collective bargaining has in some cases been abandoned and human resources management (HRM) practices are being widely used. The new chief executives report to their parent departments and to Parliament for the performance of their agencies and for the ways that they are managed.

In local government, the main impact of managerialism has been to remove the monopolies of local authorities and to force them to take on an 'enabling' rather than a 'service provider' role. The old patterns of 'bureaucratic paternalism' have given way to privatisation, subcontracting and CCT which has been applied more extensively in local government than in other areas. The impact of these changes on the way that local government is now organised and managed has been significant. Clouston (1991), for example, cites the case of Liverpool's privatised refuse collection service where the contract was won by the French owned company, Onyx, which undercut the council's in-house bid by £4 million. In consequence, the work-force was reduced by 240 and those who were rehired by Onyx were required to work six hours longer per week for £27 less pay. In addition there was no pension scheme, shorter paid holidays, reduced sick pay and a shorter lunch break. Numerous similar examples are to be found across local authorities, not all of them involving external contracts.

In addition to CCT, local authorities have been forced to introduce a mixed economy of welfare by the government's community care policy. Resource cutbacks and constraints have also forced local authorities to look for economies and to the efficient use of resources. Externally-imposed performance indicators have established targets to be aimed at by individual service areas. Chief executives and their supporting officers are now emerging as strategic managers, seeking to identify the needs within the community and to develop business plans as frameworks for service developments.

The changes in the NHS are some of the most far reaching. After the introduction of general managers in 1984, there followed a major programme of decentralisation and devolution of budgets down to 'areas' within the community services and individual 'services' within the hospitals. This was followed, after 1990, by the introduction of internal markets and the creation of purchasers and providers. This is intended to simulate the price and product competition found in private markets. Newly-created self-governing trusts have been given managerial freedoms previously unknown within the NHS. These include owning their own buildings and land, being permitted to break from nationally negotiated terms and conditions and rights to borrow money. Within months of the creation of the first trusts, it was evident that there were those that supported them arguing that the greater freedom would lead to better patient care and more efficient use of resources. Bedford (1991) argues that those criticising trusts should ask:

Why I and hundreds of other health service managers, who have devoted our careers to public service, should have put in voluntarily all the extra work necessary for trust applications. The answer is that we believe that the increased local freedoms will lead to higher quality patient services. To suggest we have more unseemly motives is a misjudgement of those who are wholly committed to the National Health Service.

Opponents (Brindle, 1991a), however, point to the cuts in staff to avoid budget overspend and, more significantly, to the wedge that is being driven between NHS staff by the changes being forced through by the government. One doctor stated 'we are fighting each other to survive. No innovation, no integration, no planning and no progress is possible under this regime'.

John Chawner, Chair of the British Medical Association's consultants' committee claims that managers in the NHS are being increasingly seen as 'an alien occupying force'. He says that there had been a slump in consultant morale because of organisational and managerial changes, the underfunding of the service and 'the ascendancy of managerial values'. According to Chawner, health service managers 'have been totally absorbed with getting these sort of changes through and they are all on performance related pay. Their jobs are all up for grabs if they don't actually agree with what's happening'.

Radical changes have also taken place in the education services at every level. The local management of schools, combined with the opting out of schools to grant maintained status, not only have seen the role of heads change from teachers to 'production managers' but also have created a situation within which internal markets can develop, with local authorities or central government as the purchasers and the schools as the providers. With the introduction of 'managerialism' and 'market forces' into schools, headteachers are increasingly seeing their 'educational units' in terms of inputs, production processes and outputs. In this model, teachers become one element in the production process and the search for greater school productivity. Symptomatic of this new culture, one teacher suggests (Bornett, 1991), 'is the way headteachers are flocking to attend courses, put on by the new breed of education/business consultants, with give-away titles like, How to manage Parent Meetings, and How to Sell Your School'. Teacher energies, in consequence, are directed away from classroom activities to public relations and the promotion of glossy brochures and newsletters. In this new culture, he argues, teacher appraisal and accounting procedures typify the new managerialist priorities.

A similar pattern exists in higher education. Within these institutions, management techniques and systems have been imported from the private sector along with the language of marketing, purchasing, public relations and accounting. Similar debates to those taking place in health emerged in higher education. A group of university vice-chancellors went on record in the academic press in 1990–91 condemning the government for pushing too hard in making them pay their own way. They warned that further squeezes on their finances could lead to a demoralised and run-down higher education system. As the vice-chancellor of the University of Kent said, 'universities are in no way comparable to nationalised industries, whose success or failure may be measured by looking at a balance sheet, and whose income can be increased by raising the cost of the product' (Meikle, 1990).

Kogan (1988), in analysing the growth of managerialism in universities, puts forward two models of university governance. The first is collegial which is founded on the idea of self-governing institutions, where authority is not imposed by 'hierarchy working through management systems'. The second model is that 'to which government policy is now leading us', that of a 'dependent institution'. It is predicated on the premise that higher education is no different from any other public service and that it is there to meet national economic needs in terms of human resources skills and useful knowledge for society. 'It is a system in which the objectives are not set by the inhabitants but by the [governmental] sponsors'. It has led to managerialism in higher education which Kogan sees as based on the assumption:

> that the institutions and the system to which it becomes subordinate can specify objectives within which those of the basic units can be subsumed. It further assumes that the ability to determine and control the pursuit of objectives can be distributed hierarchically. Its moral justification is that higher education outcomes should or ought to be determined and judged outside itself and in terms of social rather than intellectual criteria.

Kogan questions whether government can be certain that 'the most productive academics are those that state their objectives, convert their Vice-Chancellors into Chief Executives, call the Deans middle managers and the Heads of Departments first line managers?'

It is in the former polytechnics and institutes of higher education that the managerialist thrust in higher education has become most institutionalised. Wagner (1989), Director and 'Chief Executive' of what was then the Polytechnic of North London writes that 'this whole business of being a Chief Executive instead of a Director is of very recent origin'. In distinguishing the 'managerial' from the 'representational' model of governance in this sector, Wagner argues that the managerial model takes its cue from the limited liability companies in the industrial and commercial sectors. It produces 'governing bodies' comprising both executive directors (that is, senior managers) and non-executive directors (that is, lay members). Staff are the 'employees' of the 'company' with students exercising their rights as 'consumers' through the 'market' process, not as 'of right' as junior members of a diverse academic community. Wagner, unlike some of his directorial colleagues, disagrees with the 'so called managerial model', where staff and students have no rights to participate in the governance of the institution in which they work and study. For him staff are 'the real capital stock of our institutions' and 'the key to their intellectual health'. Only by 'treating staff as partners in the enterprise and not as the opposition' will higher education flourish.

These new managerialist orientations across the new public services have been introduced by a variety of means including political imposition, propaganda and changing public service cultures. The political means have involved every one of the instruments available to government, including legislation, administrative directives, departmental circulars and financial controls such as cash limits and new accounting procedures. Propaganda has involved government departments stressing how more efficient, better managed and more accountable public service organisations need to be to their users or 'clients', compared with the past.

The changing of public service cultures has been initiated by a variety of measures. These include: using language to create new images and values; implanting new symbols and logos, ceremonies and folk heroes with which members of the organisation can identify; rewarding those who accept the new culture and penalising those that do not; using training as a vehicle, for not only developing new skills but also changing people's perceptions of their roles and those of their organisations. Management training has been given top priority in the public services and is illustrated clearly in the civil service publication *Management Matters* which highlights managerial developments and innovations, features articles each month on successful 'new managers', runs competitions to 'reward' achievements in improving customer service, gaining a 'chartermark' or increasing productivity. Civil servants, along with other public service employees now appear to identify with a new managerial culture, although there are still some disbelievers.

Cultural change has also been achieved by organisational restructuring, decentralising and localising certain managerial decisions and providing rewards packages to motivate public service managers. Most now have performance related pay, non-pay benefits such as private medical insurance, 'company' cars and individualised contracts of employment. It was reported at the end of 1991, for example, that regional managers in the NHS had salaries of up to £75,000, with district managers earning up to £67,000 and unit managers up to £58,000. In April 1992 three chief executives in local government were recorded as earning in excess of £100,000 per year. This matched the growing consensus across the public and private sectors that pay for all groups of staff, but especially managers, 'must be determined by performance factors – profits, productivity, quality and service – rather than inflationary factors such as the RPI [Retail Price Index] and skills shortages' (Gilbert, 1991).

There are many positive outcomes and potential benefits of the changes in the new public services. First, public organisations are 'leaner' and 'meaner'. They are no longer over-staffed and they are more efficient, more productive and more business-like enterprises. People at all levels are now cost conscious, more conservative of resources and more rational in their allocation of scarce economic inputs. There is less waste and higher productivity has been shown in a number of Audit Commission reports. The public services also appear to be more rational in their approach to decision-making and in determining their strategic direction. They have developed a contractual approach to service provision, resulting in more precise delivery of outcomes. They are also using more sophisticated techniques to evaluate their own performance and to control and monitor their activities.

Second, public service organisations are also attempting to be more responsive to those using their services. They are providing more open access to information to the public and are having to account in some detail for their expenditures, use of resources and quality of services. Third, the curbing of the traditional powers of public officials, and their unions and professional bodies, is making professional workers in the public services more accountable to both their managers and their client groups. The power of the public sector unions has been reduced and this has enabled management to have more control over wages and staff costs. It has also resulted in more continuity and reliability of services to the public. Fourth, with more flexibility, there is greater opportunity for managers to innovate and adapt their organisational policies and activities to local circumstances and needs. It has been argued by C. Painter (1991) that 'the dynamism applicable to an "enterprise culture" is permeating the public as well as private sector, in the process abandoning inflexible organisational modes, transforming an anachronistic culture, and most crucially counteracting bureaucratic obstacles to change'.

The criticisms and claimed negative consequences and weaknesses of these changes are, first, that managerialism is an ideology which provides a very limited version and model of managing. It is essentially a directive and potentially authoritarian mode of management which minimises, if not excludes, union and collective participation in managerial processes. It is not based on a philosophy of management by consent. It is also an élitist view of management, defensive of the 'right to manage' in a sector where professional groups of staff have traditionally been involved in contributing to the management function. Second, the 'new managerialism' is a result of governmental initiatives and political policy-making. Collectively, public service managers, especially those in senior positions, have been agents of political and economic change and in this sense management has been politicised. Such managers may claim that they are neutral professionals, carrying out policy made by the politicians and committed to organisational effectiveness and efficiency. In fact, they have been responsible for driving through a series of extensive and sometimes contentious programmes of political reforms in the public services in the name of managerial competence. With few exceptions, they have provided little resistance to these changes and, some would add, many of them have been rewarded handsomely for their efforts in doing so.

Third, the impact of organisational and managerial change has not been without its adverse consequences for staff. There are repeated claims of a lowering of staff morale, deterioration in their terms and conditions of employment and the infringement of health and safety regulations, amongst a wide range of staff groups, across the public services. Edwards and Whitson (1991) show, as a result of changes of working practices during the 1980s, that people are now working harder in the face of assertive and sometimes aggressive workplace management. In the NHS, their study demonstrates that hospital workers in a large general hospital were convinced that they were having to work harder, under pressure for increased efficiency, notably in association with competitive tendering. The harsher aspects of the new management regimes may have been felt by only a minority of workers 'but they nonetheless constitute an important part of the changing nature of work'.

Fourth, the question arises, are these public service management reforms, focused on improving efficiency and lowering unit costs, being used to cover up lack of investment and the effective renewal of public service infrastructures? Furthermore, with more devolved managerial structures, it seems probable that this will fragment the public services and lead to wide variations in standards of provision and quality of service to their users and in the terms and conditions of employment they provide to staff. This could diminish the distinctiveness of the public services as providers to the community and their attractiveness as potential employers to the best qualified and most skilled members of the work-force.

It may be conjectured that the 'winners' of the new public service managerialism include governments, some high income taxpayers, some citizens as clients and a number of managerial careerists. The 'losers' include: some of the staff of the new public services; those who have lost their jobs; trade union and professional associations; those managers who have not identified with the new public service orientation; and the underclass who have fallen through the safety net of the new enabling state. The new public services may well be more efficient than the old 'welfare' sector was. Whether they are more effective in achieving the goals for which they were originally created, and whether they even have the same goals, is debateable.

There were many changes in the pipeline when the Conservative government went to the electorate for a renewed mandate in April 1992 and these will go ahead over the next few years. The boundaries between the public and private sectors will become even less distinct, as the mixed economy of welfare becomes the key characteristic of social policy and the government carries out its manifesto commitments on further economic reform. The future therefore looks set for 'more of the same'. The Conservative government is committed to reducing taxes, to reducing the share of GDP taken up by the public sector and to encouraging 'enterprise'. The government is further pledged to:

- privatise a number of remaining public corporations and local authority commercial services;
- bring private sector enterprises into the public services by encouraging contracting-out and competitive tendering throughout government;
- require all government departments to report annually on their plans for market testing;
- ensure that competitive tendering is extended to white-collar local authority services such as those offered by lawyers, accountants, architects and surveyors.

The Conservative government is committed to carrying through its Citizen's Charter and extending 'citizens rights' to standards of service clearly set out in advance. Managers and staff will be personally identifiable and called to account for decisions and actions taken. There will be further Next Steps agencies created, including the Prison Service and the decentralisation and deconcentration of central government departments will continue. There will be more opting out of schools and hospitals and the extension of the internal market to community services. Although the government is committed to increasing the number of uniformed police officers, there are plans for further civilianisation and the appointment of lay inspectors, with management experience, to the police inspectorate.

It is difficult to predict where new developments will take place but there are some signs and pointers. The trend away from vertically-integrated hierarchical organisations towards market-directed forms of resource allocation and exchange between separate purchasers and providers is likely to continue unabated. It is envisaged that by April 1994 provider units within the NHS, whether independently managed trusts or still under health authority management, will be operating under contract. The drawing up and monitoring of contracts will become major growth areas, creating new occupations and, of course, consuming resources. The Audit Commission's conservative estimate of 250 additional accountants in the NHS over the next two years seems likely to be exceeded some three or four times. Increases in numbers of accountants in local and central government, especially in the Next Step agencies, can also be predicted. A more interesting outcome to monitor will be the extent to which the high levels of transaction costs, involved in contracting, will offset the expected gains in efficiency associated with internal market competition and management flexibility and autonomy.

Another area of further innovation and change will be that of Information Technology (IT). IT offers scope for not only changing the way that things are done but also what is done. There is great potential for improved service delivery, better management decisions and both more decentralisation and central control. There is likely to be great advances in the development of expert systems and executive information in the major service areas during the 1990s. However, the management of IT information systems calls for considerable skills which, at the moment, few public sector managers have. This will be a major area for education and training.

Another growth area is likely to be in marketing. Walsh (1991) has illustrated the many developments that have already taken place in marketing health, education and local authority services like tourism, leisure, housing and museums. Marketing is also now being used by the police in public opinion surveys. The thrust of the Citizen's Charter is to constantly monitor consumer satisfaction, whilst the new approaches to local social services will require surveys of 'need' to form the basis of planning for community care. There have been many positive results from the use of marketing techniques including more awareness of public and consumer views. There is a danger, however, as Pollitt (1990) and others (Walsh, 1991; Stewart and Ranson, 1989) point out, in these commercial approaches to management and marketing which see the public solely as consumers and encourage a view of the public services as 'supermarkets'. These writers question whether it is ethical to market public goods like 'soap powders', or to incite people to see themselves solely as consumers.

More surveys, market research and feedback exercises will occur. But there is scope to use some marketing techniques to extend citizen participation in the policy-making process and there are likely to be developments in this field. A higher profile for marketing, in all public organisations, can be expected and more marketing staff will be recruited and trained. Other specialist areas of public services management which will offer new career structures are likely to be in purchasing and public relations.

Further changes can be expected in employment patterns, personnel management and industrial relations. The unified career civil service is likely to be replaced by a small élite of higher civil servants located in a core of central policy departments which may employ as little as 10 per cent of the total central government work-force. There will also be a series of executive agency services, with some mobility both between agencies and between agencies and the central core. But careers will be increasingly determined by individuals seeking advancement through changes of job, rather than by planned career structures. In this sense the civil service will become more like local government and other public services. Pay and conditions of service will become more agency specific and be based at the higher levels on short term contracts and performance pay.

Similar patterns are likely to emerge in the NHS and local government, along with more extensive use of contractors, consultants and private firms. A core of permanent employees will co-exist with peripheral workers. The police may well continue for some time yet as a 'career profession', although civilianisation will make inroads into non-operational areas like personnel, training, IT, research and support services. It is likely to have proceeded towards being an all graduate profession by 2000.

Trade unions are likely to continue to decline in importance across the public services as HRM practices further individualise employment relationships. Some of the agencies, health service trusts and grant-maintained schools may derecognise unions or seek to limit the scope of collective bargaining. These moves would lead to a fall in trade union membership, further weakening union power and influence.

What, then, are some of the issues facing public service managers as the 'managerialist revolution' moves into its second decade? And how far does the new public management satisfy the needs of governance and politics? One of the greatest challenges will be to meet the rising demands being made for public services by their citizens in the light of declining real resources. Unless increased resources are provided in health, education and social services, the level and quality of service will fall. And this will be at a time when the 'citizen's charters' will be encouraging higher expectations and demands for service delivery and provision. Even with more resources, it is likely that there would be unmet needs, since these are infinite but resources are finite.

Second, quality of service also depends on front line workers. If public employees continue to be demoralized, frustrated and over-worked, their co-operation and collaboration with management will only be reluctantly given. As Christine Hancock, the General Secretary of the Royal College of Nursing (RCN), said at its annual congress in 1992, there is the danger of a macho culture taking root in the NHS and 'you can't build a good, corporate image on top of underlying problems over staffing and resources' (Brindle, 1992, p. 4). Performance-related pay, personal contracts and flexible modes of employment are not easily reconcilable with long service, committed staff and teamworking.

Third, public management in the 1980s was largely inward looking, focusing on operational management, cost reduction and increasing productivity. The focus now should shift outwards towards strategic management, identifying social needs, ensuring policies are achieving their objectives and being alert to the unintended consequences of governmental action or inaction. In the 1990s, strategic choice must balance the previous emphasis on strategic implementation.

Fourth, public sector choices are, however, political choices and these are usually contested, challengeable and disputed. It is the task of public service managers, together with politicians, to seek some degree of consensus amongst the different interests and stakeholders within the 'policy community'. In practice, managing the public services *is* different from managing in the market sector. There *are* distinct differences between managing a supermarket, say, and a public service. Public managers are exercising public power and they are ultimately accountable for how they use it. To quote the General Secretary of the RCN again: 'commonly nurses perceive that [NHS] managers have absorbed the culture of competition and commercial confidence and forgotten that they are managing an accountable public service' (Brindle, 1992, p. 4). Since they are constantly in the proverbial goldfish bowl, the public services have to be more open to their 'clients', citizens and staff than do market-led organisations.

Fifth, because political decisions are matters of judgement, they have been guided in the past by a 'public service ethic'. This acted as a defence against the abuse of power or the unrepresentativeness of these judgements. Equity, fairness, honesty, probity, altruism and trust combined with the ethics of the public service professions to protect 'the public interest.' Since the 1980s the public service ethic has, in part at least, been abandoned to a new managerial ethic, focusing on the three 'Es'. This is complemented by the belief that managers must be 'in control', claiming, as professionals, organisational legitimacy and authority. Looking to the future, we would argue that public service management should reflect a revived public service culture, balancing citizen needs, ethical considerations and resource availability. Top-down, hierarchic management is inconsistent with public service professionalism, flexible and responsive service provision and political participation by citizens.

Finally, in carrying through radical, market-led governmental policies, the new public service managers have to some degree politicised the managerial role in their organisations. At the same time, governments have contracted the scope of politics by privatising, marketising and managerialising the public sector. This is neither good for public management nor for democratic politics. It makes public management a powerful political force and weakens the principle of political neutrality in the public services. It also weakens democracy, by narrowing the scope of politics and by limiting citizen participation in the political process.

Bibliography

Abel-Smith, B. (1990) 'The First Forty Years', in Carrier, J. and Kendall, I. (eds) *Socialism and the NHS* (Farnborough: Gower).

Armstrong, Sir W. (1987) 'Taking Stock of Our Achievement', in Royal Institute of Public Administration, *Future Shape of Reform in Whitehall* (London: Royal Institute of Public Administration).

Audit Commission Report (1990) *Taking Care of the Coppers*, Paper no. 7 (London: HMSO).

Audit Commission (1984) *The Impact on Local Authorities' Economy, Efficiency and Effectiveness of the Block Grant Distribution System* (London: HMSO).

Audit Commission (1986) *Making a Reality of Community Care* (London: HMSO).

Audit Commission (1988) *Better Financial Management* (London: HMSO).

Audit Commission (1989) Management Paper no. 3, *Better Financial Management* (London: HMSO).

Bacon, R. and Eltis, W. (1976) *Britain's Economic Problem* (London: Macmillan).

Bains Report (1972) *The New Local Authorities: Management and Structure* (London: HMSO).

Banfield, E.C. (1961) *Political Influence* (Glencoe, Ill.: The Free Press).

Barratt, J. and Downs, J. (1988) *Organising for Local Government: A Local Political Responsibility* (London: Longman).

Barrett, S. and Fudge, C. (eds) (1982) *Policy and Action* (London: Methuen).

Bedford, A. (1991) 'For NHS freedom', *The Guardian*, 14 October.

Beveridge, Sir W. (1942) *Social Insurance and Allied Services* (Cmnd 6404) (London: HMSO).

Bittner, E. (1970) *The Functions of the Police in Modern Society* (Chevy Chase, Maryland: National Institute of Mental Health).

Blackstone, T. and Plowden, W. (1988) *Inside the Think Tank: Advising the Cabinet, 1971–1983* (London: Heinemann).

Blackwell, R. and Lloyd, P. (1989) 'New Managerialism in the Civil Service: Industrial Relations under the Thatcher Administration', in Mailly, R. *et al. Industrial Relations in the Public Services* (London: Routledge).

Booth, S. and Pitt, D. (1984) 'Continuity and Discontinuity: IT as a Force for Organisational Change', in Pitt, D. and Smith, B.C. (eds), *The Computer Revolution in Public Administration* (Brighton: Wheatsheaf Books).

Bornett, C. (1991) Letter to *The Guardian*, 19 October.

Bottomley, K. and Pease, K. (1986) *Crime and Punishment: Interpreting the Data* (Milton Keynes: Open University Press).

Bowman, C. (1990) *The Essence of Strategic Management* (Englewood Cliffs, NJ: Prentice Hall).

Brindle, D. (1991a) 'Opted-out NHS Trust Offers 21 per cent', *The Guardian*, 8 March 1991.

Brindle, D. (1991b) 'Ignored Warnings that Backfired', *The Guardian*, 30 April, p. 2.

Brindle, D. (1992) 'Bottomley rejects nurses plea to ban gagging clause', *The Guardian*, 20 April, p. 4.

Brooke, R. (1989) *Managing the Enabling Authority* (London: Longman).

Brown, R.G.S. (1978) *Reorganising the National Health Service* (Oxford: Basil Blackwell).

Bryson, J.M. (1988) 'Strategic Planning: Big Wins and Small Wins', *Public Money and Management*, 8 (3), pp. 11–15.

Buchanan, J. and Tullock, G. (1962) *The Calculus of Consent* (Ann Arbor: Michigan University Press).

Buchanan, M. (1975) *The Limits of Liberty: Between Anarchy and Leviathan* (Chicago: University of Chicago Press).

Bull, R. and Horncastle, P. (1989) 'An Evaluation of Human Awareness Training', in Morgan, R. and Smith, D. (eds) *Coming to Terms with Policing* (London: Routledge).

Butler, A.J. (1984) *Police Management* (London: Gower).

Cabinet Office (OMP)/Treasury (FMO) (1985) *Policy Work and FMI* (London: HMSO).

Cabinet Office Efficiency Unit (1991) *Making the Most of Next Steps: The Management of Ministers' Departments and their Executive Agencies*, Report to the Prime Minister (London: HMSO).

Carr, F. (1990) 'Foreign and Defence Policy: The Impact of Thatcherism', in Savage, S. and Robins, L. (eds) *Public Policy under Thatcher* (London: Macmillan).

Carrier, J. and Kendall, I. (1986) 'The Griffiths Report', in Brenton, M. and Ungerson, C. (eds) *Yearbook of Social Policy 1985–6* (London: Routledge & Kegan Paul).

Cassels Report (1983) *Review of Personnel Work in the Civil Service: Report to the Prime Minister* (London: HMSO).

Caulfield, I. and Shulz, J. (1989) *Planning for Change: Strategic Planning in Local Government* (London: Longman, Local Government Training Board).

Central Office of Information (1989) *Our Business in Service* (London: HMSO).

Central Statistical Office (1991) 'Employment in the Public and Private Sectors', *Economic Trends*, 458 (December) (London: HMSO).

Cervi, B. (1992) 'DoH Stretches Timetable for Community Care Reforms', *Social Work Today*, 12 March 1992.

Chapman, B. (1963) *British Government Observed* (London: Allen & Unwin).

Charlton, J. and Martlew, C. (1987) 'Stirling District Council', in Elcock, H. and Jordan, A.G. (eds) *Learning from Local Authority Budgeting* (Aldershot: Avebury Press).

Christie, L. (1991) 'Next Steps: A Union Critique', *Public Money and Management*, 11, 3.

Clarke, M. and Stewart, J. D. (1988) *Managing Tomorrow* (Birmingham: Local Government Training Board).

Clarke, R. and Hough, M. (1980) *The Effectiveness of Policing* (Farnborough: Gower).

Clouston, E. (1991) 'Private Sector binmen junk their old image', *The Guardian*, 30 July 1991, p.2.

Cmnd 8616 (1982) *Efficiency and Effectiveness in the Civil Service* (London: HMSO).

Cmnd 9058 (1983) *Financial Management in Government Departments* (London: HMSO).

Collins, B. (1987) 'The Rayner Scrutinies' in Harrison, A. and Gretton, J. (eds) *Reshaping Central Government* (Bristol: Policy Journals).

Collins, B. (1991) 'Central Government', in Jackson, P. and Terry, F. (eds) *Public Domain* (London: Public Finance Foundation with Peat, Marwick, McLintock).

Collins, K. (1985) 'Some Issues in Police Effectiveness and Efficiency', *Policing*, 1 (2).

Conservative Party Manifesto (1992) *The Best Future for Britain* (London: Conservative Central Office).

Corby, S. (1991) 'Civil Service Decentralisation: Reality or Rhetoric?', *Personnel Management*, February.

Crewe, I. (1982) 'The Labour Party and the Electorate', in Kavanagh, D. (ed.) *The Politics of the Labour Party* (London: Allen & Unwin).

Crosland, A. (1956) *The Future of Socialism* (London: Cape).

Daniel, W. W. and Millward, N. (1983) *Workplace Industrial Relations in Britain* (London: Heinemann).

Deal, T. E. and Kennedy, A. A. (1982) *Corporate Culture* (Reading, Mass.: Addison-Wesley).

Department of the Environment (DoE) (1974) Circular 98/74 *Structure Plans* (London: HMSO).

Department of the Environment (1983) *Streamlining the Cities*, Cmd 9005 (London: HMSO).

Department of the Environment (DoE) (1991a) *The Internal Management of Local Authorities in England: A Consultation Paper* (London: HMSO).

Department of the Environment (DoE) (1991b) *The Structure of Local Government in England: A Consultation Paper* (London: HMSO).

Department of the Environment and Welsh Office (1986) *The Future of Development Plans: A Consultation Paper* (London: HMSO).

Department of the Environment, Welsh and Scottish Office (1991) *A New Tax for Local Government: A Consultation Paper* (London: HMSO).

Department of Health (DoH) (1989a) *Working for Patients* (the NHS Review) (Cm 555) (London: HMSO).

Department of Health (1989b) *Caring for People: Community Care in the Next Decade and Beyond* (White Paper) (Cm 849) (London: HMSO).

Department of Health (DoH) (1990) *NHS Trusts: A Working Guide* (London: HMSO).

Department of Health and Social Security (DHSS) (1972a) *National Health Service Reorganisation: England* (Cm 5055) (London: HMSO).

Department of Health and Social Security (DHSS) (1972b) *Management Arrangement for the Reorganised NHS* (the 'Grey Book') (London: HMSO).

Department of Health and Social Security (DHSS) (1976) *Regional Chairman's Enquiry into the Working of the NHS in Relation to Regional Health Authorities* (The Three Chairmen's Report) (London: HMSO).

Department of Health and Social Security (DHSS) (1983) *NHS Management Enquiry* (The Griffith's Report) (London: HMSO).

Department of Health and Social Security (DHSS) (1986) *Neighbourhood Nursing: a focus for care* (The Cumberlege Report) (London: HMSO).

Department of Transport (DOT) (1990) *Driver and Vehicle Licensing Agency Framework Document* (London: HMSO).

Dixon, R. (1991) 'Local Management of Schools', *Public Money and Management*, 11 (3).

Downs, A. (1957) *An Economic Theory of Democracy* (New York: Harper & Row).

Drewry, G. (ed.) (1989) *The New Select Committees: A Study of the 1979 Reforms* (Oxford: Clarendon Press).

Drewry, G. and Butcher, T. (1988) *The Civil Service Today* (Oxford: Blackwell).

Drucker, P. (1954) *Principles of Management* (London: Heinemann).

Drucker, P. (1974) *Management: Tasks, Responsibilities, Practices* (London: Heinemann).

Drucker, P. (1989) *The Practice of Management* (Oxford: Heinemann).

Dunsire, A. (1973) *Administration: The Word and the Science* (London: Martin Robertson).

Dunsire, A. (1982) 'Challenges to Public Administration in the 1980s', *Public Administration Bulletin*, 39 (August).

Eckstein, H. (1958) *The English Health Service* (Harvard, Mass.:   Harvard University Press).

Eddison, Tony (1973) *Local Government: Management and Corporate Planning* (Birmingham: INLOGOV).

Edwards, P. and Whitson, C. (1991) 'Workers are Working Harder: Effort and Shop Floor Relations in the 1980s', *British Journal of Industrial Relations*.

Elcock, H.J. (1975) 'English Local Government Reformed: The Politics of Humberside', *Public Administration*, 53, pp. 159–66.

Elcock, H.J. (1979a) *Strategic Planning Processes in Regional and Local Government*, Hull Papers in Politics no. 5, University of Hull.

Elcock, H.J. (1979b) 'Politicians, Organisations and the Public: The Provision of Gipsy Sites', *Local Government Studies*, May/June, pp. 43–54.

Elcock, H.J. (1985) 'Theory and Practice of Structure Planning: Writing the Humberside Structure Plan', Chapter 5 of Stephenson, M. and Elcock, H. (eds), *Public Policy and Management: Case Studies in Improvement* (Newcastle upon Tyne: Polytechnic Products).

Elcock, H.J.(1986a) *Local Government: Politicians, Professionals and the Public, in Local Authorities*, 2nd edn (London: Methuen).

Elcock, H. J.(1986b) 'Going Local in Humberside: Decentralisation as a Tool for Social Services Management', *Local Government Studies*, July/August, pp. 35–49.

Elcock, H. J. (1987) 'Modelling the Budgetary Process in Local Government', *Local Authority Management Unit Discussion Paper*, 872 (Newcastle upon Tyne Polytechnic).

Elcock, H. (1988) 'Alternatives to Representative Democracy: Going Local', *Public Policy and Administration*, 3 (2), pp. 38–50.

Elcock, H. (1991) *Change and Decay* (London: Longman).

Elcock, H., Fenwick, J. and Harrop, K.J. (1988) '*Partnerships for Public Service*', *Local Authority Unit Discussion Paper*, 88/2 (Newcastle upon Tyne Polytechnic).

Elcock, H. J. and Haywood, S. (1980) *The Buck Stops Where? Accountability and Control in the National Health Service* (Hull: Institute for Health Studies, University of Hull).

Elcock, H. and Jordan, A.G. (eds) (1987) *Learning from Local Authority Budgeting* (Aldershot: Avebury Press).

Elcock, H., Jordan A.G. and Midwinter, A.F. (1989) *Budgeting in Local Government: Managing the Margins* (London: Longman).

Etzioni, A. (1968) *The Active Society* (London: Free Press).

Fabian Society (1964) *The Administrators*, Fabian Tract 355 (London: The Fabian Society).

Farnham, D. (1978) 'Sixty years of Whitleyism', *Personnel Management*, July.

Farnham, D. (1990) 'Trade Union Policy 1979–1989: Restriction or Reform?', in Savage, S. and Robins, L. (eds) *Public Policy under Thatcher* (London: Macmillan).

Farnham, D. (1992) 'Citizens' Charter', *Talking Politics*, Winter 1991/2.

Fatchett, D. (1989) 'Workplace Bargaining in Hospitals and Schools or Opportunity for the Unions', *Industrial Relations Journal*, 4, pp. 253–59.

Fayol, H. (1949) *General and Industrial Management* (London: Pitman).

Fenwick, J. and Harrop, K. (1988) 'Consumer Responses to Local Authority Services: Notes Towards an Operational Model', *Local Authority Management Unit Discussion Paper*, 88/1 (Newcastle upon Tyne Polytechnic).

Flynn, N. (1990) *Public Sector Management* (Brighton: Harvester Wheatsheaf).

Freeman, M. (1981) 'Controlling Police Discretion', *Poly Law Review*, 6 (2), spring.

Friedman, M. (1962) *Capitalism and Freedom* (Chicago: University of Chicago Press).

Friend, J. K. and Hickling, A. (1987) *Planning under Pressure: The Strategic Choice Approach* (Oxford: Pergamon Press).

Friend, J. K. and Jessop, W.N. (1969) *Local Government and Strategic Choice* (London: Tavistock Press).

Friend, J. K., Power, J.M. and Yewlett, C. J. L. (1977) *Public Planning: The Inter-Corporate Dimension* (London: Tavistock Press).

Fry, G. (1984) 'The Development of the Thatcher Government's "Grand Strategy" for the Civil Service: A Public Policy Perspective, *Public Administration*, 62 (3), pp. 322–35.

Fulton, Lord (1968) *The Civil Service*, 1, Report of the Committee (Cmnd 3638) (London: HMSO).

Gamble, A. (1985) *Britain in Decline* (London: Macmillan).

Gamble, A. (1988) *The Free Economy and the Strong State: The Politics of Thatcherism* (London: Macmillan).

Game, C. (1987) 'Birmingham City Council', in Elcock, H. and Jordan, A. G. (eds) *Learning from Local Authority Budgeting* (Avebury Press).

Gilbert, R. (1991) 'Need to Focus on Performance Factors when Determining Pay', *Financial Times*, 5 November 1991, p. 19.

Glennester, H., Matsaganis, M. and Owens, P. (1992) *A Foothold for Fundholding* (London: Kings Fund).

Gough, I. (1979) *The Political Economy of the Welfare State* (London: Macmillan).

Gower Davies, J. (1973) *The Evangelistic Bureaucrat* (London: Tavistock Press).

Gray, A. and Jenkins, B. (eds) (1982) 'Policy Analysis in British Central Government: The Experience of PAR', *Public administration*, 60, pp. 429–50.

Gray, A. and Jenkins, B. (eds) (1983) *Policy Analysis and Evaluation in British Government* (London: Royal Institute of Public Administration).

Gray, A. and Jenkins, B. (1985) *Administrative Politics in British Government* (Brighton: Wheatsheaf).

Gray, A. and Jenkins, B. (1986) 'Accountable Management in British Government: Some Reflections on the Financial Management Initiative', *Financial Accountability and Management*, 2 (3), pp. 171–87.

Greenwood, J. (1992) 'Local Government Reform', *Talking Politics*, Winter 1991/2.

Greenwood, J. and Wilson, D. (1989) *Public Administration in Britain Today* (London: Unwin Hyman).

Greenwood, R. (1983) 'Changing Patterns of Budgeting in English Local Government', *Public Administration*, 61, pp. 149–68.

Greenwood, R. (1987) 'Managerial Strategies in Local Government', *Public Administration*, 65, pp. 295–312.

Greenwood, R. and Stewart, J. D. (eds) (1974) *Corporate Planning in English Local Government* (INLOGOV and Charles Knight).

Greenwood, R. Walsh, K., Hinings, C.R. and Ranson, S. (1978) *Patterns of Management in Local Government* (London: Martin Robertson).

Gyford, J. (1984) *The Politics of Local Socialism* (London: Allen & Unwin).

Hague, B. (1989) 'Local Authorities and a Public Service Orientation: Ideas into Action', *Local Authority Management Unit Discussion Paper*, 89/3 (Newcastle upon Tyne Polytechnic).

Hall, S. and Jacques, M. (1983) *The Politics of Thatcherism* (London: Lawrence & Wishart).

Hall, S. and Jacques, M. (eds) (1990) *New Times: The Changing Face of Politics in the 1990s* (London: Lawrence & Wishart).

Hampton, W.A., (1991) *Local Government and Urban Politics*, 2nd edn (London: Longman).

Hansard (1979) *House of Commons Budget Statement* 12 June 1979 (Parliamentary Debates Commons 1979–80, 968) (London: HMSO).

Harrop, K. Mason, T., Vielba, C. A. and Webster, B. (1978) *The Implementation and Development of Area Management* (Institute of Local Government Studies: University of Birmingham).

Hayek, F. A. (1944) *The Road to Serfdom* (London: Routledge & Kegan Paul).

Hayek, F. A. (1973) *Law Legislation and Liberty, Vol. 1: Rules and Order* (London: Routledge & Kegan Paul).

Hayek, F. A. (1976) *Law, Legislation and Liberty* (London: Routledge & Kegan Paul).

Haynes, R. J. (1980) *Organisation Theory and Local Government* (London: Allen & Unwin).

Hayward, J. E. S. (1975) 'The Politics of Planning in Britain and France', *Comparative Politics*, 7, pp. 285–98.

Hayward, S. and Aleszewski, A. (1980) *Crisis in the Health Service* (London: Croom Helm).

Heclo, H. and Wildavsky, A. V. (1973) *The Private Government of Public Money* (London: Macmillan).

Hennessy, P. (1989) *Whitehall* (London: Secker & Warburg).

Herzberg, F. W. *et al.* (1959) *The Motivation to Work* (New York: Wiley).

Heseltine, M. (1980) 'Ministers and Management in Whitehall', *Management Services in Government*, 35.

Hill, D. and Rockley, L.E. (1990) *The Secrets of Successful Financial Management* (London: Heinemann).

HMSO (Merrison Report) (1979) *Royal Commission on the National Health Service* (Cm 7615) (London: HMSO).

HMSO (1983) Home Office Circular No. 114/1983, Manpower: *Effectiveness and Efficiency in the Police Force* (London).

HMSO (1988–9) Home Office Circular No. 106/1988 and 31/1989 *Application for Increase in Police Force Establishments* (London).

HMSO (1988) Home Office Circular No. 105/1988, *Civilian Staff in the Police Service* (London).

HM Treasury (1990) Management Matters, June.

Hoggett, P. and Hambleton, R. (1987) *Decentralisation and Democracy* (School of Advanced Urban Studies, University of Bristol).

Hogwood, B. and Gunn, L. (1984) *Policy Analysis for the Real World* (Oxford: Oxford University Press).

Hood, C. and Jones, G. (1990) 'Progress in the Government's Next Step Initiative', memorandum submitted to the *Treasury and Civil Service Committee. 8th Report Progress in the Next Steps Initiative*, 1989–90 (London: HMSO).

Home Office (1989) *Police Manpower*, Home Office/Treasury Police Manpower Study, Circular 1989/91.

Hopper, T. (1986) 'Private Sector Problems Posing as Public Sector Solutions', *Public Finance and Accountancy*, 3 October.

Horton, C. (1989) 'Good Practice and Evaluation Policy' in Morgan, R. and Smith, P. S. (eds) *Coming to Terms with policing* (London: Routledge).

Horton, S. (1990) 'Local Government 1978–89: A Decade of Change', in Savage, S. and Robins, L. (eds) *Public Policy under Thatcher* (London: Macmillan).

Hough, M. (1989) 'Demand for Policing and Police Performance: Progress and Pitfalls in Public Surveys', in Weatheritt, M. (ed.), *Police Research: Some Future Prospects* (Aldershot: Gower).

House of Commons Expenditure Committee (1977) Eleventh Report of the Expenditure Committee, *The Civil Service* (English Report), HC 535 (1977) (London: HMSO).

House of Commons Social Services Committee (1989) *Third Report* (London: HMSO).

Humphrey, C. (1991) 'Accountable Management in the Public Sector', in Ashton, D. *et al.* (eds) *Issues in Management Accounting* (Englewood Cliffs, NJ: Prentice Hall).

Institute of Personnel Management and Incomes Data Services Public Sector Unit (IPM-IDS) (1986) *Competitive Tendering in the Public Sector* (London: IPM/IDS).

Isaac-Henry, K. and Painter, C. (1991) 'The Management Challenge in Local Government: Emerging Themes and Trends', *Local Government Studies*, May-June, pp. 69–90.

Jenkins, K., Caines, K. and Jackson, A. (1988) Efficiency Unit: *Improving Management in Government: The Next Steps* (London: HMSO).

Johnson, G. and Scholes, K. (1988) *Exploring Corporate Strategy* (Englewood Cliffs, NJ: Prentice Hall International, 2nd edn.)

Joint Consultative Committee (1990) Operational Policy Review (Surbiton).

Joint Management Unit (1987) *Policy Evaluation* (London: HMSO).

Joubert, C. and Derwent, H. (1981) *Report on Rayner Study of Non-staff Running Costs in the Department of the Environment* (Central) 1, Main Report (London: Department of Environment).

Kavanagh, D. (1987) *Thatcherism and British Politics* (Oxford: Clarendon Press).

Keeling, D. (1972) *Management in Government* (London: Allen & Unwin).

Kendall, I. and Moon, G. (1990) 'Health Policy', in Savage, S. P. and Robins, L. (eds) *Public Policy under Thatcher* (London: Macmillan).

Kessler, I. (1989) 'Bargaining Strategies in Local Government', in Mailly, R. *et al. Industrial Relations in the Public Services* (London: Routledge).

King, D. and Pierre, J. (1990) *Challenges to Local Government* (London: Sage Press).

Kinsey, R., Lea, J. and Young, J. (1986) *Losing the Fight Against Crime* (Oxford: Basil Blackwell).

Klein, R. (1983) *The Politics of the National Health Service* (London: Longman).

Knight, P. (1984) 'The 1984/1985 NAB Planning Exercises: How Great a Failure?' *Higher Education Review*, 17, pp. 19–28.

Kogan, M. (1988) *Managerialism in Higher Education*, paper presented at London Institute of Education, March.

Krieger, J. (1986) *Reagan, Thatcher and the Politics of Decline* (Cambridge: Polity Press).

Laffin, M. (1989) *Managing under Pressure* (London: Macmillan).

Lansley, S., Goss, S. and Wolmar, C. (1989) *Councils in Conflict: The Rise and Fall of the Municipal Left* (London: Macmillan).

Lavery, K. and Hume, C. (1991) 'Blending Planning and Pragmatism: Making Strategic Management Effective in the 1990s', *Public Money and Management*, Winter.

Lawrence, P. R., and Lorsch, J. W. (1969) *Organisation and Environment* (London: Irwin-Dorsey).

Lawton, A. and Rose, A. (1991) *Organisation and Management in the Public Sector* (London: Pitman).

Leech, Bob (1988) 'Conservatism, Thatcherism and Local Government', *Local Government Policy Making*, 14, 4, March, p. 12.

Likierman, A. (1988) *Public Expenditure* (London: Penguin).

Lindblom, C. (1959) 'Incrementalism: The Science of Muddling Through', *Public Administration Review*, 19, pp. 78–88.

Lindblom, C. (1977) *Politics and Markets* (New York: Basic Books).

Lipsky, M. (1980) *Street Level Bureaucracy* (London: Russell Sage).

Lubans, V. and Edgar, J. (1979) *Policing by Objectives* (Hartford: Social Development Corporation).

McCarthy, M. (ed.) (1989) *The New Politics of Welfare* (London: Macmillan).

McGregor, D. (1960) *The Human Side of Enterprise* (New York: McGraw-Hill).

Maguire, M. and Corbett, C. (1989) 'Patterns and Profiles of Complaints Against the Police', in Morgan, R. and Smith, D. (eds) *Coming to Terms with Policing* (London: Routledge & Kegan Paul).

Mailly, R. (1986) 'The Impact of Contracting Out in the NHS', *Employee Relations*, 8 (1).

Mailly, R., Dimmock, S.J and Sethi, A.S. (1989) 'Industrial Relations in the NHS since 1979', in *Industrial Relations in the Public Services* (London: Routledge).

Major, J. (1989) Address to the Audit Commission, *The Impact of General Economic Developments on Public Service Management* (London: HMSO).

Mallabar, N. (1991) *Local Government Administration in a Time of Change* (Business Education Publishers).

Marquand, D. (1988) *The Unprincipled Society* (London: Fontana).

Marwick, A. (1968) *Britain in the Century of Total War* (London: Bodley Head).

Marwick, A. (1990) *British Society since 1945* (London: Penguin).

Maud Report (1967) *Report of Committee: The Management of Local Government* (London: HMSO).

Mayhew, P., Elliott, D. and Dowds, L. (1988) *The 1988 British Crime Survey* (London: HMSO).

Mead, G. (1990) 'The Challenge of Police Leadership – The Centralisation of the Special Course', *Management Education and Development*, 21, pp. 406–14.

Meikle, J. (1990) 'Universities jib at "balance sheet" stance?' *The Guardian*, 12 November 1990, p. 6

Metcalfe, L. and Richards, S. (1987a) 'The Efficiency Strategy in Central Government: An Impoverished Concept of Management?' *Public Money*, June.

Metcalfe, L. and Richards, S. (1987b) *Improving Public Management* (London: Sage).

Midwinter, A. (1988a) 'Local Budgetary Strategies in a Decade of Retrenchment', *Public Money, and Management*, 8 (3), pp. 21–8.

Midwinter, A. (1988b) *Margins* (London: Longman).

Millward, N. and Stevens, M. (1986) *British Workplace Industrial Relations 1980–84* (Aldershot: Gower).

Minford, P. (1984) 'State Expenditure: A Study in Waste' supplement to *Economic Affairs*, April-June.

Ministry of Health (1967) *Report of the Joint Working Party on the Organisation of Medical Work in Hospitals* (The First Cogwheel Report) (London: HMSO).

Minzberg, H. (1973) *The Nature of Managerial Work* (New York: Harper & Row).

Mueller, D. (1979) *Public Choice* (London and New York: Cambridge University Press).

Murlis H. (1987) 'Performance-Related Pay in the Public Sector', *Public Money*, March, pp. 29–33.

NHS/DHSS (1982) *First Report to the Secretary of State: Steering Group on Health Services Information* (London: HMSO).

Niskanen, W. A. (1971) *Bureaucracy and Representative Government* (Chicago: Aldine Atherton).

Norris, G. M. (1989) 'The Organisation of the Central Policy Capability in Multi-Functional Public Authorities', *Local Authority Management Unit Discussion Paper*, 98/1 (Newcastle upon Tyne Polytechnic).

Norris, P. (1982) 'Who Should Decide? The Experts versus the Public', in Elcock, H. (ed.) *What Sort of Society? Economic and Social Policy in Modern Britain* (Martin Robertson), pp. 223–32.

Norton, P. (1991) *British Polity* (London: Longman).

O'Connor, J. (1973) *The Fiscal Crisis of the State* (New York: St Martin's Press).

Painter, J. (1991) 'Compulsory Competitive Tendering in Local Government: The First Round', *Public Administration*, 69, pp. 191–210.

Painter, C. (1991) 'The Public Sector and Current Orthodoxies: Revitalisation or Decay?' *Political Quarterly*, 62, pp. 75–89.

Parkinson, M. (1985) *Liverpool on the Brink* (Bristol: Policy Journals).

Parkinson, M. (1986) 'Financial Ingenuity in Local Government', *Public Money*, 6.

Parkinson, M. (1987a) *Reshaping Local Government* (Bristol: Policy Journals).

Parkinson, M. (1987b) 'Liverpool City Council', in Elcock, H. and Jordan, A. G. (eds) *Learning from Local Authority Budgeting* (Aldershot: Avebury Press).

Peacock, A. and Wiseman, J. (1961) *Growth of Public Expenditure in the UK* (Princeton, New Jersey: Princeton University Press).

Perry, J. and Kraemer, K. L. (1983) *Public Management: Public and Private Perspectives* (California: Mayfield).

Peters, T. (1987) *Thriving on Chaos* (New York: Harper & Row).

Peters, T. and Austin, N. (1985) *A Passion for Excellence* (New York: Harper & Row).

Peters, T. and Waterman, L. (1982) *In Search of Excellence* (New York: Harper & Row).

Phyrr, P. A. (1970) 'Zero-base budgeting', *Harvard Business Review*, Nov-Dec.

Plowden, Lord (1961) *Control of Public Expenditure* (Cm 1432) (London: HMSO).

Plumridge, M. (1985) 'Management and Organisation Development in the Police Service: The Role of Bramshill', in Southgate, P. (ed.) *New Directions in Police Training* (London: HMSO).

Pollitt, C. (1985) 'Measuring Performance: A New System for the National Health Service', *Policy and Politics*, 13 (1), pp. 1–15.

Pollitt, C. (1986) 'Beyond the Management Model: The Case for Broadening Performance Assessment in Government and the Public Services', *Financial Accountability and Management*, 2 (3), pp. 171–87.

Pollitt, C. (1989) 'Performance Indicators in the Long Term', *Public Money and Management*, 9 (3).

Pollitt, C. (1990) *Managerialism and the Public Services* (Oxford: Blackwell).

Pressman, J. and Wildavsky, A. V. (1973) *Implementation* (California: University of California Press).

Price Waterhouse (1990) *Executive Agencies: Facts and Trends, Vols 1 and 2.* (London: Price Waterhouse).

Priestley Report (1956) *Royal Commission on the Civil Service* (London: HMSO).

Prime Minister's Office (1991) *The Citizen's Charter* (London: HMSO).

Public Money (1984) 'Public Sector as Employer: How Industrial Relations Compares with the Private Sector', 1 and 2, March and June.

Ranson, S. and Stewart, J. (1989) 'Citizenship and Government: Management in the Public Domain', *Political Studies*, XXXVII.

Reed, D. and Ellis, V. (1987) 'A Union Assessment', in Harrison, A. and Gretton, J., *Reshaping Central Government* (Policy Journals).

Reiner, R. (1991) *Chief Constables* (Oxford: Oxford University Press).

Reiner, R. (1985) *The Politics of the Police* (Brighton: Wheatsheaf).

Rice, A. K. (1963) *The Enterprise and its Environment: A System Theory of Management Organisation* (London: Tavistock Publications).

Richards, S. (1987a) 'The Financial Management Initiative', in Harrison, A. and Gretton, J. (eds) *Reshaping Central Government* (Bristol: Policy Journals).

Richards, S. (1987b) 'Cultural Change in the Civil Service', paper given at Public Administration Conference, University of York.

Richards, S. (1990) 'Central Government' in Jackson, P. and Terry, F. (eds) *Public Domain*, (London: Public Finance Foundation with Peat, Marwick, McLintock).

Riddell, P. (1983) *The Thatcher Government* (Oxford: Robertson).

Rose, R. and Peters, G. (1978) *Can Government go Bankrupt?* (New York: Basic Books).

Salmon Report (1966) *Report of Committee on Senior Nursing Staff Structure* Ministry of Health, Scottish Home and Health Department (London: HMSO).

Salter, B. and Tapper, T. (1981)   *Education, Politics and the State: The Theory and Practice of Educational Change* (London: Grant McIntyre).

Savage, S. P. (1990)   'A War on Crime? Law and Order Policies in the 1980s', in Savage, S. and Robins, L. (eds) *Public Policy under Thatcher* (London: Macmillan).

Scarman, Lord (1982)   *The Brixton Disorders 10–12 April 1982, Report of an Inquiry by the Rt. Hon the Lord Scarman* (Cmnd 8427) (London: HMSO).

Schein, E. H. (1985)   *Organisational Culture and Leadership* (London: Jossey-Bass).

Schon, D. (1975)   *Beyond the Stable State* (London: Penguin Books).

Seabrook, J. (1984)   *The Idea of Neighbourhood: What Local Politics should be About* (London: Pluto Press).

Seebohm Report (1968)   *Report of the Committee on the Local Authority and Allied Personal Social Services* (Cmnd 3703) (London: HMSO).

Seldon, A. (1990)   *Capitalism* (Oxford: Blackwell).

Self, P. (1965)   *Bureaucracy or Management* (London: London School of Economics).

Self, P. (1971)   'Tests of Efficiency: Public and Business Administration', *PAC Bulletin*, 11, pp. 28–41.

Self, P. (1990)   'What's Wrong with Government? The Problem of Public Choice', *Political Quarterly*, 61(1).

Shaw, K. (1987)   'Training for Local Economic Development: The Contribution of Educational Institutions', *Local Authority Management Unit Discussion Papers*, 87/1 (Newcastle upon Tyne Polytechnic).

Sheaff, M. (1988)   'NHS Ancillary Services and Competitive Tendering', *Industrial Relations Journal*, 19.2, pp. 93–105. 1987.

Skeffington Report (1969)   *Participation in Planning* (London: HMSO).

Smith, D. and Gray, J. (1985)   *Police and People in London* (Aldershot: Gower).

Smith, D. and Horton, C. (1988)   *Evaluating Police Work* (London: Policy Studies Institute).

Starks, M. (1991)   *Not for Profit Not for Sale: The Challenge of Public Sector Management* (Bristol: Policy Journals).

Stead, P. (1985)   *The Police of Britain* (London: Macmillan).

Stewart, J. and Ranson, S. (1989)   'Citizenship and Government. The Challenge for Management in the Public Domain', *Political Studies*, XXXVII.

Stewart, J. and Stoker, G. (1989)   *The Future of Local Government* (London: Macmillan).

Stewart, J. D. (1986)   *The New Management of Local Government* (London: Allen & Unwin).

Stoker, G. (1991)   *The Politics of Local Government*, 2nd edn (London: Macmillan).

Storey, J. (1989)   'Human Resource Management in the Public Sector', *Public Money and Management*, Autumn, pp. 19–24

Taylor, F. (1911)   *Principles of Scientific Management* (New York: Harper Press).

Taylor, S. (1987) 'Radical Structures and Systems', in Royal Institute of Public Administration, *Future Shape of Reform in Whitehall* (London: Royal Institute of Public Administration).

Thomas, H. (ed.) (1959) *The Establishment* (London: Anthony Blond).

Thomas, R. (1978) *The British Philosophy of Administration* (London: Longman).

Thornley, A. (1990) *Urban Planning Under Thatcherism: The Challenge of the Market* (London: Routledge).

Tomkins, C. R. (1987) *Achieving Economy, Efficiency and Effectiveness in the Public Sector* (London: Kegan Paul).

Treasury and Civil Service Committee (1982) *Third Report: Efficiency and Effectiveness in the Civil Service*, HC 236–1 (London: HMSO).

Tyson, S. (1987) 'Personnel Management', in Harrison, A. and Gretton, J. *Reshaping Central Government* (New Brunswick: Transaction Books).

Urwick, L. (1944) *The Elements of Administration* (London: Pitman).

Vidal, John (1990) 'Searching for Heseltown', *The Guardian*, 23 November.

Waddington, P. (1986) 'Defining Objectives: A Reply to Tony Butler', *Policing*, 2 (1).

Wagner, L. (1989) 'From Director to Chief Executive', *NATFHE Journal*, January/February.

Walker, A. (1990) 'The Strategy of Inequality: Poverty and Income Distribution in Britain 1979–89', in Taylor, I. (ed.) *The Social Effects of Free Market Policies* (Hemel Hempstead: Harvester Wheatsheaf).

Walsh, K. (1991) 'Citizens and Consumers: Marketing and Public Sector Management', *Public Money and Management*, Summer.

Weatheritt, M. (1986) *Innovations in Policing* (Aldershot: Gower).

Weatheritt, M. (1989) 'Why Should the Police Use Police Research?', in Weatheritt, M. (ed.) *Police Research: Some Future Prospects* (Aldershot: Gower).

White, L. D. (1933) *Whitley Councils in the British Civil Service* (Chicago: Chicago University Press).

Widdicombe, D. (1986) *Report of Committee Inquring into the Conduct of Local Authority Business: The Conduct of Local Authority Business* (Cmnd 9797) (London: HMSO).

Wildavsky, A. (1973) 'If Planning is Everything, then Maybe It's Nothing', *Policy Sciences*, 4, pp. 127–53.

Wildavsky, A. (1979) *Implementation* (London: University of California Press).

Wildavsky, A. (1980) *The Art and Craft of Policy Analysis* (London: Macmillan).

Wintour, P. (1983) 'Breaking the Chains', *New Statesman*, 14 January, pp. 8–10.

Wolff Ohlins (1988) *A Force for Change* (London: Metropolitan Police).

Wolman, H. (1984) 'Understanding Local Government Responses to Fiscal Pressure: A Cross-national Analysis', *Journal of Public Policy*, 3, pp. 245–64.

Index

Abel-Smith, B.   173
accountability   171
  civil service   136, 139, 145, 147
  financial   81, 96–7
  and metropolitan councils'
      abolition   158
  and new managerialism   248
  of organisations   32; private   32,
      34; public   37–9, 41–2, 51, 88
  responsibility budgets   91–2
Adam Smith Institute   13
administration   see management/
    managerialism
Aleszewski, A.   176
ambulance personnel dispute   122
appraisal   see staff appraisal
armed forces   4
Armstrong, W.   111
Audit Commission   156
  and financial management   94–5,
      96
  functions of   154
  and local government   171
  on NHS   250
  performance measures   72, 94–5
  on police   215, 218, 220, 223,
      225–6, 231
  on results of new
      managerialism   247
Austin, N.   35

Bacon, R.   12
Bains Report   68, 151, 152, 169, 239
Banfield, E. C.   63
bankruptcies   24
Barratt, J.   164, 169
Barrett, S.   61
Bedford, A.   243
benefits   see welfare benefits
Beveridge, W./Report   10, 11
Bittner, E.   219

Blackstone, T.   67
Blackwell, R.   110, 119
Boer War   4
Booth, S.   169
Bornett, C.   244
Bottomley, K.   221
Bowman, C.   55
Bradbeer Committee   174, 175
Bradley Report   135
Brent Council   164
Brindle, D.   119, 244, 253
British Gas   see gas
British Medical Association   244
British Telecom   see
    telecommunications
Brixton public disorder   213
Broadwater Farm   215
Brooke, R.   164, 170
Brown, R. G. S.   57
Bryson, J. M.   58
Buchanan, J.   15
budget/budgeting
  construction of   82–4
  control   92
  incremental   82–4
  as information   82
  line-item   82
  police service   217
  responsibility   91–2
  schools   197–8, 199
  zero-based   84–5
Bull, R.   227
bureaucracy   see management/
    managerialism
Burnham Committee   115
bus services   21, 100
Butcher, T.   4
Butler, A. J.   218, 219, 220
Butler, Robin   138, 139

Cabinet Office   137, 141
  Efficiency Unit   139

Callaghan, James 189
capital markets deregulation 19–20
capital ownership 19
capitalism
  economic crisis of 239
  popular 23–4, 25
Carr, F. 139
Carrier, J. 179
Cassels Report 140, 141
Caulfield, I. 65
CBI 10
central government
  employment 4–5, 102, 104
  strengthening 21–3
Central Policy Review Staff 131
Centre for Policy Studies 13
Cervi, B. 160
Chapman, B. 129
Charlton, J. 69
Chawner, John 244
choice/s
  consumer 18, 23, 24
  and education 194, 210
  political 253
  public 15, 16
Citizen's Charter 32, 39, 50, 168,
    171, 250, 251
  and police 223
  and resources 252
citizen's rights, post-war 10
City Technology Colleges 195, 202
civil service 127–49
  accountability 139, 145, 147
  administrative management
    of 41, 43, 44
  changes 127
  collective bargaining 117, 142,
    143
  and Conservative
    Government 89
  contracting out 120
  decentralisation 136
  delivery of services 138
  departmental
    responsibilities 128–9
  departmental reviews 135
  economy, efficiency and
    effectiveness 127

Efficiency Unit 135
employment 4–5, 100, 102, 103,
    148
  and financial management 131,
    133, 134, 135–9, 145–6
  flexible working 114
  Fulton legacy 128–33
  functions of 129–30
  future changes 251–2
  Management Matters 114, 119,
    246
  management/managerialism 49,
    116–117, 129, 130, 131, 132–9,
    141–2, 242
  MINIS 135, 146
  as model employers 104–5
  Pay Research Unit 142
  pay structures 132
  performance indicators 130,
    136–7, 138, 142, 143, 148
  personnel management and
    industrial relations 140–3
  PES 130, 131, 133, 136
  planning 131
  private sector values 127
  promotion 141
  PRP 112
  recruitment 140–1
  right to manage 110
  scrutinies 90, 91, 134–5, 143
  size of 128, 134, 242
  staff appraisal 142, 143
  strike 142
  and Thatcher policies 127
  value for money 133, 135, 136–7
Clarke, M. 68, 69, 74, 164
Clarke, R. 222
Clegg, H. 142
Clouston, E. 243
Cogwheel Report 180
collective bargaining 99, 105, 108
  abandoned 242
  changes in 117–21
  civil service 142, 143
  and Conservative
    Governments 19
  decentralised 123, 124
  power shift in 46

collective bargaining (*cont.*)
  teachers   202–3
  see also human resources
    management
collectivism, decline of   12, 13
Collins, B.   93, 135, 217
community care   21, 243
  in 1970s   176, 177
  implementation   166–7; delay
    in   160
  and reticulists   62
  see also Griffiths Report
community charge   22, 155–6
  replacement of   171
competition, business   18, 19–20
competitive tender   *see* compulsory
    competitive tendering
compulsory competitive
    tendering   20, 96, 120–1, 158–9,
    241, 243
  and DSOs   165–6
  extension   of 171
  problems   167
  responses to   165–6
Confederation of British
    Industry   10
consensus   3
  defined   10–11
  weakening of   11, 12, 24, 26
Conservative governments
  cuts in expenditure   192–3
  economic solution   240
  effects of   3
  future changes   249–50
  and local government   154–60;
    erosion of power   193–6
  and New Right   16–17, 25
  policies   127; for enterprise
    culture   18–24
  see also Labour; New Right; New
    Urban Left; politics, new
consumers
  clients as   167–8
  and public organisations   39
contracting out   20, 30, 120, 122,
    123
  and reticulists   62
Corbett, C.   224

Corby, S.   123
Créwe, I.   154
Crosland, A.   11
culture/cultural
  of administrative and managerial
    systems   40–1
  change   49, 50, 123; civil
    service   142, 144–5, 147;
    methods of   246, 247
  corporate   34–5, 238
  creation of new managerial   111
  education   209
  local government   162, 169
  and management success   88
  NHS   179
  public service   246, 247, 253–4
  and strategic management   55
Cumberlege Report   181

Deal, T. E.   35
Dear, Geoffrey   216
debt
  national   9
  private   24
decision-making
  and enterprise culture   18
  and financial information   78, 79
  improvements in   89
  private sector   31, 34
  public participation   251, 254
  public sector   43
  and responsibility budgets   91–2
  see also strategic management
defence
  budget   23
  expenditure   9
  Ministry of   91, 96
  state provision   30
demographic changes   12–13, 24
  and new managerialism   239
  and planning   58
dependency culture   18
  reducing   23
  and Welfare State   15
Derwent, H.   135
development corporations   20
discrimination
  and local government   163–4

positive 163
see also equal opportunities
District Management Teams
      (NHS) 65, 66, 67, 175
Dixon, R. 197, 200
Downs, A. 15
Downs, J. 164, 169
Drewry, G. 4, 39
Driver and Vehicle Licensing
      Agency 48–9
Drucker, P. 34
Dunsire, A. 29, 42

Eckstein, H. 172
economic development agencies 161
economic planning *see* planning
economics, supply side 20
economy
      deregulation 19–21
      growth 11
Eddison, Tony 62
Edgar, J. 218
education 4, 7, 166, 188–210
      Assisted Places 24, 194
      collective bargaining 118
      competition in 209
      comprehensive 189
      and Conservative
            governments 19, 191–6; cuts
            in expenditure 192–3;
            weakening local
            government 193–6
      criticisms in 1970s 189–90
      effective schools 201
      employment 101, 103, 104
      grant-maintained schools 195,
            209
      heads, role of 244; as
            managers 195, 209
      HMIs 191
      institutional management 200–4
      internal markets 209, 244–5
      LEAs 190, 191; new role of 203,
            208, 209
      Local Management of
            Schools 97, 195, 196–200,
            244
      management pre-1979 190–1

and management training 202
and market mechanisms 16,
      209–10
new managerialism 49
and New Right 189–90
and parental choice 194
pay policies 113–14, 114, 115–16
performance indicators for
      staff 208, 209
policy implementation 37
post-war consensus 10, 188–9
private sector management
      in 203–4
public relations 244–5
reforms 159, 241, 244–5; and role
      of state 210
tradition of autonomy 190–1
see also further education; higher
      education; Local Management
      of Schools
Education Act (1944) 188
Education Reform Act (1988) 192,
      194, 196, 204
Edwards, P. 249
effectiveness and strategic
      planning 72
efficiency 48, 51, 110
      and performance indicators 87
      and strategic planning 72
Efficiency Unit 137, 139
Eland Report 116
Elcock, H. 55–77, 150–71
electricity
      collective bargaining 117
      privatisation 9, 100
Ellis, V. 123
Eltis, W. 12
employment
      flexible 124
      future patterns 251
      model employers 104–7
      in public services 4–5, 100–4; sex
            and employment status 104
Employment Acts 1980, 1982, 1988,
      1989, 1990 20
enterprise culture 3, 17–19, 23, 25,
      110, 111, 248
see also markets

enterprise zones   20
Environment, Department of   69,
       161, 170
   management accounting   135
   MINIS   60, 137
environmental issues   69, 76–7
equal opportunities   106–7
   local government   163
   police service   216
Etzioni, A.   64
Europe, police service   231
European Community   23
   and CCT   166
excellence, private sector
       management   34, 35
expenditure, public   4–5
   as an evil   240
   composition of   7
   and Conservative
       governments   19, 20, 240
   on education   192–3
   increases in   9, 25
   and Labour Governments   11–12
   and new managerialism   110
   as percentage of GGE   6–7, 9
   on police   217
   restructuring   94
   transfer payments   7, 9

Fabian Society   129
Fair Trading, Office of   32
Family Practitioner Services   *see*
   General Practitioners; National
   Health Service
Farnham, D.   3–26, 27–52, 99–124,
       237–54
Farquharson-Lang Report   174, 175
Fatchett, D.   118
Fayol, H.   33, 239
Fenwick, J.   70, 74, 75, 154, 155,
       156, 168
financial management   68, 69, 78–98,
       237
   accountability   81
   and civil service   131, 133, 134,
       135–9, 145–6
   and control   78–9

defined   79
delegation   93
importance of feedback   79
information   78–9, 82–7, 88;
       deficient   89
Initiative (FMI)   90–2, 93, 96–7,
       131, 135–9, 215, 217; and
       police service   215, 217
   performance indicators   81, 86–8
   problems   97
   since 1979   89–95, 111
Financial Management Unit   92
Flynn, N.   3, 9
FMI   *see* financial management
   initiative
forecasting   *see* planning
Fraser Report   116
free enterprise   240
   see also enterprise
Freeman, M.   211
Friedman, M.   13, 15
Friend, J. K.   58, 59, 61, 153
Fry, G.   134
Fudge, C.   61
Fulton, Lord/Report   41, 60, 127,
       128–33, 138, 140, 148, 239
further education colleges   21
   incorporation   193–4, 195
   institutional autonomy   203
   and role of LEAs   203
Further and Higher Education Act
   1992   196

Gamble, A.   17, 23
Game, C.   157
gas   29
   collective bargaining   117
   privatisation   9, 20, 100
GCHQ   *see* General
   Communications Headquarters
General Communications
   Headquarters (GCHQ)   117–18,
       143
General Practitioners   45
   and 1991 reforms   184–5
   and creation of NHS   173
   Doctors' Charter   174

FPCs 176, 177, 181
as fundholders 185–6, 187
and Griffiths Report 180
Gilbert, R. 247
Glennester, H. 186
Gough, I. 11
Gower Davies, J. 67
Gray, A. 64, 131, 136
Greater Manchester Police 216
Greenwood, J. 136, 170
Greenwood, R. 73–4, 151, 152, 154,
156, 157
Griffiths Report 93, 172, 178–80
and PRP 112
growth, post-war 11
Gunn, L. 44
Gyford, J. 150, 160

Hague, B. 155
Hall, S. 17
Hambleton, R. 69, 154, 164
Hampton, W. A. 57, 150, 161, 163,
164
Hancock, Christine 252
Handsworth riots 215
Harrop, K. 70, 74, 75, 154, 155,
156, 161, 168
Hayek, F. A. 13, 14, 16
Haynes, R. J. 68, 152
Hayward, J. E. S. 64
Hayward, S. 176
Haywood, S. 57, 65, 66, 72
Health Authorities 65, 66–7, 175–9,
182–3
health care
and market mechanisms 16
private 19
see also National Health Service
Health and Social Security,
Department of 122
Heath, Edward 130, 144, 240
Heclo, H. 64
Hennessy, P. 60
Herzberg, F. W. 34
Heseltine, Michael 46, 60, 69, 91,
146, 170

Hickling, A. 58, 59
higher education
growth of 188
incorporation 159, 193–4;
commercial activities 207–8;
and competition 196, 209–
10; funding 207–8; impact
of 206–8; new personnel
required 205–6; and role of
LEAs 203, 208, 209; staff as
managers 206–7, 209, 245–6
institutional autonomy 203
management techniques 245
new managerialism 204–8, 245–6;
new management
functions 204–6
performance indicators 208
pre-1979 191
Hill, D. 79
Hoggett, P. 69, 154, 164
Hogwood, B. 44
Hood, C. 147
Hopper, T. 111
Horncastle, P. 227
Horton, C. 215, 219
Horton, S. 3–26, 27–52, 127–49,
237–54
Hough, M. 220, 222
housing 7
associations 166
sale of council 158
Howe, G. 117
human resources management 99–
124, 238, 242
disputes 106, 122, 142, 142–3
features of 108–9
flexibility in pay 113
flexible working 114
innovations 113–17
management development
schemes 116–17
market-centred approach 99
model employers 104–7
pay review bodies 114–16
recent developments 109–21
right to manage 109–12
social cost 122

Hume, C.   71, 76
Humphrey, C.   90

Ibbs Report   137
ILEA abolition   193
industrial relations
  civil service   140–3, 142
  and Conservative
      governments   22
  defined   107–8
  disputes   106, 122, 142, 142–3
  education   202
  future changes   251
  and model employers   105
  Whitley model   99
  Winter of Discontent   154, 155
  see also human resources
      management; trade unions
inflation   12
  and Conservative
      governments   20
information
  budget as   82, 85, 88
  and uncertainty   59–60
information technology   47, 49, 251
  civil service   141
  and local government   169
  and NHS   181, 186
Institute of Economic Affairs   13
Institute of Health Services
    Management   182, 186
international role of Britain   23
Isaac-Henry, K.   68, 74, 76, 152,
    154, 168
Islington Council   162

Japan   35
  police service   231
Jaques, M.   17
Jenkins, B.   64, 131, 136
Jenkins, K.   137
Jessop, W. N.   58
Johnson, G.   73
Joint Management Unit   72, 76
Jones, G.   147
Jordan, A. G.   68, 72, 156, 157
Joubert, C.   135

Kavanagh, D.   11
Keeling, D.   40, 41
Kemp, P.   123, 138
Kendall, I.   172–87
Kennedy, A. A.   35
Kent County Council   71
Kessler, I.   120
Keynes, J. M./Keynesian
    policies   10, 11, 240
  abandoned   131
  and Conservative government   13,
      24
  criticisms as inefficient   16
  decline of   12, 17, 20
King, D.   161
Kinsey, R.   222
Klein, R.   174
Knight, P.   192
Kogan, M.   245
Korner Reports   94, 180
Kraemer, K. L.   27
Krieger, J.   11

labour
  deregulation of labour market   20
  size of labour force   100–4
Labour governments   11
  and civil service   129, 130, 131
  and local government   156
  nationalisation   5
  and NHS   174
  and public expenditure   12
  see also New Urban Left
Laffin, M.   155, 165
laissez-faire policies   5, 9–10
land use   32, 38
Lansley, S.   163
Lavery, K.   71, 76
law and order   9
  and Conservative
      governments   22–3
  see also police service
Law Society   39
Lawrence, P. R.   34
Lawton, A.   38
Lea, J.   222
Leech, B.   94

legislation
  education 191–2
  and local authority power 21–3
  pollution 33
Leishman, F. 211–33
Liberal Party 4
Likierman, A. 87
Lindblom, C. 13, 14, 57, 144
Lipsky, M. 169
Lloyd, P. 110, 119
LMS *see* Local Management of
  Schools
local government 4, 150–71
  agenda for change 164–5
  budget controls 156–7
  catering 159, 166
  chief executive officer 151–2, 153
  clients as customers 155, 167–8,
    170
  complaints centres 168
  compulsory competitive
    tendering 120–1, 159
  and consumer research 168
  creative accountancy 156, 157
  culture of 169
  decentralisation 161–3, 169, 170
  direct service organisations 165–6
  economy, efficiency and
    effectiveness 154
  employment 100–4
  as enabling 164–70, 170, 171
  erosion of power 193–6, 209
  expansion of 5, 7
  financial management 93–4,
    155–7
  future 252
  general managers 169–70
  governmental role 152–3
  grant allocation 157
  impact of managerialism 242–3
  limits to power 21–3
  management 44–5, 111, 151–4,
    170–1; consequences 153–4;
    corporate 151–2;
    evaluation 76; reactive and
    proactive 74–5;
    responsibilities of 160; since
    1987 164–70; strategies 74–6,
  under
    Conservatives 154–60
  market-based solutions 164–7
  neighbourhood offices 162–3
  New Right 164–5
  New Urban Left 160–4, 164
  overspending 22
  pay bargaining 119–10
  performance indicators 72, 171
  personal social services 175, 176
  planning 58, 65, 68, 69
  matrix analysis 73–4
  short-term 44
  policy and resources
    committees 151
  public service orientation 168–9
  refuse collection 158, 243
  relationship to central
    government 22
  responsiveness 170
  reticulists 153
  service cuts 156
  service delivery 158–60
  standstill strategies 156, 157
  street-level bureaucrats 169
  structural change 157–8
  and uncertainty 68–9
  see also New Urban Left; public
    sector
Local Management of Schools 195,
  196–200, 244
  objectives 197
  responsibilities of
    management 199–200
  and role of LEA 197–9, 200
Lorsch, J. W. 34
Lubans, V. 218

McGoldrick case 164
McGregor, D. 34
McKinsey Report 239
McNee, David 214
McVicar, M. 188–210
Maguire, M. 224
Mailly, R. 115, 121
Major, J. 17, 25, 118, 134, 147, 237,
  240, 241
Mallabar, N. 158, 159, 168

management/managerialism
  accountancy 110
  accounting systems 135
  and administration 27
  assessed 237–54
  crisis management 55; in local
    government 68–9
  defined 27, 128
  and democracy 254
  development schemes 116–17,
    141–2
  evaluation 76
  information systems *see* MINIS
  line management
    strengthening 47, 49, 142
  management training: civil
    service 141–2
  new managerialism 26, 110,
    123–4; defined 45, 237; as
    economic solution 239, 240;
    emergence of 45–6, 51, 52;
    features of 237–8, 241–2;
    ideology 238; methods of
    implementation 246–7; and
    New Right 25; origins
    of 239; results of 247–9
  private sector 30–5; criteria for
    success 31, 32, 33;
    culture 34–5; economistic
    approach 33, 35; generic
    approach 33, 34, 35; goals
    and accountabilities 31–3;
    managerial function 33–5; as
    market-driven 30–1;
    principles of 33–5;
    rationalist approach 33–4,
    35; as superior 46
  proactive 49; model 74–5
  public sector 27–8; and
    administration 40–2; as
    bureaucratic 42, 43; criteria
    for success 28, 36, 40, 41, 51;
    culture 40–1; as
    economistic 47; efficiency
    indicators 48; financial
    planning 44; generic 47,
    49; goals and
    accountabilities 36–45;

  improvements 92–3; as
    incrementalist 42, 44; line
    management functions 47,
    108; management
    systems 40–1; managerial
    function 42–5; as
    particularist 43, 44–5;
    political agenda 36, 37–8,
    46–7, 51, 254; as
    rationalist 47, 48–9;
    requirements 88
  reactive 55; model 74–5
  right to manage 18, 109–12, 119,
    248
  terminology 51, 123, 147, 241,
    245, 246
  see also education; financial
    management; strategic
    management
Manpower Services
  Commission 193
market individualism 18–19
marketing 251
  see also higher education; Local
    Management of Schools
markets 3, 24, 29
  advantages of 13–14, 16
  and Conservative
    governments 19
  as economic solution 240, 241
  and education 16
  and efficiency 16
  and health 16
  internal 30; NHS 183, 184, 187,
    243
  and New Right 13, 14
Marquand, D. 10
Martlew, C. 69
Marwick, A. 5, 10
Matsaganis, M. 186
Maud Report 151, 169, 239
Mayhew, P. 221
Mayne, Richard 227–8
Mead, G. 229
Meikle, J. 245
Metcalfe, L. 89, 145, 146
metropolitan councils' abolition 22,
  65, 69, 157–8, 164

Midwinter, A. 72, 76, 156, 157
Minford, P. 240
MINIS (Management Information
  for Ministers) 89–90, 135,
  137–8
  introduction of 60
  purpose of 91, 146
minority groups 150, 162, 163
Minzberg, H. 34
mission statements 48, 71, 242
  and local government 170
  and police 220, 233
monetarism 20, 131
Monopolies and Mergers
  Commission 21
Moon, G. 172–87
Morrison, Herbert 228
Mueller, D. 13, 14
Murlis, H. 112

national curriculum 22, 209
National Health Service 4, 172–87
  1974 reorganisation 176
  1991 reorganisation 166–7,
    183–7, 241, 243–4
  budgetary control 93–4
  collective bargaining 118–19
  complaints 39
  compulsory competitive
    tendering 121, 122
  consensus years 172–87;
    management of 173–4
  Conservative governments
    and 22, 24, 174–5
  creation of 7, 172–3
  criticisms of changes 244
  cultural change 179
  employment 100–1, 103, 104
  expenditure on 174
  financial issues 78
  future changes 250–1, 252
  Griffiths Report 178–80
  Health Investment Plans 183
  internal markets 182, 183, 184,
    187, 243
  management: in 1980s 177–83;
    ethos 180, 185;
    professionals 43, 45

managers 49, 111, 243–4; rewards
  for 247
new managerialism 49; adverse
  results of 249
Patients First 177
pay dispute 122
pay review 115
performance indicators 72, 180,
  184, 187
planning 57, 58, 65–7, 69–70,
  71–2
primary health care teams 174
private sector management
  consultants 186–7
professionals involved in decision-
  making 180, 186
purchaser–provider functions 30,
  182, 183–6, 243
resource allocation 243
reviews of 182
right to manage 119
trusts 97, 185, 187, 243–4, 250
nationalised industries 4
neighbourhood offices 162–3
New Management Strategy 92
New Right 13–16, 25–6, 239
  and Conservative
    governments 16–17
  and education 189–90
  ideology 13, 16, 24
  and local government 164–5
  and new managerialism 47, 239,
    240
  and public goods 15
New Urban Left 160–4, 164
  economic development
    agencies 161
  reforms of 161
Newman, Kenneth 218
Next Steps agencies 49, 77, 146,
  147, 148
  and FMI 93, 96
  future 147, 250
  output targets 139
  pay policies 113
  results of 138–9
  and unions 123, 143
Niskanen, W. A. 13, 15

Norris, G. M.   153, 154
Norris, P.   155
Northcote Trevellyan reforms   144
Norton, P.   152

O'Connor, J.   239
oil   7, 11
organisations
    goals of   32, 55, 56
    private   28–30;
        accountabilities   32, 33;
        regulated   29–30
    public: accountabilities   28; and
        complaints   39; control of
        spending   47–8; customer
        awareness   50; financial
        responsibilities   47–8; public
        service orientation   238; use
        of resources   40, 42, 51
    responsibilities   32
    typology   28–30
    see also management/
        managerialism; public
Owens, P.   186

Painter, C.   68, 74, 76, 152, 154, 168
Painter, J.   159, 166, 248
parent power   194
Parkinson, M.   154, 156, 157
Patients' Charter   187
Patten, C.   69
Pay Comparability, Standing
    Commission on   9
pay review bodies   114–16, 118
pay   *see* performance-related pay;
    wage/s
PBSR   9
Peach, L.   112
Peacock, A.   5
Pease, K.   221
Peat Marwick McLintock   111
performance indicators   123, 238
    and Audit Commission   72
    civil service   136–7, 142, 143, 148
    and economy, efficiency and
        effectiveness   87

financial   81, 86–8
higher education   208
local government   171, 243
NHS   180, 184, 187
in public organisations   47
performance-related pay   111, 122,
    247
    civil service   141
    features of   112
    NHS   244
Perry, J.   27
personnel management
    civil service   140–3
    future changes   251
    traditional   107
    see also human resources
        management
PES system   136, 144
Peters, G.   15
Peters, T.   35, 146
Phyrr, P. A.   84
Pierre, J.   161
Pitt, D.   169
planning
    and financial management   81
    horizons   63–4
    long-term   60, 67
    National Health Service   65–7,
        69–70
    private sector   31–2, 34
    in public sector   44, 45, 47, 48;
        criticisms of   45
    role of state   10
    and strategic management   55, 56,
        57–8, 61–2, 70–6
    and uncertainty   68
Plowden Report   63, 128, 129, 130,
    144
Plowden, W.   67
Plumridge, M.   229
police service   4, 211–33
    and black people   213, 214
    career development   214
    changes in   23
    Circular 105/1988   226
    Circular 106/1988   218
    Circular 114/1983   216, 217, 218
    Circular 81/1989   218

civilianisation 212, 225–6, 250
crime screening 225
criticisms of 214–15
effect on clear-up rate 222
effect on crime rates 221–2
effectiveness, efficiency and
    economy 224–5
employment 103, 104
equal opportunities issues 216,
    227, 232
and FMI 215, 217
graded response 225
HMIs 217–18, 223
management as authoritarian 215
management functions 212
management training 213, 227–
    30, 232; Metropolitan
    Police 227–8
objective setting 219–20, 223
Operational Review 225, 226
OSPRE 214
performance measurement 218,
    220–4; matrix of
    indicators 223
policing by objectives 218
pressures for change 213–16, 218,
    231; objections to 231–2
promotion process 214, 227–8,
    229–30
and public confidence 224, 225
purchaser–provider
    separation 226
rank structure and decision-
    making 212, 213
reactive characteristic 211, 219
recruitment 227–9, 231; adequacy
    of 230; fast-tracking 228,
    229, 230; possible changes
    in 231, 232
research 224
resource allocation 215
and RUC 216
state provision 30
towards planned policing 217–26
and value for money 224–6
work as symbolic 221, 223
Policy Analysis Reviews 131
Policy Studies Institute 213–14, 215

politics, new 16–24
defined 17
popular capitalism 23–4
strong state 21–3
see also Conservative; Labour;
    New Right; New Urban Left
poll tax *see* community charge
Pollitt, C. 36, 45, 46, 72, 137, 251
pollution control 32–3, 77
Polytechnics and Colleges Funding
    Council 204
polytechnics *see* further education;
    higher education
position statements *see* mission
    statements
post-war settlement 3, 9–13
critique of 13
weakening of 24
poverty 12
Power, J. M. 58, 61, 153
Pressman, J. 61
Price Waterhouse 139
Priestley Report 105, 143
Prison Service 250
private sector *see* management/
    managerialism; organisations
privatisation 9, 20
as economic solution 240, 241
extension of 16
property ownership 23
see also housing
public disorder 213, 215
Public Expenditure Survey
    (PES) 63–4, 130, 131, 133
public goods and New Right 15
public health 4
consensus years 173
public interest 29, 38
public sector 5, 241
employment 100–4
facilitating change 49
fragmentation of 249
growth of 4–9
managers 111–12
as model employers 104–5;
    decline of 122
public service orientation 168–9
size of 25

public sector (*cont.*)
    see also civil service; education,
        local government;
        management/managerialism;
        National Health Service;
        organisations; police service
public sector borrowing
    requirement 9
public utilities 5
    privatisation 9, 20, 100

quality 123
    and demoralised workers 252–3
    as new concern 50
    and NHS 184
    and police service 223, 232
    private sector management 34
    and scrutinies 91

Ranson, S. 251
rate-capping 22, 155, 164
Rayner, D. 134–5, 137, 140, 143,
    148
recession 9, 24
    world 7, 11, 25
Reed, D. 123
refuse collection 158
    Liverpool 243
Reiner, R. 211, 233
resource allocation
    and budget 85
    and FMI 135
    future changes 250
    and markets 3
    NHS 243
    police service 215, 225
    policies for 76
    see also markets
Resource Management Initiative 93
responsibility, personal 23
reticulists 61–2, 153
Rice, A. K. 34
Richards, S. 89, 93, 145, 146
Riddell, P. 17
Ridley, Nicholas 67, 69, 155
Robbins Report 188
Rockley, L. E. 79
Rose, A. 38

Rose, R. 15
Rowan, Charles 227–8
Royal College of Nursing 253
Royal Ulster Constabulary 216

Salmon Report 174, 180, 239
Salter, B. 189
Savage, S.P. 22, 211–33
Scarman, Lord/Report 213, 227
Schein, E. H. 35
Scholes, K. 73
Schon, D. 62
School Management Task
    Force 201, 202
    see also education; Local
        Management of Schools
Scott, Harold 228
scrutinies programme 89–91
Seabrook, J. 162
Seebohm Report 152
Self, P. 27, 42
shareholders
    employee 23
    private sector 32
Shaw, K. 152
Sheaff, M. 121
Shulz, J. 65
Skeffington Report 67, 168
Smith, D. 214, 215
social security benefits *see* welfare
    benefits
Social Security, Department of,
    performance indicators 137
social services 7, 9
    and Conservative
        Government 25
    employment 103, 104
    post-war 10
    universal 12
socialism, and Conservative
    governments 18
Southend Council 158
staff appraisal 47, 114, 122
    civil service 140, 141, 142, 143
    teachers 203, 245; and
        incorporation 207
Stalker, John 216
Starks, M. 240

state
  cases for intervention 14
  enabling 26
  and new politics 21–3
  role of 4, 5, 18; and Conservative
    government 67
  see also civil service; local
    government; public sector
statistical services 60
Stead, P. 228
Stewart, J. D. 68, 69, 74, 151, 152,
  164, 193, 251
Stirling District Council 69
Stoker, G. 193
Storey, J. 109, 140
strategic management 55–77
  choices 55, 63–4, 70; and public
    sector 57
  defined 55
  evaluation 76
  failures 65–70
  implementation 55, 70;
    improving 75–6; and public
    sector 57
  as learning cycle 63
  monitoring and control 56
  need for 253
  objective setting 56
  PES system 67, 70, 71
  in public sector 57
  rational model 56
  requirements 77
  and reticulists 61–2
  strategic planning 55, 56, 57–8,
    61–2, 70–6; approaches 72;
    cycle 70–1; decline 65;
    matrix analysis 73–4;
    problems 72–3;
    requirements 73
  and uncertainty 57–63, 76, 77
SWOT analysis 57, 70, 73

Tapper, T. 189
taxation
  and Conservative
    Governments 20
  and public organisations 38
Taylor, F. 33, 239

Taylor, S. 111
Teachers' Pay and Conditions Act
  1987 113, 115, 202–3
telecommunications privatisation 9,
  20, 24, 29, 100
Thatcher, Margaret *see*
  Conservative governments
Thomas, H. 129
Thomas, R. 242
Thornley, A. 155
Tomkins, C. R. 29, 30
Tomlin Commission 104
Tonge, R. 78–98
total quality management 35, 146
  NHS 186
  see also quality
town and country planning, public
  participation 155
Town and Country Planning
  Acts 57, 64, 65, 153
Trade Union Act 1984 20
trade unions 3
  changing role 117–21, 122–3
  civil service 142
  and Conservative
    governments 18
  and DSOs 165
  future of 252
  marginalised 110, 123, 248
  and model employers 105–6
  and new managerialism 238
  recognition of 105–6, 117
  teacher 190, 202, 206
  and Wapping 215–16
  and Winter of Discontent 155
Trades Union Congress 10
Trading Funds Act 1973 130
training programmes 193
transport
  bus services 21, 24, 100
  planning 57
  public infrastructure 30
Transport, Department of 48–9
Treasury 92, 139
  and financial management 97
  Management Matters 114, 119,
    246
  PES 131

Treasury (*cont.*)
  role of   129
Trenchard, Lord   228, 229
Tullock, G.   15
Tyson, S.   116

ultra vires, and public
    organisations   38
uncertainty
  about environment   59–60
  about related organisations   61–3
  about values   60–1
  as good   68
  managing   59
  and planning   68
  reduction of   57–63
  and strategic management   70, 76,
    77
underclass   249
unemployment   9, 24, 25
  and Conservative
    governments   20, 21
  and training programmes   193
unions   *see* trade unions
United States   23
  management practices   122, 240
universities   *see* higher education
University of Kent   245
Urwick, L.   33

value for money   97–8, 110, 242
  civil service   133, 135, 136–7
  as cost-cutting   95
  police   224–6
Vidal, J.   65
voluntary sector, and local
    government   156, 160, 170

Waddington, P.   211
wage/s
  flexible arrangements   111, 112–14

  market determination of   20
  PRP   111, 112
  social   12
Wagner, L.   246
Walker, A.   18, 19
Walsall Council   161–2
Walsh, K.   251
Wandsworth Council   158, 167
Wapping print unions   215–16
water privatisation   9, 20
Waterman, L.   35, 146
Weatheritt, M.   217, 219, 224
welfare benefits   10, 241
welfare and markets   3
Welfare State   10, 11
  criticisms of   12, 15–16
  and new managerialism   239
  weakening   23
West Midlands Serious Crime
    Squad   216
West Wiltshire District Council   165
White, L. D.   104
Whitley Report   105, 115, 117, 130,
    142
Whitson, C.   249
Widdicombe, D.   152, 153
Wildavsky, A.   58, 61, 64, 67, 76
Wilson, D.   136
Wilson, H.   129, 144
Wintour, P.   162
WIRS   105–6
Wiseman, J.   5
Wolff Ohlins   215
Wolman, H.   156
Woodcock, John   230
Workplace Industrial Relations
    Survey   105–6

Yewlett, C. J. L.   58, 61, 153
Young, J.   222
Youth Training Scheme   193